COLLECTED LETTERS

OF A

RENAISSANCE FEMINIST

THE
OTHER VOICE
IN
EARLY MODERN
EUROPE

A Series Edited by
Margaret L. King and
Albert Rabil, Jr.

Laura Cereta

COLLECTED LETTERS
OF A
RENAISSANCE FEMINIST

و

Transcribed, Translated, and Edited
by
Diana Robin

THE UNIVERSITY OF CHICAGO PRESS
Chicago and London

Laura Cereta, born in Brescia in 1469, was educated by nuns at a local convent. She was married at the age of fifteen and widowed at sixteen. Her first book—a collection of autobiographical Latin letters—appeared three years after her husband's death.

Diana Robin is professor of classics and director of comparative literature and cultural studies at the University of New Mexico. She is the author of *Filelfo in Milan: Writings 1451–1477* (Princeton).

The University of Chicago Press, Chicago 60637
The University of Chicago Press, Ltd., London
© 1997 by The University of Chicago
All rights reserved. Published 1997
Printed in the United States of America
06 05 04 03 02 01 00 99 98 97   1 2 3 4 5

ISBN: 0-226-10011-1 (cloth)
ISBN: 0-226-10013-8 (paper)

Library of Congress Cataloging-in-Publication Data

Cereta, Laura, 1469–1499.
    [Correspondence. English]
    Collected letters of a Renaissance feminist / edited and translated by Diana Robin.
       p.   cm. — (The other voice in early modern Europe)
    Translated from Latin.
    Includes bibliographical references (p.   ) and index.
    ISBN 0-226-10011-1 (cloth : acid-free paper). — ISBN 0-226-10013-8 (pbk.)
    1. Cereta, Laura, 1469–1499—Correspondence.   2. Authors, Latin (Medieval and modern)—Italy—Correspondence.   3. Women—Italy—History—Renaissance, 1450–1600—Sources.   4. Humanists—Italy—Correspondence.   5. Feminists—Italy—Correspondence.   I. Robin, Diana Maury.   II. Title.   III. Series.
PA85.C4A4   1997
001.3′092—dc20
[B]   96-45730
                                         CIP

This translation was supported by a generous grant from the NEH.

CONTENTS

INTRODUCTION TO THE SERIES

THE OLD VOICE AND THE OTHER VOICE

In western Europe and the United States women are nearing equality in the professions, in business, and in politics. Most enjoy access to education, reproductive rights, and autonomy in financial affairs. Issues vital to women are on the public agenda: equal pay, child care, domestic abuse, breast cancer research, and curricular revision with an eye to the inclusion of women.

These recent achievements have their origins in things women (and some male supporters) said for the first time about six hundred years ago. Theirs is the "other voice," in contradistinction to the "first voice," the voice of the educated men who created western culture. Coincident with a general reshaping of European culture in the period 1300 to 1700 (called the Renaissance or early modern period), questions of female equality and opportunity were raised that still resound and are still unresolved.

The "other voice" emerged against the backdrop of a three-thousand-year history of misogyny—the hatred of women—rooted in the civilizations related to western culture: Hebrew, Greek, Roman, and Christian. Misogyny inherited from these traditions pervaded the intellectual, medical, legal, religious, and social systems that developed during the European Middle Ages.

The following pages describe the misogynistic tradition inherited by early modern Europeans, and the new tradition which the "other voice" called into being to challenge reigning assumptions. This review should serve as a framework for the understanding of the texts published in the series "The Other Voice in Early Modern Europe." Introductions specific to each text and author follow this essay in all the volumes of the series.

THE MISOGYNIST TRADITION, 500 B.C.E.–1500 C.E.

Embedded in the philosophical and medical theories of the ancient Greeks were perceptions of the female as inferior to the male in both mind and body. Similarly, the structure of civil legislation inherited from the ancient Romans was biased against women, and the views on women developed by Christian thinkers out of the Hebrew Bible and the Christian New Testament were negative and disabling. Literary works composed in the vernacular language of ordinary people, and widely recited or read, conveyed these negative assumptions. The social networks within which most women lived—those of the family and the institutions of the Roman Catholic church—were shaped by this misogynist tradition and sharply limited the areas in which women might act in and upon the world.

GREEK PHILOSOPHY AND FEMALE NATURE. Greek biology assumed that women were inferior to men and defined them merely as childbearers and housekeepers. This view was authoritatively expressed in the works of the philosopher Aristotle.

Aristotle thought in dualities. He considered action superior to inaction, form (the inner design or structure of any object) superior to matter, completion to incompletion, possession to deprivation. In each of these dualities, he associated the male principle with the superior quality and the female with the inferior. "The male principle in nature," he argued, "is associated with active, formative and perfected characteristics, while the female is passive, material and deprived, desiring the male in order to become complete."[1] Men are always identified with virile qualities, such as judgment, courage, and stamina; women with their opposites—irrationality, cowardice, and weakness.

The masculine principle was considered to be superior even in the womb. Man's semen, Aristotle believed, created the form of a new human creature, while the female body contributed only matter. (The existence of the ovum, and the other facts of human embryology, were not established until the seventeenth century.) Although the later Greek physician Galen believed that there was a female component in generation, contributed by "female semen," the followers of both Aristotle and Galen saw the male role in human generation as more active and more important.

In the Aristotelian view, the male principle sought always to reproduce itself. The creation of a female was always a mistake, therefore, resulting from an imperfect act of generation. Every female born was considered a "de-

---

1. Aristotle, *Physics*, 1.9 192a20–24 (*The Complete Works of Aristotle*, ed. Jonathan Barnes, rev. Oxford translation, 2 vols. [Princeton, 1984], 1:328).

fective" or "mutilated" male (as Aristotle's terminology has variously been translated), a "monstrosity" of nature.[2]

For Greek theorists, the biology of males and females was the key to their psychology. The female was softer and more docile, more apt to be despondent, querulous, and deceitful. Being incomplete, moreover, she craved sexual fulfillment in intercourse with a male. The male was intellectual, active, and in control of his passions.

These psychological polarities derived from the theory that the universe consisted of four elements (earth, fire, air, and water), expressed in human bodies as four "humors" (black bile, yellow bile, blood, and phlegm) considered respectively dry, hot, damp, and cold, and corresponding to mental states ("melancholic," "choleric," "sanguine," "phlegmatic"). In this schematization, the male, sharing the principles of earth and fire, was dry and hot; the female, sharing the principles of air and water, was cold and damp.

Female psychology was further affected by her dominant organ, the uterus (womb), *hystera* in Greek. The passions generated by the womb made women lustful, deceitful, talkative, irrational, indeed—when these affects were in excess—"hysterical."

Aristotle's biology also had social and political consequences. If the male principle was superior and the female inferior, then in the household, as in the state, men should rule and women must be subordinate. That hierarchy did not rule out the companionship of husband and wife, whose cooperation was necessary for the welfare of children and the preservation of property. Such mutuality supported male preeminence.

Aristotle's teacher, Plato, suggested a different possibility: that men and women might possess the same virtues. The setting for this proposal is the imaginary and ideal Republic that Plato sketches in his dialogue of that name. Here, for a privileged elite capable of leading wisely, all distinctions of class and wealth dissolve, as do consequently those of gender. Without households or property, as Plato constructs his ideal society, there is no need for the subordination of women. Women may, therefore, be educated to the same level as men to assume leadership responsibilities. Plato's Republic remained imaginary, however. In real societies, the subordination of women remained the norm and the prescription.

The views of women inherited from the Greek philosophical tradition became the basis for medieval thought. In the thirteenth century, the supreme scholastic philosopher Thomas Aquinas, among others, still echoed

---

2. Aristotle, *Generation of Animals*, 2.3 737a27–28 (Barnes, 1:1144).

Aristotle's views of human reproduction, of male and female personalities, and of the preeminent male role in the social hierarchy.

ROMAN LAW AND THE FEMALE CONDITION. Roman law, like Greek philosophy, underlay medieval thought and shaped medieval society. The ancient belief that adult, property-owning men should administer households and make decisions affecting the community at large is the very fulcrum of Roman law.

Around 450 B.C.E., during Rome's republican era, the community's customary law was recorded (legendarily) on Twelve Tables erected in the city's central forum. It was later elaborated by professional jurists whose activity increased in the imperial era, when much new legislation, especially on issues affecting family and inheritance, was passed. This growing, changing body of laws was eventually codified in the *Corpus of Civil Law* under the direction of the Emperor Justinian, generations after the empire ceased to be ruled from Rome. That *Corpus*, read and commented upon by medieval scholars from the eleventh century on, inspired the legal systems of most of the cities and kingdoms of Europe.

Laws regarding dowries, divorce, and inheritance most pertain to women. Since those laws aimed to maintain and preserve property, the women concerned were those from the property-owning minority. Their subordination to male family members points to the even greater subordination of lower-class and slave women, about whom the laws speak little.

In the early Republic, the *paterfamilias*, "father of the family," possessed *patria potestas*, "paternal power." The term *pater*, "father," in both these cases does not necessarily mean biological father, but householder. The father was the person who owned the household's property and, indeed, its human members. The *paterfamilias* had absolute power—including the power, rarely exercised, of life or death—over his wife, his children, and his slaves, as much as over his cattle.

Male children could be "emancipated," an act that granted legal autonomy and the right to own property. Males over the age of fourteen could be emancipated by a special grant from the father, or automatically by their father's death. But females never could be emancipated; instead, they passed from the authority of their father to a husband or, if widowed or orphaned while still unmarried, to a guardian or tutor.

Marriage under its traditional form placed the woman under her husband's authority, or *manus*. He could divorce her on grounds of adultery, drinking wine, or stealing from the household, but she could not divorce him. She could possess no property in her own right, nor bequeath any to her children upon her death. When her husband died, the household property passed not to her but to his male heirs. And when her father died, she had no claim to any family inheritance, which was directed to her brothers or more remote male relatives. The effect of these laws was to exclude women from civil society, itself based on property ownership.

In the later Republican and Imperial periods, these rules were significantly modified. Women rarely married according to the traditional form, but according to the form of "free" marriage. That practice allowed a woman to remain under her father's authority, to possess property given her by her father (most frequently the "dowry," recoverable from the husband's household in the event of his death), and to inherit from her father. She could also bequeath property to her own children and divorce her husband, just as he could divorce her.

Despite this greater freedom, women still suffered enormous disability under Roman law. Heirs could belong only to the father's side, never the mother's. Moreover, although she could bequeath her property to her children, she could not establish a line of succession in doing so. A woman was "the beginning and end of her own family," growled the jurist Ulpian. Moreover, women could play no public role. They could not hold public office, represent anyone in a legal case, or even witness a will. Women had only a private existence, and no public personality.

The dowry system, the guardian, women's limited ability to transmit wealth, and their total political disability are all features of Roman law adopted, although modified according to local customary laws, by the medieval communities of western Europe.

CHRISTIAN DOCTRINE AND WOMEN'S PLACE. The Hebrew Bible and the Christian New Testament authorized later writers to limit women to the realm of the family and to burden them with the guilt of original sin. The passages most fruitful for this purpose were the creation narratives in Genesis and sentences from the Epistles defining women's role within the Christian family and community.

Each of the first two chapters of Genesis contains a creation narrative. In the first "God created man in his own image, in the image of God he created him; male and female he created them" (NRSV, Genesis 1:27). In the second, God created Eve from Adam's rib (2:21–23). Christian theologians relied principally on Genesis 2 for their understanding of the relation between man and woman, interpreting the creation of Eve from Adam as proof of her subordination to him.

The creation story in Genesis 2 leads to that of the temptations in Genesis 3: of Eve by the wily serpent, and of Adam by Eve. As read by Christian theologians from Tertullian to Thomas Aquinas, the narrative made Eve responsible for the Fall and its consequences. She instigated the act; she deceived her husband; she suffered the greater punishment. Her disobedience made it necessary for Jesus to be incarnated and to die on the cross. From the pulpit, moralists and preachers for centuries conveyed to women the guilt that they bore for original sin.

The Epistles offered advice to early Christians on building communities of the faithful. Among the matters to be regulated was the place of women. Paul offered views favorable to women in Galatians 3:28: "There is neither Jew nor Greek, there is neither slave nor free, there is neither male nor female; for you are all one in Christ Jesus." Paul also referred to women as his coworkers and placed them on a par with himself and his male coworkers (Phil. 4:2–3; Rom. 16:1–3; I Cor. 16:19). Elsewhere Paul limited women's possibilities: "But I want you to understand that the head of every man is Christ, the head of a woman is her husband, and the head of Christ is God" (I Cor. 11:3).

Biblical passages by later writers (though attributed to Paul) enjoined women to forego jewels, expensive clothes, and elaborate coiffures; and they forbade women to "teach or have authority over men," telling them to "learn in silence with all submissiveness" as is proper for one responsible for sin, consoling them however with the thought that they would be saved through childbearing (I Tim. 2:9–15). Other texts among the later Epistles defined women as the weaker sex, and emphasized their subordination to their husbands (I Peter 3:7; Col. 3:18; Eph. 5:22–23).

These passages from the New Testament became the arsenal employed by theologians of the early church to transmit negative attitudes toward women to medieval Christian culture—above all, Tertullian ("On the Apparel of Women"), Jerome (*Against Jovinian*), and Augustine (*The Literal Meaning of Genesis*).

THE IMAGE OF WOMEN IN MEDIEVAL LITERATURE. The philosophical, legal, and religious traditions born in antiquity formed the basis of the medieval intellectual synthesis wrought by trained thinkers, mostly clerics, writing in Latin and based largely in universities. The vernacular literary tradition which developed alongside the learned tradition also spoke about female nature and women's roles. Medieval stories, poems, and epics were infused with misogyny. They portrayed most women as lustful and deceitful, while praising good housekeepers and loyal wives, or replicas of the Virgin Mary, or the female saints and martyrs.

There is an exception in the movement of "courtly love" that evolved in southern France from the twelfth century. Courtly love was the erotic love between a nobleman and noblewoman, the latter usually superior in social rank. It was always adulterous. From the conventions of courtly love derive modern western notions of romantic love. The phenomenon has had an impact disproportionate to its size, for it affected only a tiny elite, and very few women. The exaltation of the female lover probably does not reflect a higher evaluation of women, or a step toward their sexual liberation. More likely it gives expression to the social and sexual tensions besetting the knightly class at a specific historical juncture.

The literary fashion of courtly love was on the wane by the thirteenth century, when the widely read *Romance of the Rose* was composed in French by two authors of significantly different dispositions. Guillaume de Lorris composed the initial four thousand verses around 1235, and Jean de Meun added about seventeen thousand verses—more than four times the original— around 1265.

The fragment composed by Guillaume de Lorris stands squarely in the courtly love tradition. Here the poet, in a dream, is admitted into a walled garden where he finds a magic fountain in which a rosebush is reflected. He longs to pick one rose but the thorns around it prevent his doing so, even as he is wounded by arrows from the God of Love, whose commands he agrees to obey. The remainder of this part of the poem recounts the poet's unsuccessful efforts to pluck the rose.

The longer part of the *Romance* by Jean de Meun also describes a dream. But here allegorical characters give long didactic speeches, providing a social satire on a variety of themes, including those pertaining to women. Love is an anxious and tormented state, the poem explains, women are greedy and manipulative, marriage is miserable, beautiful women are lustful, ugly ones cease to please, and a chaste woman is as rare as a black swan.

Shortly after Jean de Meun completed *The Romance of the Rose,* Mathéolus penned his *Lamentations,* a long Latin diatribe against marriage translated into French about a century later. The *Lamentations* sum up medieval attitudes toward women, and they provoked the important response by Christine de Pizan in her *Book of the City of Ladies.*

In 1355, Giovanni Boccaccio wrote *Il Corbaccio,* another antifeminist manifesto, though ironically by an author whose other works pioneered new directions in Renaissance thought. The former husband of his lover appears to Boccaccio, condemning his unmoderated lust and detailing the defects of women. Boccaccio concedes at the end "how much men naturally surpass women in nobility"[3] and is cured of his desires.

WOMEN'S ROLES: THE FAMILY. The negative perception of women expressed

3. Giovanni Boccaccio, *The Corbaccio or The Labyrinth of Love,* trans. and ed. Anthony K. Cassell (Binghamton, N.Y.; rev. paper ed., 1993), 71.

in the intellectual tradition are also implicit in the actual roles that women played in European society. Assigned to subordinate positions in the household and the church, they were barred from significant participation in public life.

Medieval European households, like those in antiquity and in non-western civilizations, were headed by males. It was the male serf, or peasant, feudal lord, town merchant, or citizen who was polled or taxed or who succeeded to an inheritance or had any acknowledged public role, although his wife or widow could stand on a temporary basis as a surrogate for him. From about 1100, the position of property-holding males was enhanced further. Inheritance was confined to the male, or agnate, line—with depressing consequences for women.

A wife never fully belonged to her husband's family or a daughter to her father's family. She left her father's house young to marry whomever her parents chose. Her dowry was managed by her husband and normally passed to her children by him at her death.

A married woman's life was occupied nearly constantly with cycles of pregnancy, childbearing, and lactation. Women bore children through all the years of their fertility, and many died in childbirth before the end of that term. They also bore responsibility for raising young children up to six or seven. That responsibility was shared in the propertied classes, since it was common for a wet nurse to take over the job of breastfeeding, and servants took over other chores.

Women trained their daughters in the household responsibilities appropriate to their status, nearly always in tasks associated with textiles: spinning, weaving, sewing, embroidering. Their sons were sent out of the house as apprentices or students, or their training was assumed by fathers in later childhood and adolescence. On the death of her husband, a woman's children became the responsibility of his family. She generally did not take "his" children with her to a new marriage or back to her father's house, except sometimes in artisan classes.

Women also worked. Rural peasants performed farm chores, merchant wives often practiced their husband's trade, the unmarried daughters of the urban poor worked as servants or prostitutes. All wives produced or embellished textiles and did the housekeeping, while wealthy ones managed servants. These labors were unpaid or poorly paid, but often contributed substantially to family wealth.

WOMEN'S ROLES: THE CHURCH. Membership in a household, whether a father's or a husband's, meant for women a lifelong subordination to others. In western Europe, the Roman Catholic church offered an alternative to the career of wife and mother. A woman could enter a convent parallel in function to the monasteries for men that evolved in the early Christian centuries.

In the convent, a woman pledged herself to a celibate life, lived according to strict community rules, and worshiped daily. Often the convent offered training in Latin, allowing some women to become considerable scholars and authors, as well as scribes, artists, and musicians. For women who chose the conventual life, the benefits could be enormous, but for numerous others placed in convents by paternal choice, the life could be restrictive and burdensome.

The conventual life declined as an alternative for women as the modern age approached. Reformed monastic institutions resisted responsibility for related female orders. The church increasingly restricted female institutional life by insisting on closer male supervision.

Women often sought other options. Some joined the communities of laywomen that sprang up spontaneously in the thirteenth century in the urban zones of western Europe, especially in Flanders and Italy. Some joined the heretical movements, flourishing in late medieval Christendom, whose anticlerical and often antifamily positions particularly appealed to women. In these communities, some women were acclaimed as "holy women" or "saints," while others often were condemned as frauds or heretics.

In all, though the options offered to women by the church were sometimes less than satisfactory, sometimes they were richly rewarding. After 1520, the convent remained an option only in Roman Catholic territories. Protestantism engendered an ideal of marriage as a heroic endeavor, and appeared to place husband and wife on a more equal footing. Sermons and treatises, however, still called for female subordination and obedience.

THE OTHER VOICE, 1300–1700

Misogyny was so long-established in European culture when the modern era opened that to dismantle it was a monumental labor. The process began as part of a larger cultural movement that entailed the critical reexamination of ideas inherited from the ancient and medieval past. The humanists launched that critical reexamination.

THE HUMANIST FOUNDATION. Originating in Italy in the fourteenth century, humanism quickly became the dominant intellectual movement in Europe. Spreading in the sixteenth century from Italy to the rest of Europe, it fueled the literary, scientific, and philosophical movements of the era, and laid the basis for the eighteenth-century Enlightenment.

Humanists regarded the scholastic philosophy of medieval universities as out of touch with the realities of urban life. They found in the rhetorical discourse of classical Rome a language adapted to civic life and public speech. They learned to read, speak, and write classical Latin, and eventually classical Greek. They founded schools to teach others to do so, establishing the pattern for elementary and secondary education for the next three hundred years.

In the service of complex government bureaucracies, humanists employed their skills to write eloquent letters, deliver public orations, and formulate public policy. They developed new scripts for copying manuscripts and used the new printing press for the dissemination of texts, for which they created methods of critical editing.

Humanism was a movement led by males who accepted the evaluation of women in ancient texts and generally shared the misogynist perceptions of their culture. (Female humanists, as will be seen, did not.) Yet humanism also opened the door to the critique of the misogynist tradition. By calling authors, texts, and ideas into question, it made possible the fundamental rereading of the whole intellectual tradition that was required in order to free women from cultural prejudice and social subordination.

A DIFFERENT CITY. The other voice first appeared when, after so many centuries, the accumulation of misogynist concepts evoked a response from a capable woman female defender: Christine de Pizan. Introducing her *Book of the City of Ladies* (1405), she described how she was affected by reading Mathéolus's *Lamentations*: "Just the sight of this book . . . made me wonder how it happened that so many different men . . . are so inclined to express both in speaking and in their treatises and writings so many wicked insults about women and their behavior."[4] These statements impelled her to detest herself "and the entire feminine sex, as though we were monstrosities in nature."[5]

The remainder of the *Book of the City of Ladies* presents a justification of the female sex and a vision of an ideal community of women. A pioneer, she has not only received the misogynist message, but she rejects it. From the fourteenth to seventeenth century, a huge body of literature accumulated that responded to the dominant tradition.

The result was a literary explosion consisting of works by both men and women, in Latin and in vernacular languages: works enumerating the achievements of notable women; works rebutting the main accusations made against women; works arguing for the equal education of men and women;

---

4. Christine de Pizan, *The Book of the City of Ladies*, trans. Earl Jeffrey Richards; Foreword Marina Warner (New York, 1982), I.1.1., pp. 3–4.

5. Ibid., I.1.1–2, p. 5.

works defining and redefining women's proper role in the family, at court, and in public; and works describing women's lives and experiences. Recent monographs and articles have begun to hint at the great range of this phenomenon, involving probably several thousand titles. The protofeminism of these "other voices" constitute a significant fraction of the literary product of the early modern era.

THE CATALOGUES. Around 1365, the same Boccaccio whose *Corbaccio* rehearses the usual charges against female nature wrote another work, *Concerning Famous Women.* A humanist treatise drawing on classical texts, it praised 106 notable women—one hundred of them from pagan Greek and Roman antiquity, and six from the religious and cultural tradition since antiquity—and helped make all readers aware of a sex normally condemned or forgotten. Boccaccio's outlook, nevertheless, was misogynist, for it singled out for praise those women who possessed the traditional virtues of chastity, silence, and obedience. Women who were active in the public realm, for example, rulers and warriors, were depicted as suffering terrible punishments for entering into the masculine sphere. Women were his subject, but Boccaccio's standard remained male.

Christine de Pizan's *Book of the City of Ladies* contains a second catalogue, one responding specifically to Boccaccio's. Where Boccaccio portrays female virtue as exceptional, she depicts it as universal. Many women in history were leaders, or remained chaste despite the lascivious approaches of men, or were visionaries and brave martyrs.

The work of Boccaccio inspired a series of catalogues of illustrious women of the biblical, classical, Christian, and local past: works by Alvaro de Luna, Jacopo Filippo Foresti (1497), Brantôme, Pierre Le Moyne, Pietro Paolo de Ribera (who listed 845 figures), and many others. Whatever their embedded prejudices, these catalogues of illustrious women drove home to the public the possibility of female excellence.

THE DEBATE. At the same time, many questions remained: Could a woman be virtuous? Could she perform noteworthy deeds? Was she even, strictly speaking, of the same human species as men? These questions were debated over four centuries, in French, German, Italian, Spanish, and English, by authors male and female, among Catholics, Protestants, and Jews, in ponderous volumes and breezy pamphlets. The whole literary phenomenon has been called the *querelle des femmes*, the "Woman Question."

The opening volley of this battle occurred in the first years of the fifteenth century, in a literary debate sparked by Christine de Pizan. She exchanged letters critical of Jean de Meun's contribution to the *Romance of the Rose* with two French humanists and royal secretaries, Jean de Montreuil and

Gontier Col. When the matter became public, Jean Gerson, one of Europe's leading theologians, supported de Pizan's arguments against de Meun, for the moment silencing the opposition.

The debate resurfaced repeatedly over the next two hundred years. *The Triumph of Women* (1438) by Juan Rodríguez de la Camara (or Juan Rodríguez del Padron) struck a new note by presenting arguments for the superiority of women to men. *The Champion of Women* (1440–42) by Martin Le Franc addresses once again the misogynist claims of *The Romance of the Rose*, and offers counterevidence of female virtue and achievement.

A cameo of the debate on women is included in *The Courtier,* one of the most read books of the era, published by the Italian Baldassare Castiglione in 1528 and immediately translated into other European vernaculars. *The Courtier* depicts a series of evenings at the court of the Duke of Urbino in which many men and some women of the highest social stratum amuse themselves by discussing a range of literary and social issues. The "woman question" is a pervasive theme throughout, and the third of its four books is devoted entirely to that issue.

In a verbal duel, Gasparo Pallavicino and Giuliano de' Medici present the main claims of the two traditions—the prevailing misogynist one, and the newly emerging alternative one. Gasparo argues the innate inferiority of women and their inclination to vice. Only in bearing children do they profit the world. Giuliano counters that women share the same spiritual and mental capacities as men and may excel in wisdom and action. Men and women are of the same essence: just as no stone can be more perfectly a stone than another, so no human being can be more perfectly human than others, whether male or female. It was an astonishing assertion, boldly made to an audience as large as all Europe.

THE TREATISES. Humanism provided the materials for a positive counter-concept to the misogyny embedded in scholastic philosophy and law, and inherited from the Greek, Roman, and Christian pasts. A series of humanist treatises on marriage and family, on education and deportment, and on the nature of women helped construct these new perspectives.

The works by Francesco Barbaro and Leon Battista Alberti, respectively *On Marriage* (1415) and *On the Family* (1434–37), far from defending female equality, reasserted women's responsibilities for rearing children and managing the housekeeping while being obedient, chaste, and silent. Nevertheless, they served the cause of reexamining the issue of women's nature by placing domestic issues at the center of scholarly concern and reopening the pertinent classical texts. In addition, Barbaro emphasized the companionate nature of marriage and the importance of a wife's spiritual and mental qualities for the well-being of the family.

These themes reappear in later humanist works on marriage and the education of women by Juan Luis Vives and Erasmus. Both were moderately sym-
pathetic to the condition of women, without reaching beyond the usual
masculine prescriptions for female behavior.

An outlook more favorable to women characterizes the nearly unknown
work *In Praise of Women* (ca. 1487) by the Italian humanist Bartolommeo
Goggio. In addition to providing a catalogue of illustrious women, Goggio
argued that male and female are the same in essence, but that women (re-
working from quite a new angle the Adam and Eve narrative) are actually
superior. In the same vein, the Italian humanist Mario Equicola asserted the
spiritual equality of men and women in *On Women* (1501). In 1525, Galeazzo
Flavio Capra (or Capella) published his work *On the Excellence and Dignity of
Women*. This humanist tradition of treatises defending the worthiness of
women culminates in the work of Henricus Cornelius Agrippa, *On the Nobility
and Preeminence of the Female Sex*. No work by a male humanist more succinctly
or explicitly presents the case for female dignity.

THE WITCH BOOKS. While humanists grappled with the issues pertaining
to women and family, other learned men turned their attention to what they
perceived as a very great problem: witches. Witch-hunting manuals, explora-
tions of the witch phenomenon, and even defenses of witches are not at first
glance pertinent to the tradition of the other voice. But they do relate in this
way: most accused witches were women. The hostility aroused by supposed
witch activity is comparable to the hostility aroused by women. The evil
deeds the victims of the hunt were charged with were exaggerations of the
vices to which, many believed, all women were prone.

The connection between the witch accusation and the hatred of women
is explicit in the notorious witch-hunting manual, *The Hammer of Witches*
(1486), by two Dominican inquisitors, Heinrich Krämer and Jacob Sprenger.
Here the inconstancy, deceitfulness, and lustfulness traditionally associated
with women are depicted in exaggerated form as the core features of witch
behavior. These inclined women to make a bargain with the devil—sealed
by sexual intercourse—by which they acquired unholy powers. Such bizarre
claims, far from being rejected by rational men, were broadcast by intellectuals. The German Ulrich Molitur, the Frenchman Nicolas Rémy, the Italian
Stefano Guazzo coolly informed the public of sinister orgies and midnight
pacts with the devil. The celebrated French jurist, historian, and political
philosopher Jean Bodin argued that, because women were especially prone
to diabolism, regular legal procedures could properly be suspended in order
to try those accused of this "exceptional crime."

A few experts, such as the physician Johann Weyer, a student of
Agrippa's, raised their voices in protest. In 1563, Weyer explained the witch

phenomenon thus, without discarding belief in diabolism: the devil deluded foolish old women afflicted by melancholia, causing them to believe that they had magical powers. His rational skepticism, which had good credibility in the community of the learned, worked to revise the conventional views of women and witchcraft.

WOMEN'S WORKS. To the many categories of works produced on the question of women's worth must be added nearly all works written by women. A woman writing was in herself a statement of women's claim to dignity.

Only a few women wrote anything prior to the dawn of the modern era, for three reasons. First, they rarely received the education that would enable them to write. Second, they were not admitted to the public roles—as administrator, bureaucrat, lawyer or notary, university professor—in which they might gain knowledge of the kinds of things the literate public thought worth writing about. Third, the culture imposed silence upon women, considering speaking out a form of unchastity. Given these conditions, it is remarkable that any women wrote. Those who did before the fourteenth century were almost always nuns or religious women whose isolation made their pronouncements more acceptable.

From the fourteenth century on, the volume of women's writings crescendoed. Women continued to write devotional literature, although not always as cloistered nuns. They also wrote diaries, often intended as keepsakes for their children; books of advice to their sons and daughters; letters to family members and friends; and family memoirs, in a few cases elaborate enough to be considered histories.

A few women wrote works directly concerning the "woman question," and some of these, such as the humanists Isotta Nogarola, Cassandra Fedele, Laura Cereta, and Olimpia Morata, were highly trained. A few were professional writers, living by the income of their pen: the very first among them Christine de Pizan, noteworthy in this context as in so many others. In addition to *The Book of the City of Ladies* and her critiques of *The Romance of the Rose*, she wrote *The Treasure of the City of Ladies* (a guide to social decorum for women), an advice book for her son, much courtly verse, and a full-scale history of the reign of King Charles V of France.

WOMEN PATRONS. Women who did not themselves write but encouraged others to do so boosted the development of an alternative tradition. Highly placed women patrons supported authors, artists, musicians, poets, and learned men. Such patrons, drawn mostly from the Italian elites and the courts of northern Europe, figure disproportionately as the dedicatees of the important works of early feminism.

For a start, it might be noted that the catalogues of Boccaccio and Alvaro de Luna were dedicated to the Florentine noblewoman Andrea Acciaiuoli and to Doña María, first wife of King Juan II of Castile, while the French translation of Boccaccio's work was commissioned by Anne of Brittany, wife of King Charles VIII of France. The humanist treatises of Goggio, Equicola, Vives, and Agrippa were dedicated, respectively, to Eleonora of Aragon, wife of Ercole I d'Este, duke of Ferrara; to Margherita Cantelma of Mantua; to Catherine of Aragon, wife of King Henry VIII of England; and to Margaret, duchess of Austria and regent of the Netherlands. As late as 1696, Mary Astell's *Serious Proposal to the Ladies, for the Advancement of Their True and Greatest Interest* was dedicated to Princess Ann of Denmark.

These authors presumed that their efforts would be welcome to female patrons, or they may have written at the bidding of those patrons. Silent themselves, perhaps even unresponsive, these loftily placed women helped shape the tradition of the other voice.

THE ISSUES. The literary forms and patterns in which the tradition of the other voice presented itself have now been sketched. It remains to highlight the major issues about which this tradition crystallizes. In brief, there are four problems to which our authors return again and again, in plays and cata-logues, in verse and in letters, in treatises and dialogues, in every language: the problem of chastity; the problem of power; the problem of speech; and the problem of knowledge. Of these the greatest, preconditioning the others, is the problem of chastity.

THE PROBLEM OF CHASTITY. In traditional European culture, as in those of antiquity and others around the globe, chastity was perceived as woman's quintessential virtue—in contrast to courage, or generosity, or leadership, or rationality, seen as virtues characteristic of men. Opponents of women charged them with insatiable lust. Women themselves and their defenders— without disputing the validity of the standard—responded that women were capable of chastity.

The requirement of chastity kept women at home, silenced them, iso-lated them, left them in ignorance. It was the source of all other impedi-ments. Why was it so important to the society of men, of whom chastity was not required, and who, more often than not, considered it their right to vio-late the chastity of any woman they encountered?

Female chastity ensured the continuity of the male-headed household. If a man's wife was not chaste, he could not be sure of the legitimacy of his offspring. If they were not his, and they acquired his property, it was not his household, but some other man's, that had endured. If his daughter was not chaste, she could not be transferred to another man's household as his wife, and he was dishonored.

The whole system of the integrity of the household and the transmission of property was bound up in female chastity. Such a requirement only pertained to property-owning classes, of course. Poor women could not expect to maintain their chastity, least of all if they were in contact with high-status men to whom all women but those of their own household were prey.

In Catholic Europe, the requirement of chastity was further buttressed by moral and religious imperatives. Original sin was inextricably linked with the sexual act. Virginity was seen as heroic virtue, far more impressive than, say, the avoidance of idleness or greed. Monasticism, the cultural institution that dominated medieval Europe for centuries, was grounded in the renunciation of the flesh. The Catholic reform of the eleventh century imposed a similar standard on all the clergy, and a heightened awareness of sexual requirements on all the laity. Although men were asked to be chaste, female unchastity was much worse: it led to the devil, as Eve had led mankind to sin.

To such requirements, women and their defenders protested their innocence. More, following the example of holy women who had escaped the requirements of family and sought the religious life, some women began to conceive of female communities as alternatives both to family and to the cloister. Christine de Pizan's city of ladies was such a community. Moderata Fonte and Mary Astell envisioned others. The luxurious salons of the French *précieuses* of the seventeenth century, or the comfortable English drawing rooms of the next, may have been born of the same impulse. Here women might not only escape, if briefly, the subordinate position that life in the family entailed, but they might make claims to power, exercise their capacity for speech, and display their knowledge.

THE PROBLEM OF POWER. Women were excluded from power: the whole cultural tradition insisted upon it. Only men were citizens, only men bore arms, only men could be chiefs or lords or kings. There were exceptions which did not disprove the rule, when wives or widows or mothers took the place of men, awaiting their return or the maturation of a male heir. A woman who attempted to rule in her own right was perceived as an anomaly, a monster, at once a deformed woman and an insufficient male, sexually confused and, consequently, unsafe.

The association of such images with women who held or sought power explains some otherwise odd features of early modern culture. Queen Elizabeth I of England, one of the few women to hold full regal authority in European history, played with such male/female images—positive ones, of course—in representing herself to her subjects. She was a prince, and manly, even though she was female. She was also (she claimed) virginal, a condition absolutely essential if she was to avoid the attacks of her opponents. Catherine de' Medici, who ruled France as widow and regent for her sons, also adopted such imagery in defining her position. She chose as one symbol the figure of Artemisia, an androgynous ancient warrior-heroine, who combined a female persona with masculine powers.

Power in a woman, without such sexual imagery, seems to have been indigestible by the culture. A rare note was struck by the Englishman Sir Thomas Elyot in his *Defence of Good Women* (1540), justifying both women's participation in civic life and prowess in arms. The old tune was sung by the Scots reformer John Knox in his *First Blast of the Trumpet against the Monstrous Regiment of Women* (1558), for whom rule by women, defects in nature, was a hideous contradiction in terms.

The confused sexuality of the imagery of female potency was not reserved for rulers. Any woman who excelled was likely to be called an Amazon, recalling the self-mutilated warrior women of antiquity who repudiated all men, gave up their sons, and raised only their daughters. She was often said to have "exceeded her sex," or to have possessed "masculine virtue"—as the very fact of conspicuous excellence conferred masculinity, even on the female subject. The catalogues of notable women often showed those female heroes dressed in armor, armed to the teeth, like men. Amazonian heroines romp through the epics of the age—Ariosto's *Orlando Furioso* (1532), Spenser's *Faerie Queene* (1590–1609). Excellence in a woman was perceived as a claim for power, and power was reserved for the masculine realm. A woman who possessed either was masculinized, and lost title to her own female identity.

THE PROBLEM OF SPEECH. Just as power had a sexual dimension when it was claimed by women, so did speech. A good woman spoke little. Excessive speech was an indication of unchastity. By speech women seduced men. Eve had lured Adam into sin by her speech. Accused witches were commonly accused of having spoken abusively, or irrationally, or simply too much. As enlightened a figure as Francesco Barbaro insisted on silence in a woman, which he linked to her perfect unanimity with her husband's will and her unblemished virtue (her chastity). Another Italian humanist, Leonardo Bruni, in advising a noblewoman on her studies, barred her not from speech, but from public speaking. That was reserved for men.

Related to the problem of speech was that of costume, another, if silent, form of self-expression. Assigned the task of pleasing men as their primary occupation, elite women often tended to elaborate costume, hairdressing, and the use of cosmetics. Clergy and secular moralists alike condemned these practices. The appropriate function of costume and adornment was to announce the status of a woman's husband or father. Any further indulgence in adornment was akin to unchastity.

THE PROBLEM OF KNOWLEDGE. When the Italian noblewoman Isotta Nogarola had begun to attain a reputation as a humanist, she was accused of incest—a telling instance of the association of learning in women with unchastity. That chilling association inclined any woman who was educated to deny that she was, or to make exaggerated claims of heroic chastity.

If educated women were pursued with suspicions of sexual misconduct, women seeking an education faced an even more daunting obstacle: the assumption that women were by nature incapable of learning, that reason was a particularly masculine ability. Just as they proclaimed their chastity, women and their defenders insisted upon their capacity for learning. The major work by a male writer on female education—*On the Education of a Christian Woman,* by Juan Luis Vives (1523)—granted female capacity for intellection, but argued still that a woman's whole education was to be shaped around the requirement of chastity and a future within the household. Female writers of the following generations—Marie de Gournay in France, Anna Maria van Schurman in Holland, Mary Astell in England—began to envision other possibilities.

The pioneers of female education were the Italian women humanists who managed to attain a Latin literacy and knowledge of classical and Christian literature equivalent to that of prominent men. Their works implicitly and explicitly raise questions about women's social roles, defining problems that beset women attempting to break out of the cultural limits that had bound them. Like Christine de Pizan, who achieved an advanced education through her father's tutoring and her own devices, their bold questioning makes clear the importance of training. Only when women were educated to the same standard as male leaders would they be able to raise that other voice and insist on their dignity as human beings morally, intellectually, and legally equal to men.

THE OTHER VOICE. The other voice, a voice of protest, was mostly female, but also male. It spoke in the vernaculars and in Latin, in treatises and dialogues, plays and poetry, letters and diaries and pamphlets. It battered at the wall of misogynist beliefs that encircled women and raised a banner announcing its claims. The female was equal (or even superior) to the male in essential nature—moral, spiritual, intellectual. Women were capable of higher education, of holding positions of power and influence in the public realm, and of speaking and writing persuasively. The last bastion of masculine supremacy, centered on the notions of a woman's primary domestic responsibility and the requirement of female chastity, was not as yet assaulted—although visions of productive female communities as alternatives to the family indicated an awareness of the problem.

During the period 1300 to 1700, the other voice remained only a voice, and one only dimly heard. It did not result—yet—in an alteration of social patterns. Indeed, to this day, they have not entirely been altered. Yet the call for justice issued as long as six centuries ago by those writing in the tradition of the other voice must be recognized as the source and origin of the mature feminist tradition and of the realignment of social institutions accomplished in the modern age.

We would like to thank the volume editors in this series, who responded with many suggestions to an earlier draft of this introduction, making it a collaborative enterprise. Many of their suggestions and criticisms have resulted in revisions of this introduction, though we remain responsible for the final product.

Margaret L. King
Albert Rabil, Jr.

PROJECTED TITLES IN THE SERIES

Henricus Cornelius Agrippa, *Declamation on the Nobility and Preeminence of the Female Sex*, translated and edited by Albert Rabil, Jr.

Tullia d'Aragona, *Dialogue on the Infinity of Love*, edited and translated by Rinaldina Russell and Bruce Merry

Laura Cereta, *Collected Letters of a Renaissance Feminist*, edited and translated by Diana Robin

Cassandra Fedele, *Letters and Orations*, edited and translated by Diana Robin

Cecilia Ferrazzi, *Autobiography of an Aspiring Saint*, transcribed, translated, and annotated by Anne Jacobson Schutte

Moderata Fonte, *The Worth of Women*, edited and translated by Virginia Cox

Veronica Franco, *Selected Poems and Letters*, edited and translated by Margaret Rosenthal and Ann Rosalind Jones

Lucrezia Marinella, *The Nobility and Excellence of Women*, edited and translated by Anne Dunhill

Antonia Pulci, *Florentine Drama for Convent and Festival*, annotated and translated by James Wyatt Cook

Anna Maria van Schurman, *Whether a Christian Woman Should Be Educated and Other Writings from Her Intellectual Circle*, edited and translated by Joyce Irwin

Arcangela Tarabotti, *Paternal Tyranny*, edited and translated by Letizia Panizza

ACKNOWLEDGMENTS

I would like to express my gratitude to the friends and colleagues and the institutions and fellowships that made it possible for me to complete this project. My thanks go to the Newberry Library in Chicago and the Gladys Krieble Delmas Society for research in Venice for the fellowships they awarded me in the summer of 1991, and to the National Endowment for the Humanities for two years of support from 1993–95. No words can possibly convey my indebtedness to Al Rabil, Margaret King, and Ira Jaffe for talking me through the most nerve-racking phases of this project, day after day for well over two years now. I also want to thank a few friends without whom this book would never have been written and who so generously provided me with advice and encouragement over the several years it has taken to finish the manuscript: Dale Kent, Tom Mayer, Ken Gouwens, Paul Gehl, Beverly Burris, Shane Phelan, Minrose Gwin, Ruth Salvaggio, Pamela Becker-Koch, Amy Richlin, Judy Hallett, Barbara Gold, Patricia Labalme, Jennifer Rondeau, Don Jackson, Jack Holtsmark, Roger Hornsby, Nancy Jaicks, Lynette Cofer, and Nina Wallerstein. And finally and most importantly my thanks to Jo Ann Kiser, the editor without whom this book would not exist.

COLLECTED LETTERS
OF A
RENAISSANCE FEMINIST

LAVRA CERETA BRIXIENSIS
LITERIS ORNATISSIMA

TRANSLATOR'S INTRODUCTION

T hough a finished manuscript of Laura Cereta's *Epistolae familiares* was already circulating among prominent scholars in Brescia, Verona, and Venice by 1488–92, her work remained outside the mainstream of humanist letters in her own lifetime and did not find a publisher until the middle of the seventeenth century.[1] The mingling in her epistolary essays of themes characteristic of fifteenth-century humanist discourse with those anticipating modern feminism marks her work as different from that of any other writer of her time.[2] Unlike the standard humanist letterbook of the period, which was geared to attract patrons by showcasing the author's learning and social connections, her book addressed family members and friends, an unusual proportion of them women.[3]

1. Laura Cereta, *Laurae Ceretae Brixiensis Feminae Clarissimae Epistolae iam primum e MS in lucem productae*, ed. Jacopo Filippo Tomasini (Padua: Sebastiano Sardi, 1640), hereafter cited as Tom.; two manuscripts of her *Epistolae* are extant: Vatican City, Biblioteca Apostolica Vaticana, Vat. lat. 3176, the most complete text, hereafter cited as Vat.; Venice, Biblioteca Nazionale Marciana, Marc. lat. 4186, hereafter cited as Ven. Albert Rabil, Jr., *Laura Cereta: Quattrocento Humanist* (Binghamton, N.Y.: Medieval and Renaissance Texts and Studies, 1981), contains a biography and all Latin texts not in Tom.; for selected letters in translation see Margaret L. King and Albert Rabil, Jr., eds., *Her Immaculate Hand: Selected Works by and about the Women Humanists of Quattrocento Italy* (Binghamton, N.Y.: Medieval and Renaissance Texts and Studies, 1983), pp. 77–86. On Cereta's life and milieu see also Carlo Pasero, "Il dominio veneto fino all'incendio della loggia," Ettore Caccia, "Cultura e letteratura nei secoli XV e XVI," and Virginio Cremona, "L'umanesimo Bresciano" in *Storia di Brescia. II, La dominazione Veneta (1426–1575)*, ed. Giovanni Reccani degli Alfieri (Brescia: Morcelliana, 1961), esp. pp. 182–222; 477–527; 542–66. See also M. Palma, "Cereto, Laura," in *Dizionario biografico degli italiani*, 23 (1979), pp. 729–30. Cereta appears to have been the humanist name she took for herself; she is referred to as Laura Cereto in the articles by Caccia, Pasero, and Cremona as well as in Palma's.

2. Palma, "Cereto, Laura," p. 730, mistakenly describes Cereta's religious beliefs as excessively orthodox while dismissing her humanism as insignificant.

3. The standard work on humanist epistolarity remains Cecil H. Clough, "The Cult of Antiq-

Many of her letters concern private, familial matters such as her difficult relationships with both her mother and her husband, subjects considered taboo in a humanist letterbook. Other letters represent Cereta's concern with such issues as the history of women's contributions to scholarship and learning, women's right to an education in literature and the sciences, and the servitude of women in marriage—themes that were to characterize the feminist thought of later centuries. At the same time, Cereta wrote epistolary essays on all the topics the humanists considered *de rigueur*—the nature of true pleasure, the role of fate versus contingency in human affairs, the problem of human greed, the threat from Turkish Islam, the brevity of human life, the randomness of death, and the bitterness of bereavement.

Her Latin style, like that of other late fifteenth-century and early sixteenth-century writers, reflects a shift away from the Ciceronian Latinity that characterized the prose of an earlier generation of humanists and a movement towards a terser, more recondite style indebted to the later Latin writers so admired by the literati of her era such as Pliny the Elder, Juvenal, Aulus Gellius, and Apuleius.[4] Key to her own style is that, like Augustine and Conrad, Cereta is working in a language foreign to her native tongue to stitch together with exotic colors and strange and jagged metaphors a self not known before in Western letters.

HER LIFE

Born into an urban, upper-middle-class family in Brescia in 1469, Laura Cereta was the first of six siblings—with three brothers and two sisters.[5] The daughter of Silvestro Cereto, an attorney and magistrate in Brescia, and Veronica di Leno, whose family bragged about the antiquity of its coat of arms, Laura was sent to a monastery at the age of seven. There she learned reading,

uity," in *Cultural Aspects of the Italian Renaissance. Essays in Honour of Paul Oskar Kristeller*, ed. Cecil H. Clough (Manchester: Manchester University Press, 1976), pp. 33–67. See also Alessandro Perosa, "Sulla pubblicazione degli epistolari degli umanisti," in *La pubblicazione delle fonti del medioevo europeo negli ultimi 70 anni (1883–1953)* (Rome: Istituto Storico Italiano per il Medio Evo, 1954), pp. 327–38; John M. Najemy, *Between Friends. Discourses of Power and Desire in the Machiavelli-Vettori Letters of 1513–1515* (Princeton: Princeton University Press, 1993), pp. 18–57; and Diana Robin, *Filelfo in Milan. Writings, 1451–1477* (Princeton: Princeton University Press, 1991), pp 11–55.

4. Cf. Angelo Poliziano, *Opera omnia*, ed. I. Maier, 3 vols. (Turin, 1971); Francesco Filelfo, *Epistolae familiares* (Venice: Gregorii, 1502); Ernst Walser, *Poggio Florentinus. Leben und Werke* (Leipzig, 1914).

5. According to Tomasini's vita of Cereta, p. 5, she had three brothers, Ippolito, Daniel, and Basilio, and two sisters, Diana and Deodata; Rabil and I have followed Tomasini and the testimony in Cereta's letters (which mention only the above-named siblings); Caccia, p. 495, on the other hand writes that Laura was the eldest of seven children.

writing, embroidery, and the rudiments of Latin from a learned nun,[6] while her brothers were sent to the prestigious humanist boarding school established by Giovanni Olivieri in Chiari.[7] When she was nine, her father brought her home from the convent, only to return her some months later to her erudite female teacher for further instruction in the Latin canon. At eleven years of age, she was sent home again, because she was needed to help care for her younger brothers and sisters. She continued to study the ancient authors in her room at night after the children were put to bed. Such an educational route for girls of Cereta's class—convent schooling at an early age followed by home schooling during the years preceding marriage—was not by any means unusual, since by the last quarter of the fifteenth century Brescia had ten monasteries for women housing a population of some eight hundred nuns.[8]

During the war of Ferrara (1482–84), when the Venetians ravaged towns and villages in Brescia, Crema, and Bergamo in an effort to retain control over their client cities in the face of Milanese and Aragonese incursions,[9] Cereta lived at Lake Iseo with her father, who had been sent there to supervise the fortification of the town.[10] After the war Cereto appears to have been forced to retire from his magistracy. It was at this time that Laura acted as her father's surrogate and amanuensis, not only with his sons but with certain of his oldest friends.[11] About her mother Cereta is mostly silent with the exception of a single short letter addressed to her, the tenor of which suggests that their relationship was filled with tension and conflict.[12]

Sometime around the end of 1484 or the beginning of 1485 Cereta left her parents' household to marry Pietro Serina, a merchant who owned a shop on the Rialto in Venice. But after eighteen months of marriage, Serina died, apparently of a species of plague.

The year after Pietro's death saw the invasion of the town of Calliano by

---

6. The biographical details that follow are from Cereta's own letter about her life addressed to Nazaria Olympica in Vat. 71 (fols. 56v–58v); Ven. 61 (fols. 100v–106); Tom. 59 (pp. 145–54); Rabil 50 (his date November 5, 1486). The text of this letter is in chapter 1.

7. Olivieri's humanist school is mentioned in Pasero, "Il dominio veneto," p. 200; Caccia, "La cultura," p. 506 n. 2; and Cremona, "L'umanesimo Bresciano," p. 590 n. 2.

8. See Caccia, "La Cultura," pp. 500–508; and Paul Grendler et al., *Schooling in Renaissance Italy. Literacy and Learning, 1300–1600* (Baltimore: Johns Hopkins University Press, 1989), pp. 96–102.

9. Pasero, "Il dominio veneto," pp. 182–189.

10. See her letter to Ludovico Cendrata of Verona in chapter 5.

11. See letters IX–XVI in chapter 1.

12. See letters about her mother (I, to Nazaria Olympica) and to her mother (III, to Veronica di Leno) in chapter 1.

the emperor of Austria, whose aim was to seize Trent.[13] In August 1487
Cereta wrote a letter to the Venetian envoy Luigi Dandolo in which she described the slaughter that had taken place when Austrian and Italian troops
clashed at Rovereto just south of Trent.[14] If, as her correspondence suggests,
Cereta met regularly with groups of scholars in Brescia and Chiari and gave
readings from her essays, the documentary-style reporting in her letter to
Dandolo would surely have had no trouble drawing an audience.[15] In fact,
many of her last letters, particularly the epistolary essays in chapters 4 and 5
would have easily lent themselves to presentation in the urban academies and
salons of late Quattrocento Brescia and its environs.

The prominent humanist teachers and professors Cereta counted
among her friends included Clemenzo Longolio, who belonged to the community of resident scholars at the monastery at Chiari; the classical scholar
and historian Lodovico Cendrata of Verona; the university professor Bonifacio Bembo, who taught at Pavia and later in Rome; and Giovanni Olivieri,
who had founded an influential private school at Chiari. Other friends were
the attorneys Francesco Prandoni, Alberto degli Alberti of Brescia, Sigismondo de Bucci of Brescia, the physicians Michele Beto of Chiari and Felicio Tadino of Brescia, and the priests fra Tommaso da Milano, fra Tommaso
da Firenze, and fra Lodovico de la Turre, a resident at the monastery at
Chiari. Though her attempt to forge a literary friendship with Cassandra
Fedele, the most famous woman scholar in Italy during the last two decades
of the fifteenth century, came to nothing, Cereta appears to have sustained a
number of intellectual friendships with women, among whom were the nuns
Nazaria Olympica, suora Veneranda (abbess at Chiari), Santa Pelegrina
(who appears to be a nun though her affiliation is not specified by Cereta),
and suora Deodata di Leno (Cereta's sister). Cereta sought the patronage of
Cardinal Ascanio Maria Sforza, a younger son of the duke of Milan, though
whether or not she was successful in her quest for the Cardinal's support is
not known.

Laura Cereta died in 1499 at the age of thirty, leaving behind an unpublished volume containing eighty-two Latin letters and a dialogue on the

---

13. See Pasero, "Il dominio veneto," pp. 194–95.

14. See Cereta's letter XLVII, chapter 5.

15. Cereta's letters LI–LV in the appendix to chapter 5 paint a convincing picture of her own
relationships as an insider/outsider in literary circles in both Brescia and Chiari. For the perhaps
fictitious tradition, however, that Cereta and her brother Daniel frequented a literary salon at
the house of the Brescian physician Luigi Mondella see Ottavio Rossi, *Elogi istorici de'Bresciani
illustri* (Brescia: Bartolomeo Fontana, 1620); Tom., vita, pp. xi–xvii; Caccia, "Cultura," pp. 496;
Rabil, *Laura Cereta*, p. 29.

death of an ass. A funeral mass was said over her body in the church of San Domenico while the entire city mourned her passing.

WOMEN AND HUMANISM BEFORE CERETA

A century of Italian women humanists preceded Cereta and the learned female writers of her era. These first women were educated in the classics of Greco-Roman antiquity under the auspices of their fathers, brothers, and their brothers' tutors.[16] Coming almost exclusively from the ruling classes, none of these women—among whom were Maddalena Scrovegni of Padua (1356–1429), Cecilia Gonzaga of Mantua (1425–51), Battista Montefeltro Malatesta of Urbino (1383–1450), Caterina Caldiera (d. 1463), Ippolita Sforza of Milan (1445–88), and Costanza Varano of Pesaro (1428–47)—represented herself as separate from her family or wrote for causes unconnected to its interests.

A second generation of women humanists came typically from the urban, citizen classes rather than the nobility or the courts. These women, who received at least some of their humanist schooling from a teacher outside the range of the panoptic gaze of the father, were the first female writers in Italy to mobilize their talents to advance their own interests rather than those of their families. But they were working against the grain. Influential humanists such as Leonardo Bruni and Francesco Barbaro intimated that no virtuous woman would seek to publish her work or express her views in public.[17] The response from this second wave of women humanists was a relentless pairing in their writings of the theme of feminine eloquence with that of chastity. The emergence of this theme in the letters of the Veronese writer Isotta Nogarola (1418–66), for example, suggests an attempt on the part of a new generation of women scholars to counter Bruni's and Barbaro's pronouncements barring women from the literary arena with the new paradigm of the *chaste* female orator.[18] But while both Isotta and her sister Ginevra Nogarola

16. On this first generation of humanist women see King and Rabil, *Her Immaculate Hand,* and Patricia H. Labalme, ed., *Beyond Their Sex. Learned Women of the European Past* (New York and London: New York University Press, 1980).

17. See King and Rabil, *Her Immaculate Hand,* pp. 11–30; Francesco Barbaro, "On Wifely Duties," trans. Benjamin G. Kohl, in *the Earthly Republic. Italian Humanists on Government and Society,* eds. B. Kohl and Ronald G. Witt (Philadelphia: University of Pennsylvania Press, 1978), pp. 177–228; Leonardo Bruni, *On the Study of Literature,* in *The Humanism of Leonardo Bruni: Selected Texts,* ed. Gordon Griffiths, James Hankins, and David Thompson (Binghamton, N.Y.: Medieval and Renaissance Texts and Studies/Renaissance Society of America, 1987), pp. 240–50.

18. Margaret L. King, "The Religious Retreat of Isotta Nogarola (1418–1466)," *Signs* 3 (1978): 807–22; Lisa Jardine, "Isotta Nogarola: Women Humanists—Education for What?" *History of Education* 12 (1983): 231–44.

(1417-61/8) collected their Latin letters for publication, and while Isotta composed a dialogue in Latin partially exculpating Eve from sin, neither sister was able to sustain her career as a writer for very long. Ginevra abandoned her career when she married; and Isotta, who was the more prolific of the two, retreated from the public forum to a life of private study.

Antonia Pulci (1452–1501), wife of the poet and humanist Bernardo Pulci, wrote religious plays in the vernacular; chief among her supporters were Ficino's patron, Lorenzo de' Medici, and the humanist scholar and poet Angelo Poliziano.[19] Also closely connected to the literati who gravitated toward the circle of "Il magnifico" was the brilliant young Hellenist and pupil of Poliziano, Alessandra Scala (fl. 1490), who was much admired by the Florentine humanists for her Greek intonation and accent when she played the role of Sophocles' Electra at a salon performance of the play, and for the original Greek epigrams she composed.[20]

Among this second wave of women humanists, Cassandra Fedele (1465–1558) occupied center stage. A sometime correspondent of Cereta's who was certainly the best-known woman scholar living in Europe at the end of the fifteenth century, Fedele had almost as much trouble publishing her work as Cereta did, despite the fact that her vita appeared in virtually every biographical catalogue of the famous to come out in Italy between the sixteenth and seventeenth centuries.[21] Excepting her oration on the importance of the study of the humanities, the bulk of her extant works, impressive examples of Ciceronian eloquence though they are, represent little more than a record of Fedele's efforts to sustain more than superficial relationships with important scholars and aristocratic patrons. Among Fedele's correspondents were women who stood foremost among the promoters of humanism and the revival of classical studies in Europe: Eleonora of Aragon, duchess of

19. Bernard Toscani, "Antonia Pulci (?1452–?)," in Rinaldina Russell, ed., *Italian Women Writers. A Bio-Bibliographical Sourcebook* (Westport, Conn.: Greenwood Press, 1994), pp. 344–52.

20. On Alessandra Scala see Alison Brown, *Bartolomeo Scala (1430–1497), Chancellor of Florence. The Humanist as Bureaucrat* (Princeton: Princeton University Press, 1979), pp. 226–29; and G. Pesenti, "Lettere inedite del Poliziano," *Athenaeum* 3 (1915): 299–301.

21. Cassandra Fedele, *Clarissimae Feminae Cassandrae Fidelis venetae epistolae et orationes*, ed. Jacopo Filippo Tomasini (Padua: Franciscus Bolzetta, 1636), contains three of her orations and 123 of her Latin letters; the only work of Fedele's to appear in print before her death was her fourteen-page chapbook *Oratio pro Bertucio Lamberto* (printed in Modena in 1487; Venice, 1488; Nuremberg, 1489). See also Cesira Cavazzano, "Cassandra Fedele eurdita veneziana del Rinascimento," *Ateneo veneto* 29.2: 73–91, 249–75, 361–97; for selected texts in translation see King and Rabil, *Her Immaculate Hand*, pp. 48–50, 69–77, 87–88; and Diana Robin, "Cassandra Fedele's Epistolae (1488–1521): Biography as Ef-facement," in *The Rhetorics of Life-Writing in Early Modern Europe: Forms of Biography from Cassandra Fedele to Louis XIV*, ed. Thomas Mayer and Daniel Woolf (Ann Arbor, Mich.: University of Michigan Press, 1995), pp. 187–203.

Ferrara, Isabella d'Este, marquise of Mantua, Beatrice d'Este, duchess of Milan, Beatrice of Aragon, queen of Hungary, and Isabella of Aragon, queen of Spain.[22]

The patronage of such powerful noblewomen as these—and their support of such writers as Sabadino degli Arienti, Bartolommeo Goggio, Agostino Strozzi, and Baldassare Castiglione who by the mid-1480s were espousing in their treatises and dialogues the virtues of the female sex and the ideal of the educated women—had a significant impact on the literary world to which Cereta found herself drawn.[23]

HUMANIST AND ANTI-HUMANIST THEMES IN THE LETTERS

Chapter 1 presents Cereta's most patently autobiographical letters. To put one's character, one's ideas about philosophy and literature, and one's friendships on display in a collection of Latin letters was an obligatory step in the *cursus honorum* of a fifteenth-century humanist.[24] Petrarch, Salutati, Bruni, Beccadelli, Barbaro, Filelfo, Poliziano, and Ficino had all circulated books of their collected correspondence. Differing sharply from the works of her male humanist contemporaries, Cereta's letters present a self pointedly self-conscious about its femininity. While male humanist letters typically focus on objects, events, ideas, and literary and intellectual relationships, Cereta's letters expose the details of her intimate relationships with her mother, father, husband, and close friends. The self-portrait she fashions is amoebic, elusive, and unparalleled in humanist letters: she paints herself by turns as a struggling young artist, a compliant daughter of demanding parents, an antiwar protester, a frustrated young bride, a woman humanist attempting to make a name for herself in a man's world, and in the end a griefstricken widow ready to scrap her literary career and take up a life of religious seclusion.

Essentially a conversion narrative, Cereta's letter to Nazaria Olympica (I) is an autobiography that begins with her actual birth and culminates in her

---

22. See Werner L. Gundersheimer, "Women, Learning, and Power: Eleonora of Aragon and the Court of Ferrara," in Labalme, *Beyond Their Sex*, pp. 43–65; C. Malcolm Brown, "'Lo insaciabile desiderio nostro de antique': New Documents on Isabella d'Este's Collection of Antiquities," in Clough, *Cultural Aspects of the Italian Renaissance*, pp. 324–53; Massimo Felisatti, *Isabella d'este, la primadonna del Rinascimento* (Milan: Bompiani, 1982).

23. On these works see Pamela Joseph Benson, *The Invention of the Renaissance Woman. The Challenge of Female Independence in the Literature and Thought of Italy and England* (University Park: Pennsylvania State University Press, 1992), pp. 65–90.

24. See Stephen J. Greenblatt, *Renaissance Self-Fashioning from More to Shakespeare* (Chicago: University of Chicago Press, 1980); Robin, *Filelfo in Milan*, pp. 11–55.

spiritual rebirth after the death of her husband. In her letter to Sigismondo de Bucci (II), Cereta presents herself as a fledgling writer torn between her duties as wife and daughter and her commitment to her own intellectual goals. While letter III reveals her ambivalence towards her mother, letters IX–XVI depict the unusual and complex role she played as her father's sometime amanuensis, apologist, and surrogate. In letters IV and V Cereta delineates her artistic and philosophical development in a bid to persuade the prominent humanist patron Cardinal Ascanio Sforza to take her on as his client. While in letter VI Cereta assumes the voice of an outraged citizen, letters VII and VIII provide testimony of her descent from landed gentry, at least on her mother's side.

The letters in chapter 2 represent Cereta's most impassioned feminist statements. Both letters, XVII on the plight of women in marriage and XVIII on women and education, draw upon, and are responses to, Boccaccio's misogynistic representation of the history of women and his use of the *viri illustres* (lives of famous men) tradition—known in Renaissance Italian literature as the "donne famose" (famous women) or "uomini illustri" (celebrated men) theme—in his *De claris mulieribus (Concerning Famous Women)*.[25] Like Christine de Pizan's *Book of the City of Ladies* (1405),[26] letters XVII and XVIII take issue with Boccaccio's *De mulieribus* because he uses the exceptionality of a few women to argue the moral and intellectual inferiority of the majority of the female sex.[27] Just as Christine de Pizan uses the metaphor of the founding and building of a city to suggest that women have a tradition of their own,

25. Boccaccio's *De claris Mulieribus* is available in an English translation by Guido A. Guarino entitled *Concerning Famous Women* (New Brunswick, N.J.: Rutgers University Press, 1963); it is hereafter cited as *CFW*. The *donne famose, uomini illustri* (catalogue of famous women and men) tradition becomes especially important in Italian literature after Boccaccio; the tradition can be traced back to the ancient biographers and mythographers, Nepos, Valerius Maximus, Ovid, Diogenes Laertius, Plutarch, and others.

26. Christine's *Cité des dames*, though translated into English in 1521 by Brian Anslay (*Boke of the Cyte of Ladyes*), remained virtually unknown until the eighteenth century when her works appeared in *Collection des meilleurs ouvrages français composées par des femmes*, 14 vols., ed. Mlle. de Keralio (Paris, 1786–89). An English translation of the *Cité* is available in Christine de Pizan, *The Book of the City of Ladies*, trans. by Earl Jeffrey Richards with a foreword by Marina Warner (New York: Persea Books, 1982). Despite likenesses between Cereta's and Christine's works, Cereta is unlikely to have known Christine's *Cité*; nor have I found any textual evidence that leads me to think she knew the work firsthand.

27. On the theme of exceptionality see Constance Jordan, "Boccaccio's In-famous Women: Gender and Civic Virtue in the *De claris mulieribus*," in *Ambiguous Realities. Women in the Middle Ages and Renaissance*, ed. Carole Levin and Jeannie Watson (Detroit: Wayne State University Press, 1987), pp. 25–47; Valerie Wayne, "Zenobia in Medieval and Renaissance Literature," in *Ambiguous Realities*, pp. 48–65; and in Benson, *The Invention of the Renaissance Women*, as the extraordinary-woman theory.

Cereta uses the image of a noble lineage or family tree (*generositas*) of brilliant women to demonstrate that women too have had an illustrious past. Moreover, unlike Boccaccio and in opposition to the humanist tradition, Cereta links the gift of prophecy to erudition, thus connecting the irrational to the rational in her categorization of women seers as women of learning, so that the culture of divination, orality, and emotionality are consistently bound up in Cereta with the culture of literacy and book learning.

Focusing on women as a collectivity rather than as individuals in her letter to Bibolo Semproni (XVIII), Cereta is not so disturbed by her correspondent's surprise at her brilliance as she is at his low estimation of women in general, which is reflected in his judgment of her as an exception to the rule of women's inferiority. Women—Cereta argues in a way unheard of in her time—are born with the right to an education. There exists, she explains, a historically constituted "republic of women" (*respublica mulierum*), her own variation on the humanist commonplace *respublica litterarum* ("republic of letters"), a phrase that represented the humanist notion that scholars and teachers were citizens of an imaginary community, bound together by intellectual interests they held in common. But she also counsels that women—like men—will have not only to choose to become educated but will have to work hard at it; the acquisition of knowledge will not be theirs without an act of will.[28]

Cereta's letter to Pietro Zecchi (XVII) on marriage attempts to rewrite Boccaccio's catalogue of *donne famose* not only by foregrounding their exemplary deeds as faithful wives, mothers, and daughters, but by suppressing any unflattering slurs on their characters in the received traditions about them. And whereas Boccaccio's *De claris mulieribus* represents the good mother as a departure from the rule of woman's mutability and weakness, Cereta's *donne famose* feature the figure of the maternal and the symbol of the female breast in particular as emblems of fecundity, loyalty, and strength: Lucretia, Vitellia, Dido, Veturia, Agrippina, Semiramis (Semiamira in Cereta), and other morally ambiguous figurations of the mature female in Roman history are all exemplary women in Cereta's hands. In Cereta's letter to Zecchi it is the blood dripping from Lucretia's breast, for example, that becomes the instrument of her vengeance against her rapist; in another tale adapted from Boccaccio, it is the fertile breast of a young mother that nourishes and rescues both an aged

---

28. Cereta in Tom., pp. 192–93: "Donavit satis omnes natura dotibus suis: omnibus optionis suae portas aperuit, per quas ad voluntatem mittit ratio legatos a qua secum sua desideria reportent." ("Nature has granted to all enough of her bounty; she opens to all the gates of choice, and through these gates reason sends legates to the will, for it is through reason that these legates can transmit their desires.")

woman and an infant boy from death. In contrast to the usual male humanist epithalamic letters on marriage, Cereta's letter to Pietro Zecchi warns instead that marriage and children trap women into servitude. But Cereta's attitude towards contemporary women is at times ambivalent: she is angry at men for treating women not as adult equals but like dogs or children, but she is also angry at women for their complicity in their own oppression.

While the right of women to self-determination in their choice of clothing, hairstyle, cosmetics, and jewelry becomes a feminist issue for a number of women writers in an age of rigid sumptuary laws, Cereta is clearly ambivalent on this point.[29] She describes in lavish detail an elaborate shawl she has spent months embroidering in letter II, but in letters XIX and XX she lays the blame for women's overdeveloped interest in fashion and clothing and their underdeveloped concern with their intellectual growth alternately on women themselves and on men of authority who should see to it, she argues, that women do not squander their talents and resources on dress and adornment. Though like Christine de Pizan, Cereta does see women as an oppressed class, she neither focuses her anger on ills within the culture as a whole that perpetrate gender and class inequities nor calls for the overthrow of the patriarchal state. For this we will have to wait for the late sixteenth-century writer Arcangela Tarabotti.

Chapter 3 traces the development of Cereta's relationship with her husband until his death eighteen months after their marriage, when mourning and lamentation become dominant themes in Cereta's work as they have in fifteenth-century Italian literature in general.[30] Whereas letters XXI, XXII, and XXV reveal a struggle for power in the relationship and an erotic frustration on Cereta's part, letters XXIII and XXIV show another side of her role in the marriage—her moral leadership and her guidance of her husband in matters relating both to his business and his family. There is nothing else in humanist letters similar to these emotionally taut pieces, whose persona is clearly indebted to that of Ovid's female speakers in the *Heroides* and not at all to that of the mother of all humanist letterbooks, Cicero's *Epistolae familiares*. Cereta's letters mourning Pietro's death, XXVI–XXXI, form a core of the letterbook and reveal not only the depth of the wound his death has caused in her—and certainly Cereta got her figure of the wound (*vulnus*) of bereave-

29. See for example Patricia Labalme, "Venetian Women on Women: Three Early Modern Feminists," *Archivio Veneto* 5.117 (1981): 81–108, on Modesta da Pozzo and Lucrezia Marinella's insistence that women should dress in whatever manner they wished regardless of the sumptuary laws.

30. George McClure, *Sorrow and Consolation in Italian Humanism* (Princeton: Princeton University Press, 1991).

ment from Petrarch's *Familiares* 1.1—but also the deep split at times between her public and private selves, between her ritual gestures of mourning and the interior world of pain, sighing, and melancholy. While the humanist pre-scription for mourning exemplified in Petrarch's consolatory letters man-dates the expression of grief in moderation, many of Cereta's letters appear as exaggerated representations of conventionally "feminine" expressions of sorrow—unashamed floods of tears and bouts of weeping—as opposed to the more restrained "masculine" style of mourning.[31] Thus Cereta's perfor-mance of "female" rituals of mourning functions both to reinscribe her as Other (despite her humanist vocabulary) and to enable her to resist yet again the rigid conventions of male humanist discourse. The concluding letters in this chapter, XXXII–XXXIV, addressed to Cereta's priest and friend, fra Tommaso da Milano, represent her gradual healing from the sickness of her melancholy, in a process similar to what in psychoanalytic terms is known as transference.

Chapter 4, featuring her intellectual relationships with women (with the exception of one letter which is *about* her intellectual relationship with a woman, though it is addressed to a man), is of particular interest since hu-manist letters are almost never addressed to women other than female pa-trons, and none of Cereta's letters to women is a patronage letter. The second surprise is that her letters to women, with some exceptions (her letter to her mother, for example, in chapter 1) are no more intimate than those she ad-dresses to men; indeed they are often far less so. Many of these letters are of interest because of the idiosyncratic way in which Cereta treats stock hu-manist themes found in the letters of Petrarch, Salutati, and Valla. In the let-ter to her sister Deodata di Leno (XXXV) on Epicurus and the meaning of true pleasure (*voluptas*), which at first appears to be a mere imitation of Petrarch's famous letter describing his ascent of Mt. Ventoux and his Lucre-tian/Epicurean notion of *voluptas*, Cereta foregrounds her intensely sensual experience of nature—the taste of wild fruits, the sound of rushing waters, the deep shade under the apple-tree boughs—in a way that Petrarch does not do at all.[32] And in a letter she addresses to a woman she names "Europa solitaria" (XXXVI), Cereta pointedly appears to argue with the *De vita solitaria* (*On the Solitary Life*) of Petrarch, in which he praises the country life.[33] Cereta

31. McClure, *Sorrow and Consolation*, p. 76.

32. Cf. Petrarch, *Rerum familiarium. Libri I–VIII*, ed. and trans. Aldo Bernardo (Albany: State Uni-versity of New York, 1975), *fam.*, 1.4.

33. Vat. 82 (fols. 76r–77v); Ven. 72 (fols. 143r–148v); Tom. 70 (pp. 214–20); Rabil 81. Cereta to Europa, entitled "Solitaria Europa de Falsa delectatione vitae privatae admonitio" in all three editions; "solitaria" is the epithet of the addressee who becomes simply "Europa" in the body of

in her advice to Europa instead follows the famous letter in which Coluccio Salutati, then the chancellor of Florence, warned the chancellor of Bologna not to abandon the responsibilities of city governance to enter a monastery in the suburbs.[34] But Cereta's treatment of the humanist chestnut *amicitia* (friendship) is also novel. Whereas the humanist notion of *amicitia*, a euphemism for patronage, derives from Cicero's *De amicitia*, Cereta's interest is not in soliciting favors from a patron in her letter to Santa Pelegrina (XXXIX) but in the metaphor of a bond between two friends—here two women—as a growing plant that needs to be fed and watered.[35] Her letter on the Turkish menace (XL) also differs from the usual humanist call for a crusade to recapture Constantinople. She urges the Italians not to launch a costly war against the Turks, which would only bring the Turks to Italian shores and result in greater Italian casualties.[36] The Italians, she argues, should stay home and cultivate their own moral virtue.

Chapter 5 represents a continuation of Cereta's opus of public lectures, works in letter form on typical humanist themes suited for presentation to a salon or university audience. This group of lectures are all addressed to men, and each letter, like many of the essays in chapter 4, makes clear in one way or another its suitability for delivery in a public rather than private or familial setting. Because Cereta was writing at a time when debates in academic and court circles about the nature of gender were beginning to stimulate unprecedented interest in the "female point of view," it was expected that her lectures would treat even the most standard humanist topics differently, from the woman's perspective.[37] In this respect Cereta seems to have tried at least

---

the letter. On Petrarch's *De vita solitaria* see Paul Oskar Kristeller, *Eight Philosophers of the Italian Renaissance* (Stanford: Stanford University Press, 1964), p. 14.

34. McClure, *Sorrow and Consolation*, p. 89; see also Benjamin Kohl and Ronald Witt, eds., *The Earthly Republic: Italian Humanists on Government and Society* (Philadelphia, 1978), pp. 93–114, for Salutati's letter text.

35. See Cereta to Santa Pelegrina in Vat. 54 (fols. 37r–37v); Ven. 49 (fols. 48r–49r); Tom. 47 (pp. 105–7); Rabil 51. "De amicitia" is my title; the index in Vat. titles it similarly, "Querela de sopita sociae amicitia sine sui noxa." On the humanist vocabulary of the *amicitia* relationship see Robin, *Felelfo in Milan*, pp. 13–30.

36. On humanist writings on the Turkish threat to the West after 1453 see Robert Black, *Benedetto Accolti and the Florentine Renaissance* (Cambridge: Cambridge University Press, 1985), pp. 224–85.

37. On the growing interest and controversy over the nature of woman, woman's intellectual capacity, and the female point of view in the later fifteenth century see Benson, *The Invention of the Renaissance Woman;* Constance Jordan, *Renaissance Feminism. Literary Texts and Political Models* (Ithaca: Cornell University Press, 1990); Margaret L. King, *Women of the Renaissance* (Chicago: University of Chicago Press, 1991); Labalme, "Venetian Women on Women: Three Early Modern Feminists," pp. 81–109.

to meet her audience's expectations. In a learned essay on the role of fortune in human lives (XLV), after a lengthy recitation of examples from Livy, Plutarch, and Valerius Maximus, Cereta at the end of the piece speaks in a mode inconsistent with the rational and impersonal tone in which the rest of the letter is couched about her own situation as a widow struggling to overcome the loss of her husband. On the other hand, her letter to Giuliano Trosoli (XLVI) on the death of his infant daughter is clearly not a private consolatory epistle. Written in the third person rather than in the more personal *tu* form, the public context of the performance of this funerary elegy becomes obvious when Cereta calls on the mothers and fathers in her audience, who may themselves have lost a child, to come forward to the lectern and speak about their sorrow. She, Cereta tells her audience, cannot perform this role because she is childless. Two essays on war in Brescia and its environs (letters XLVII and XLIX), full of outrage and pity at the senseless loss of life and devastation of the countryside during two separate foreign invasions of the province, are so vivid in their detailed scenes of the war that they appear to be eyewitness accounts. There is a particularly interesting passage at the close of her first "war diary," on the German invasion of Brescia, in which she urges her fellow citizens not to underestimate either the benefits of Venetian protection or the dangers of ignoring Venice.[38] In her second lecture on foreign incursions into Brescia (letter XLIX), after a discourse on the history of war down through the ages, Cereta speaks also autobiographically of her life with her father at Lake Iseo after the war when he was in charge of the restoration of the town's fortifications.[39] Cereta's lecture on avarice (letter XLVIII), couched in an epistle to the fictional addressee Lupus Cynicus and crowded with learned references to Pliny and other ancient authors, demonstrates her acquaintance with the standard treatment of the subject in Roman satire from Horace to Persius and Juvenal and is the most uninspired of her public lectures. The last of the public lectures in this chapter (letter L) presents a mysterious urban vignette in which an unknown woman brandishing a snake suddenly appears out of nowhere on a street-corner; she performs a riveting dance, endures the jeers of the crowd of curiosity-seekers, and then vanishes as if into thin air. This odd woman,

38. On the invasion of Brescia and Verona by Sigismondo of Austria in 1487 see Pasero, "Il dominio veneto," pp. 194–95. On fears of Venice's imperialist aims in the late fifteenth century and early sixteenth century see Nicolai Rubinstein, "Italian Reactions to Terraferma Expansion in the Fifteenth Century," in *Renaissance Venice,* ed. J. R. Hale (Totowa, N.J.: Rowman and Littlefield, 1973), pp. 197–217. See also my *Filelfo in Milan,* pp. 56–81.

39. Cereta's letter XLIX describes the war of Ferrara (1482–84) in which the armies of Lodovico Sforza and Alfonso of Naples battled Venetian troops led by Roberto Sanseverino in Bergamo, Crema, and Brescia for hegemony over the region.

resembling in her Fury-like demeanor the spectre of fear that had earlier stalked Cereta in her dreams (letters XXVI and XLI), is perhaps a figure for Cereta herself, who—according to her own testimony—had often been injured by the Brescian public's hostility towards her and her work.

Chapter 6 introduces Cereta's comic dialogue on the death of an ass. Appearing at first to be nothing more than a farce featuring three interlocutors who eulogize a dead donkey, Cereta's only work in dialogue form turns out to be an intriguing whodunit based on a tale from an ancient novel much admired by Renaissance writers, Apuleius' *Golden Ass.*

EARLY MODERN WOMEN WRITERS AFTER CERETA

The sixteenth century saw the waning of humanism in Italy. Most women writers in the generation that followed Cereta wrote and published in the vernacular. The thriving commercial presses of Venice, Lucca, Ferrara, and Basel enabled the leading women writers of the period—Isabella Andreini, Tullia d'Aragona, Laura Battiferri Ammanati, Vittoria Colonna, Veronica Franco, Veronica Gambara, Lucrezia Marinella, Chiara Matraini, Isabella di Morra, Modesta da Pozzo, Gaspara Stampa, and Laura Terracina—to achieve fame through the printing and dissemination of their books, which included collections of *rime* and *stanze*, letters, treatises, epic poems, dialogues, and pastoral plays, all of them in Italian.[40]

A few learned women continued to publish translations of and commentaries on classical texts and to write and publish their letters and orations in Latin and Greek. Among these, Olympia Morata (1526–55), the daughter of a classical scholar at the ducal court in Ferrara, was the most prolific. The Protestant-leaning Morata, who had already written a Latin commentary on Cicero's *Stoic Paradoxes* and letters, dialogues, and poems in Greek and Latin by the time the Roman Inquisition came to Ferrara, was forced in 1550 to flee in Germany. Morata's *Opera omnia*, which reflect a gradual movement over time away from the classically inspired prose and poetry of her youth to religious and devotional works, were posthumously published in Basel in four editions (1558, 1562, 1570, 1580). Another northern Italian woman humanist a generation younger than Morata, Tarquinia Molza (1542–1617), not only wrote poetry in her native Modenese dialect but also published her Italian translations of Plato's *Charmides* and selections from the *Crito.*

The long-term influence of humanism on the literary culture of women was significant. It would be a mistake to define Renaissance humanism too

---

40. On these and other women writers see Rinaldina Russell, ed. *Italian Women Wrtiers,* Margaret King, *Women of the Renaissance;* and P. O. Kristeller, "Learned Women of Early Modern Italy: Humanists and University Scholars," in Labalme, *Beyond Their Sex.*

narrowly, associating with it only those writers who published their work in Greek or Latin or who translated from those languages, since, after the fifteenth century, most educated Italians wrote and published in the vernacular. Many of the sixteenth-century women writers who succeeded the pioneer women humanists of the fifteenth century, if not humanists themselves, were profoundly influenced by humanism. The vernacular love poet Tullia d'Aragona (1506–66) composed an Italian prose work in which she gave new life and meaning to a Neoplatonic theme that had become a humanist trope: the infinity of love. And although both Aragona's *On the Infinity of Love* and Lucrezia Marinella's (1571–1653) *The Nobility and Excellence of Women and the Defects and Deficiencies of Men* were written in Italian, each of these women chose to frame her discourse in the most characteristic of all humanist genres: the dialogue.

In assessing the impact of early modern women writers—many of whom were forced to work, through no fault of their own, in relative isolation—it is always tempting to overemphasize the novelty of their works. Despite their originality, Cereta's letters, particularly those on classical themes, are thoroughly grounded in the humanism of her age and that of her predecessors. A close reading of Cereta's letters suggests, as we have seen, that while she had a working knowledge of the ancient Roman authors who constituted the core of the humanist school curriculum, the exemplars she had at her side as she wrote were the early humanist scholars of the classics. Her writings show the impact of Petrarch's Ciceronianism, Salutati's civic republicanism, and Valla's Christian Epicureanism on her humanism. Her feminism points to still another strain of influence: her negative response to Boccaccio's *De claris mulieribus* and her positive response to the new *defensio mulierum* tradition (then in the making) represented first by Christine de Pizan and then by the later Quattrocento writers of the northern courts and cities. Whether or not Cereta knew the writings of Christine or, for that matter, those of Goggio, Vespasiano, and Sabadini, their writings which praised and defended women as a class created a new cultural climate for the reception of Cereta's feminist letters. The call for substantive institutional changes in the social, legal, and economic status of women would have to wait for the end of the sixteenth century with the Venetian feminists Modesta da Pozzo, Lucrezia Marinella, and Arcangela Tarabotti, for whose polemics Christine de Pizan and Cereta (both of them by then forgotten) had laid the groundwork.

A number of key themes associated with early feminist critics of the Enlightenment such as Joanna Baillie (1762–1851), Germaine de Staël (1766–1817), Anna Barbauld (1743–1825), Mary Wollstonecraft (1759–97), and Ann Finch (1661–1720), among others, surface first in the work of

Laura Cereta, namely: the privileging of the emotions in a genre (criticism) long assumed to be the domain of the rational faculties only; the attempt to reconstruct and redefine the concept of gender; the mutual support of women by women and the idea of a community of women; the construction of housework as a barrier to women's literary aspirations; the mainstreaming of women's writing into genres and venues that were once for men only; and the use of the culture of the salon (in Cereta's time the convent) to bridge over the borders between the private and the public spheres so often closed to women.[41]

Diana Robin

SUGGESTED READING

Virginia W. Beauchamp, Matthew Bray, et al., eds., *Women Critics, 1660–1820. An Anthology* (Bloomington and Indianapolis: Indiana University Press, 1995).

Pamela Joseph Benson, *The Invention of the Renaissance Woman. The Challenge of Female Independence in the Literature and Thought of Italy and England* (University Park: Pennsylvania State University Press, 1992).

Ettore Caccia, "Cultura e letteratura nei secoli XV e XVI," in *Storia di Brescia. II, La dominazione Veneta (1426–1575)* (Brescia: Morcelliana Editrice, 1963), pp. 477–553.

Virginio Cremona, "L'umanesimo Bresciano," in *Storia di Brescia. II, La dominazione Veneta (1426–1575)* (Brescia: Morcelliana Editrice, 1963), pp. 538–95.

Ann Rosalind Jones, *The Currency of Eros. Women's Love Lyric in Europe, 1540–1620* (Bloomington and Indianapolis: Indiana University Press, 1990).

Constance Jordan, *Renaissance Feminism. Literary Texts and Political Models* (Ithaca: Cornell University Press, 1990).

Margaret L. King, *Women of the Renaissance* (Chicago: University of Chicago Press, 1991).

Margaret L. King and Albert Rabil, Jr., eds., *Her Immaculate Hand. Selected Works by and about the Women Humanists of Quattrocento Italy* (Binghamton, N.Y.: Medieval and Renaissance Texts and Studies, 1983).

Julia Kristeva, *Desire in Language. A Semiotic Approach to Literature and Art.* Trans. Thomas Gore, Alice Jardine, and Leon S. Roudiez. Ed. Leon S. Roudiez (New York: Columbia University Press, 1980).

Patricia H. Labalme, "Venetian Women on Women: Three Early Modern Feminists," *Archivio Veneto* 5.117 (1981): 81–108.

41. *Women Critics, 1660–1820. An Anthology,* eds. the Folger Collective on Early Women Critics, Virginia W. Beauchamp, Matthew Bray, Susan Green, Susan S. Lanser, Katherine Larsen, Judith Pascoe, Katherine M. Rogers, Ruth Salvaggio, Amy C. Simowitz, Tara G. Wallace (Bloomington and Indianapolis: Indiana University Press, 1995).

Françoise Lionnet, *Autobiographical Voices: Race, Gender, Self-Portraiture* (Ithaca: Cornell University Press, 1991).

Thomas F. Mayer and Daniel R. Woolf, *The Rhetorics of Life-Writing in Early Modern Europe: Forms of Biography from Cassandra Fedele to Louis XIV* (Ann Arbor: University of Michigan Press, 1995).

Marilyn Migiel and Juliana Schiesari, eds., *Refiguring Woman. Perspectives on Gender and the Italian Renaissance* (Ithaca: Cornell University Press, 1991).

James Olney, *Metaphors of Self: The Meaning of Autobiography* (Princeton: Princeton University Press, 1972).

Carlo Pasero, "Il dominio veneto fino all'incendio della loggia," in *Storia di Brescia. II, La dominazione Veneta (1426–1575)* (Brescia: Morcelliana Editrice, 1963), pp. 3–226.

Maureen Quilligan, *The Allegory of Female Authority. Christine de Pizan's* Cité des Dames (Ithaca: Cornell University Press, 1991).

Albert Rabil, Jr., *Laura Cereta: Quattrocento Humanist* (Binghampton, N.Y.: Medieval and Renaissance Texts and Studies, 1981).

Diana Robin, *Filelfo in Milan. Writings, 1451–1477* (Princeton: Princeton University Press, 1991).

———, "Space, Woman, and Renaissance Discourse," in *Sex and Gender in Medieval and Renaissance Texts.* Ed. Gold et al. (Albany: State University of New York Press, 1996).

Nicolai Rubinstein, "Italian Reactions to Terraferma Expansion in the Fifteenth Century," in *Renaissance Venice,* ed. J. R. Hale (Totowa, N.J.: Rowman and Littlefield, 1973).

Rinaldina Russell, ed. *Italian Women Writers. A Bio-Bibliographical Sourcebook* (Westport, Conn.: Greenwood Press, 1994).

Sidonie Smith, *A Poetics of Women's Autobiography. Marginality and the Fictions of Self-Representation* (Bloomington and Indianapolis: Indiana University Press, 1987).

Ronald G. Witt, *Hercules at the Crossroads. The Life, Works, and Thought of Coluccio Salutati* (Durham, N.C.: Duke University Press, 1983).

I

AUTOBIOGRAPHY

Cereta's only letter to Nazaria Olympica, a friend and mentor she calls "sister," is presented at the head of this edition of her collected letters because a discussion of its themes is essential to an understanding of Cereta and her art.[1] Not only does the letter to Olympica contain more auto-biographical information than any other letter in her book of letters, it also introduces the reader to the major themes in Cereta's epistolary autobiography. Nazaria Olympica has asked Cereta for the story of her life. The narrative she produces in response is, in one sense, a conversion narrative: it starts with Cereta's actual birth and culminates in her spiritual death and rebirth. The narrative also includes the story of her intellectual formation as a humanist. Her life is a journey that begins with the typical humanist's quest for fame and recognition (*honor, honestas, dignitas*) and ends with her discovery of an inner, private voice she refers to as *conscientia* (consciousness, conscience, self-awareness).

Cereta's characteristic habit of thinking is to swing back and forth between extremes. Whereas in this and other letters she talks frankly about her *ingenium* (intellect, talent, genius), just as frequently she deprecates herself for her lack of talent and insufficient learning. She prefaces her autobiography with a confession of her anxieties about her writing. She fears that her work will not live up to the standards of her family, that her prose will appear un-polished and awkward, and that ultimately she will lack the energy and pas-sion it takes to be a serious scholar and writer.

The autobiography proper begins with her birth—in September

---

1. Vat. 71 (fols. 56v–58v); Ven. 61 (fols. 100v–106); Tom. 59 (pp 145–54); Rabil 50; Rabil's date November 5, 1486. [See Introduction, note 1, for full citations.]

1469—and the circumstances of her naming.[2] The issue of her name, after the laurel tree in the family garden, is important for its Petrarchan resonances as an image of poetic inspiration. The dryness of the family laurel at the time of her birth and its expected return to verdant fullness in the spring anticipates the use throughout her book of nature imagery as expressive of her own cycles of artistic fertility and drought and her desire to locate a lost utopic plenitude in nature.

After describing the childhood illnesses she suffers and the ugly nurse who serves as a surrogate in her mother's absence, Cereta tells of her father's sending her away at the age of seven to a convent to be educated. There she is taken under the wing of a woman of considerable standing in Brescia ("foeminae consilio et religione electissimae"), who appears from Cereta's account to have been the prioress of the convent and who is the first of several learned women influential in Cereta's life in their roles as her early teachers, mentors, and examples. Plagued by insomnia at the convent, Cereta is taught by the prioress to use the late night to predawn hours, while everyone else sleeps, to embroider, write, and study. This nighttime work, which Cereta comes to call *vigiliae* (night watches), will be a recurrent theme throughout the book—a theme that will allow her to represent the activities of writing and embroidery as vehicles for her artistic expression and, as such, homologous. Her narrative of her life history, she tells Olympica, will be the "simplest piece of weaving" (*historia quam simplicissime texta*). This strategy of conflating pen and spindle creates tension and ambiguity around Cereta's sexual persona since, in the fifteenth-century discourse of work, writing and needlework are coded as separate, gendered spheres: women do not write professionally and men do not do needlework for pleasure.

When Cereta is nine, after two years of living in the convent, her father brings her back to the family home. Her narrative of that return and the period following it exemplifies the ambivalence that characterizes her depiction of her position in the family. She recalls, with a certain pride, her mother's joy during the first days of her return and her doting pursuit of Laura no matter where she goes in the house. But she experiences her mother's embraces as discomforting at best ("excepit me strictioribus bracchis"). And she is silent about her mother's reaction when Silvestro Cereta decides within a year of Laura's return home to send her back to the woman who had been her teacher and adviser ("liberalium studiorum praeceptrici me meae restituit") because he fears she will become bored and lazy if she stays at home.[3] Her

2. Cereta nowhere in her letters mentions the exact date of her birth.
3. Though she doesn't name her teacher (or teachers), she does make it clear that she is being

teacher guides her through a regimen of courses in Latin grammar, a discipline to which she wholeheartedly devotes herself night and day, recalling her earlier initiation into the secret space of nighttime *vigiliae* and to the world of learning by a figure erudite and at the same time maternal.

At the age of eleven she leaves her teacher—and the disciplinary rod ("ferulae subducor," she writes)—having mastered the intricacies of Latin grammar and eager to read the ancient Roman poets and orators themselves. Barely twelve, she finds herself treated as the stepchild of the family. Given almost sole responsibility for care of the household, she is also entrusted with the supervision of her five younger siblings. "It was my lot," she writes, "to grow old when I was not far from childhood." Finding solace in her studies even during this period, she secretly gets up in the middle of the night to read and study—a theme which will surface again in other letters depicting the dissatisfaction and frustration she experiences as a wife and daughter.

The turning point in her life is not her marriage at the age of fifteen, but its abrupt end the following year, with the death of her husband. She experiences his last agony and death as a wound (*vulnus*) and a wrong done (*iniuria*), suggesting pain that is at once moral and physical. Almost all her letters subsequent to his death represent attempts, in one way or another, either to fetishize or suture over this originary wound. Her wound will need, she writes, to be restored to its rightful place in her story. After his death she hears the "sighs of his ashy dust in my ears" and comes to perceive the emptiness of life, which, like her writings and embroidered pictures, amounts to no more than a "night watch" (*vigilia*). And yet this writing represents an awakening in the sense that she struggles, in and through it, to gain a new consciousness and knowledge of self ("mens sui compos").

In the closing passages of her letter to Nazaria Olympica, who is certainly a nun or lay nun herself, Cereta's rhetoric changes key as she moves from her lamentations on the ephemerality of life into the language of the Old Testament. But there is a species of Petrarchan layering in this letter, in which several different voices can be heard, one over another: Aristotelian/Thomist, biblical, Christian, native, and humanist voices are blended, particularly in the last two pages of the letter, to create a voice uniquely Ceretan.[4] While her long, lyrical celebration of God's supreme rule

---

sent back to a former teacher ("restituit") and that her teacher was a woman ("praeceptrici"); for the view that there were no women teachers of Latin in Italy in the fifteenth century, see Paul Grendler et al., *Schooling in Renaissance Italy. Literacy and Learning, 1300–1600* (Baltimore: Johns Hopkins University Press, 1989).

4. See Françoise Lionnet, *Autobiographical Voices: Race, Gender, Self-Portraiture* (Ithaca: Cornell University Press, 1991). I am indebted to Lionnet's groundbreaking essays on Augustine's *Confessions* (especially relevant to Cereta since Augustine was also writing in a literary Latin and a second

over nature recalls the vocabulary, and sometimes even the cadences, of the Book of Psalms, in the very language she uses to renounce her former preoccupation with classical studies her syncretic, Scotist Aristotelianism also emerges: she will seek God, she writes, in order to "imitate the first cause [*primam causam*] rather than secondary ones." But yet another voice can be heard throughout the letter: Cereta's woman-centered, feminist voice, reminiscent of Christine de Pizan's works, in which the values of friendship, commonality, and community among women and of the sharing of work and thought by women are promoted and exemplified. Cereta writes that she and Olympica ought to follow God and the teachings of the Gospels, together— as two women who "sing in harmony" (*concinentes ambae*) and take counsel with one another (*commonitae*). In order to succeed in their quest, she and Nazaria will have to listen, she urges, not to voices of authority external to themselves but to the secret voice within.[5]

I

A NARRATIVE OF HER LIFE

To Nazaria Olympica

While I have worried about your request, I could not refuse to oblige you, sister, whose dear face and orderly ways I always carry with me in my heart. I have only looked after my own interests in doing so, though, for friendship demands that in matters where one's honor is concerned we should gratify our friends' wishes.[6] Your unblemished life, however, reveals what a great example of honor I have always had in you. And my mind bears witness to how much I have gained from the guidance of your virtue. But in order to fulfill my obligation I would like you to give me somewhat more time than would ordinarily be devoted to such an endeavor. And

---

language not his own) and the autobiographical texts of several other writers for her notion of the braiding and layering of voices in a text (*métissage*) in cases where a writer is writing in a language or tradition not her own, or addressing a culture other than her native one.

5. Cereta's use at the close of this letter of an abundance of of first-person plural pronouns *nos, nobis* (we, us: words that tend not to be expressed in Latin) violates the norms of male humanist decorum; and both this usage and her constant use of the verb prefixes co- and con- in her urgings to Nazaria that the two of them pray and sing together rather than in isolation demonstrate the surfacing of what I would argue is a distinctively feminine and feminist voice.

6. The phrase "in rebus honestis": literally, in honorable matters; *honestas* (honor, moral integrity, character) marks a major theme in the writings of the humanists in general as well as in Cereta's letters.

owing to your forgiveness, I'll give careful thought to the task itself despite the constraints of time.[7]

I have been plagued by three kinds of anxieties, and these I've had all my life until the present time. It disgusts me terribly and makes me ashamed to recall things that can't be compared in any measure to the past honor of the family.[8] Moreover, in those days when my mind was free from pain and I devoted all my time, which went by so quickly, to literature, I would have written these things in a better and perhaps more classical style. Now my time is frittered away in domestic leisure[9] and the happiness I found in study and the torch whose searing light once fired my every feeling has cooled. Instead of drawing on the energy and fineness of my more obvious gifts, I have let myself put in writing things that could raise me up again from the ground where I had been buried. And so, it is a strange and difficult task for me to commit to paper so coldly and gracelessly things that the common folk bruit about the town, though their foolish talk concerns a young woman who occupies a lowly position and has no public standing.[10] It necessarily follows then that my history, like the simplest piece of weaving, may well be consigned to the annals of darkness and oblivion.[11]

It is well established from our family records that I was born in the fourth month before the coming of the seventieth year in the century one thousand four-hundred of our Savior. Our laurel tree, which shaded with its bold branches a polished and burgeoning garden, had grown shriveled and dry in the wake of the icy frost that followed a brutal storm. I myself kept the name with which this tree was endowed. And thus, the whole house rang constantly with this sweet appellation, and I, who was carried around alternately in each of their arms, became for my adoring parents their most precious source of delight, for parents usually favor their firstborn child.

7. "Temporis necessitate" (literally, the scarcity or pressure of time): the theme of time—the prison of time by which all our creative efforts are constrained and shackled and the fleeting nature of time and human life—is perhaps the central concern in Cereta's letters.

8. Cereta uses another typical humanist term for honor, *dignitas*: this time she's talking about the honor of her ancestors: *dignitas maiorum*.

9. The phrase "otio domestico" (literally, in free time spent around the house) is important because *otium* (the word for leisure time, free time to write creatively, to study and read), the antithesis of *labor* (hard work, drudgery), is such a central concern in Cereta's autobiographical letters; the image of the leisurely life (*otium*) without which the lyric voice could not survive is also a major theme in the classical poets she read: Ovid, Tibullus, Propertius, and others.

10. Since her father was an attorney and a magistrate in the city of Brescia, she obviously doesn't mean to denigrate her class but rather her lack of status due to her gender.

11. It is noteworthy that she introduces the figure of needlework here ("simplicissime texta," a very simply woven fabric), which in her letters will be a recurrent metaphor for writing, the self-fashioning that she does in her autobiographical letters, and for the creative act itself. As we shall see, actual needlework and embroidery will play a formative role in her education.

Montana, who was the second nurse I had after my mother, had a throat swollen from a goiter and a face yellowed with jaundice, which she would wrinkle into a grimace when she would gasp—as though ill—for air. I remember I used to tremble at her frightening face. Though I, in my childish innocence, had not yet learned to speak, I fled her diurnal spectre more quickly than I thought I could.

As a sickly infant I often fell prey to dangerous intestinal worms. But afterwards I developed into a little girl who was charming and delicate. I was a playful, spirited child and I wandered everywhere freely, though I suffered from blistering sores on my skin of various sorts.[12] Recently, the extraction of several teeth has given me back my energy. Since then, divine providence has taken it upon herself to look after my otherwise excellent health.

But in order to move quickly beyond the trivia of the ensuing years, I shall begin with events that followed the first seven years of my life. For what can that tender age bequeath to history except precocious babble?[13] During this period, as soon as I had scarcely learned for the first time to use the letters of the alphabet to form syllables,[14] I was entrusted to a woman highly esteemed both for her counsel and sanctity, whose learning, habits, and discipline I, who was to be educated, intently absorbed.[15]

She kept me constantly at her side in the inner chambers of the convent, the doors to which were opened and shut with a hundred locks. She was the first to teach me to find a passage through my nights of insomnia by using an embroidery needle to draw pictures.[16] My hand, obedient enough after a brief period of time, committed the rudiments of my new learning to thread and fabric.[17] There was in fact no embroidery stitch so elegant or difficult that I could not master it, once I discerned its fine points through delicate and

12. These "vesicosas variolarum pustulas" sound like the highly contagious childhood skin disease impetigo.

13. The idea of history (*historia*), history as biography, and history as that which is selectively remembered, its events arranged and ordered, and thus a work consciously invented and molded by an idiosyncratic *ingenium* (mind, intelligence, genius) is a major theme throughout Cereta.

14. Evidently after children learned the alphabet they were taught to sound out syllables before they learned to read whole words.

15. "Foeminae consilio et religione electissimae credor . . . erudienda." While her biographers have emphasized her father's role in her intellectual formation, Cereta herself indicates that her first and subsequent teachers (as we shall see) were intellectual women.

16. Note the contrast between the clausura of the convent and the mobility and transgressivity suggested by her mentor's teaching her to break a trail through the terrifying nights ("transigere noctes insomnes") when she could neither sleep nor rest.

17. The analogy between writing and embroidery, between committing ideas to paper and fabric, will recur elsewhere in the letters.

gentle probings.[18] In this way a mind quite helpless and quite deficient in knowledge was able to raise itself up, once it was inspired, to those gentle breezes of hope.

With rough and trembling hands I designed, ornamented, and embroidered a tunic for the nursling baby Christchild, which was to be as precious as pearls. For trembling necklaces hung around his face with gleaming brilliance, from which hairlike threads of silver flowed down, which were surrounded by violet rosebuds on a bed of verdant grass. And little scales of many colors stood stiff with thread of gold, sewn under a knotty bough twisted and tawny with thorns, and these alone adorned the curving orb. One purple thread was braided into the weave of the fabric, but embossings, equal in size and divided by fissures and embroidered dots, embellished the many-colored threads and cloths of the decorative bands. But on the left shoulder of the tunic, a translucently burning gem cast its rays toward the embroidered likeness of a flashing star.

Once I had completed this work of art, which was like an empty simulacrum of my sleepless nights, I withdrew my idle hands from the pomp and vanity of such work.[19] The next year, which prepared me for the more tranquil work of contemplation, removed me from all things secular. After this, insofar as I could, imbued both with the fear of God and humility and kindliness toward everyone, I blamelessly devoted myself to obedience and I was always ready—like a little sparrow trained to come to one's hand—to go to the aid of those who called me.[20] In more private places I prostrated myself as I prayed that I might sacrifice my innocent heart. This was the root of a change of heart, and from this the seeds of hope soon sprouted—because of which I shall eventually sleep in the bosom of God, the king and redeemer of men, in the company of Christ, the fruit of the law redeemed.

Within a full two-year period from the time I had entered the convent, my father called for my return home and I departed, to everyone's sorrow. As soon as I crossed my father's threshold, my mother greeted me, clasping me

18. Cereta makes the point here that the way she masters intricacies of advanced needlework ("difficilis textu polities") is stereotypically "feminine": her stitches are "tenuius molliusque discreta" (literally, delicately and sensitively discerned as different from one another). Both adjectives, *tenuis* and *mollis* are conventionally linked with not only the feminine but the effeminate in Latin literature.

19. Note that she describes her hands in this passage as "full of leisure" (otiosas manus), from the noun *otium* so closely associated with the life and needs of the writer or scholar (see n. 9).

20. The motif of the sparrow (*passerculus; passer*) is indebted to Catullus (*Carm.* 2) and will be an important Ceretan metaphor for the self-destructive and inappropriate obedience of women elsewhere in her letters.

to her in an uncomfortable embrace.[21] Feeling joy for herself yet pity for me, she began to comfort me, following me wherever I went as though she did not know how to satisfy herself in her delight at my homecoming.

My father, however, the more purposeful figure in the family in his role as our governor and, above all, a man of temperate counsel, soon sent me back to my instructress in liberal studies,[22] since I had already begun to be bored with childish pursuits and he feared that at my age I might slip into indolent habits and grow dull from the free time I would have. With all the vigor of my genius depending on her, my teacher, I immersed myself night and day, blinking back my fatigue, in long vigils of study.[23] Then in my eleventh year, after I had entered into this dry diet, I was removed from the discipline of the rod;[24] for by this time I had already digested all the necessary elements in the obligatory paradigms of grammar.

At home, as though starving for knowledge, I diligently studied the eloquence of the tragic stage and the polish of Tully insofar as I was able.[25] But when scarcely a year had gone by, I assumed the responsibility for almost all of the household duties myself. Thus it was my lot to grow old when I was not far from childhood. Even so, I attended lectures on mathematics during the days I had free from toil, and I did not neglect those profitable occasions when, unable to sleep, I devoured the mellifluous-voiced prophets of the Old Testament and figures from the New Testament too. Even then, when I was

21. "Excepit me bracchis strictioribus genetrix": more literally, "she greeted me with overly constricting arms."

22. Cereta makes the point here that her teacher was a woman: "meae praeceptrici" (from *praeceptrix*, the feminine form infrequently found in classical Latin of the masculine noun *praeceptor*). While some translators have assumed that Cereta's "praeceptrici" was merely a figure of speech, her earlier reference to her instruction by a woman to whom she was sent specifically "to be educated" (*erudienda*) makes it difficult to dismiss this early evidence that there were in fact learned women who taught Latin in the mid- to late Quattrocento.

23. Vat. and Ven. read "huic innixus vigor omnis ingenii con[n]ives [Tom. reads "communes"] die noctuque vigilias ultro devovit." The *Oxford Latin Dictionary* [hereafter *OLD*] does not list con[n]ivis, -e, possibly a Ceretan neologism derived from the verb con[n]iveo, translated in *OLD* as "to close the eyes in sleep . . . to blink . . . to wink." So the choice is between "shared vigils" (communes) and "bleary-eyed vigils," (conives). The image conveyed by the second reading, that of the manuscripts, seems to me to be the better reading.

24. Note that Cereta's description of having "entered into a dry diet" (Vat., Ven.: "intraveram mensae [Tom: "mense"] ieiunae") under the auspices of her former teacher ("meae . . . praeceptrici") recalls her original "entrance" (*ingressu*) into the convent. The fennel stalk (*ferula*) was a common term for the rod that teachers used on their pupils: see Juvenal (*Sat.* 1.15).

25. "The eloquence of the tragic stage": an allusion to the ancient playwright Lucius Annaeus Seneca, whose tragedies were popular in the Renaissance; "Tullian polish" refers to Cicero, whose given name were "Marcus Tullius."

only a girl, I saw my father occupy three external magistracies, happy in my studies and full of the pleasure of peace and tranquility.

Then, when the third lustrum of my life was scarcely over, my lot destined me to be—oh sadness—the wife of a merchant whose fate wrapped him with her severe threads within the space of twelve months in a mournful end.[26] Alas, dark day. O heart struck with sorrow and pain deep within, how tearful has this wound been and how wretched has it been for me. Really, under how high a tower of troubles I lie, abandoned and overwhelmed by the burden of a widowhood that grows more bitter each day, has been said enough and more than enough times. One person has said it one way and another differently.

We have soiled our grieving faces enough. Enough has the sickness of a grieving heart afflicted this mournful life. And although no one can escape the ineluctable law of death; although she, the avenger, strikes down even the Gods; and although all things grow old and die, nonetheless it is not wrong to mourn the things we love, nor does the reason for mourning easily leave the heart.

I know: he had lived on the brink of dying, for death—the end of nature—unmakes all things. We are all dust and shadow, but the days of men are unlike one another; unlike are their misfortunes, and unlike their ends. While I have lived, my prayers have come to naught. This life will ever be the nurse of my misery, I believe. But let the injury, forgotten for a short while, be restored to its place in my history—the injury which, because of one man's death, has cruelly and unjustly pried up, lacerated, and dismembered my life, once quiet as though selected in safety.

Surely my husband's spirit now lies among the shades; and now unspeakable marble kisses his limbs. Now that ashy dust sighs in my ears, now one cave awaits me who lives among the living. For the dead, this life is a dream, whose course hangs over all humans like a brief watch in the night. And so, if I thought that it was completely unclear how the events of my life would proceed and in what order, and if you cared about these things, I would describe them more fully and at greater length—if my mind should ever become conscious of itself.[27]

For the time being, I shall give you this letter—insofar as it is that—as a

26. Cereta's husband, Pietro Serina, had a shop in Venice; they had been married for about eighteen months when Serina died, presumably from the plague.

27. The theme of consciousness, awareness of self, introspection (Cereta speaks here of the "mens sui compos") and moral awareness or conscience (*conscientia*)—the knowledge of self that causes one to take responsibility for one's thoughts and actions—is a central theme in her letters.

gift. Now, that I have diligently given you the information about my birth that you asked me for, I await your expressions of forgiveness, for these foster better intentions. I have written this letter with great care so that no concern of my own regarding the disposition of the heavenly host should cause you to be uneasy.

I myself used to enjoy these studies; now because I imitate the first cause, I consider of lesser importance secondary causes, because of their instability. Owing to this, I would prefer to be ignorant rather than to know what the fates have in store for me. In any case, among those who believe in Christ, fate—once linked to the causes of things—now has no meaning. For God is one and the same everlasting and omnipotent being, who moves and rules us in harmony with the arching vault of heaven. Because of this, I myself believe that to investigate God's judgment regarding the future is the mark of foolish curiosity rather than of a heart that is faithful. The quick, fleeting speed of the stars eludes the buried intelligences of human minds, however subtle the genius. I beg you, now that you have tasted the vanity of foolish ignorance, not to long for the certainty of promised events. You will long more reverently for God, who is the just judge of men, and in whom, while you have hope, you will always find succor. On him surely the guiding principle behind every sidereal body and all the orbiting planets depends. He causes the glacial horror of frozen snows to grow warm, the intense heat of the blazing sun to boil, and the moon to move nearer the planets. Nor is he far from the sight and slanting movements of the constellations. He sometimes causes hail to bristle from pregnant clouds, and a great flood of rain to pour down. He strikes this world with his thunderbolts and he calms the stormy, thunderstruck ocean and makes serene its waters. For him the rosy brilliance of the gleaming east spreads its rays. The evening that reddens with the cooling breeze of Zephyr, and dark night, laid to rest at last beneath the earth, applaud him. And so, in the same way, all luminous things alternatively rise and fall, day and night. All things are balanced by the hand of God.

May we follow him and may we imitate him as supplicants. May the trumpet of our heart proclaim his glory to the world with a Davidian psalm. May we sing his praises together, in harmony. May our conscience speak secretly to us, and may we regret that we sometimes walk in the darkness of our error. And let the two of us, who have taken counsel together, place our hope in higher things and in the teachings of the Gospel, so that after his long exile and wandering, Christ, the true son of God, may make open our souls to the nuptial feast of Paradise. For he is the son who has carried aloft in the eternal sanctuary of his salvation the lost souls of our fathers by the blood that he shed for us. November 5, 1486.

II

WRITER/EMBROIDERER INTO HOUSEWIFE

Cereta's letter to Sigismonda de Bucci, her father's friend and colleague, exhibits some of the key themes seen in the previous letter: the obsession with time and the homological relationship between writing and sewing among them.[28] This is the first of several letters suggesting that Cereta regularly acted as her father's surrogate (see letters IX–XVI), because he was suffering either from a debilitating illness or from emotional duress. She has left home to go to her father, hoping to have some time to herself to read and think. Instead she finds herself swamped with paperwork having to do with either her father's patrimony or his own estate. Her brief reference to her feelings of anxiety about her husband is equally vague. She may be alluding to his long absences from home or to his tangled business affairs, about which she complains in other letters, or the remark may simply indicate her general concern for him and their household.

The theme of time, dominant in Cereta's letter to Nazaria Olympica, is elaborated differently in this piece. Time (*tempus*) is a visual and tactile thing in Cereta: it is a room or a space (*spatium*) that awaits filling. The fill may be either *labor*, which refers usually to manual work in Cereta, or *otium*, the intervals in the day that allow for intellectual and artistic activity. While male humanist writers, working on the model of the Roman elegiac poets, enjoy *otium* day and night, the female writer can only experience this aspect of time as contraband: at night and furtively, while the rest of the household sleeps. A woman's day, whether at home or in the convent, is devoted to manual tasks, housekeeping, and the needs of her family.

Cereta develops in this letter her notion of time as a commodity, and indeed a luxury item. Its use is controlled and regulated by the paterfamilias during the daytime hours. It is "spent," like currency, on Cereta's family or her own work, and it is exchanged in return for other goods and services. It counts, however, as "stolen" merchandise when it is taken from the patriarchal treasury in the dead of the night, in the form of all-night binges of reading, writing, or sewing (*vigiliae* or *vigilantiae*). In its form as luxury commodity, as *otium*, it affords islands for study and creativity: "Time is the 'necklace of life,'" writes Cereta; but this time-necklace is not only an adornment; she imagines it in a later letter as a tight chain that constrains the lives of men and women, from birth to death (chapter 4, letter XXXV).

The central portion of the letter is taken up with a long ekphrasis describing in detail, as she did in the previous letter, a piece of needlework she

28. Vat. 11 (fols. 17–18); Ven. 10 (fols. 33v–36); Tom. 2 (pp 12–17); Rabil 29.

herself has designed and finished. Unlike other portrayals of landscapes in the late fifteenth century, deleted from her painting of the world is anything suggesting the human; domestic animals, cultivated fields, human figures, buildings, roads, and paths are all absent from her canvas. The primordial landscape she paints is both nurturant and hostile: while savage animals are portrayed in menacing pairs in the foreground, a verdant countryside studded with shade trees, gentle rivers, olive trees, and grapevines occupies the background of the canvas.

Cereta develops further the homology between sewing and writing, between needlework and narrative, by comparing herself to two famous women in antiquity: Arachne of Colophon, a weaver and teller of tales so brilliantly told in her tapestries that she was said to rival Pallas Athene in her art; and Pamphile of Cos, who was credited in antiquity with the invention of cotton cloth making from plants and silk production from silkworms. These women were geniuses who worked with their hands as well as their minds. In telling Bucci that this letter, which is mostly about the small masterpiece in linen she has created, will be part of a volume of letters she has just finished preparing for publication, she demonstrates palpably, with her ancient models, that a woman can be both a thinker and a spinner, both a historian and an artisan. Her references to Arachne and Pamphile also introduce an argument critical to her thinking about gender and entitlement: that she and other learned women are not exceptional figures among their sex, but belong to a long tradition of gifted women.

To Sigismondo de Bucci, doctor of laws

hough I came down to my father's magistracy so that I could have some leisure time, I still have not had even the time to catch my breath.[29] It's as though I'm being pulled in opposite directions—I'm torn between my desire to help settle my father's affairs and my responsibilities as a wife. The way things are here, opportunity beckons me to stay, but worry tugs at me to return home. And so I am troubled because I want, alternatively, to be in both places.

I have no leisure time for my own writing and studies unless I use the nights as productively as I can.[30] I sleep very little. Time is a terribly scarce commodity for those of us who spend our skills and labor equally on our

---

29. See nn. 7 and 9 on the *otium* theme and the problem of time in Cereta.
30. Again the key word *otium* is used; see nn. 7, 9, 19.

families and our own work.[31] But by staying up all night, I become a thief of time, sequestering a space from the rest of the day, so that after working by lamplight for much of the night, I can go back to work in the morning.[32] My point is that the first shadows of the waning day don't ever deprive me of the time to read and write.

I devote the first hours after dawn, however, to a little piece of linen which I've worked with a needle and thread of different hues.[33] And so, my firm rule of saving the night for forbidden work has allowed me to design a canvas that contains a harmonious composition of colors.[34] The work has taken three months of sleepless nights. But there was none of divine Alchimedon's art in it;[35] and such a loss of time is wasteful when time—the necklace of life—is spent on pointless work.[36] But the demand by women for luxury items and their fascination with the exotic—and neither India with its pearls nor Arabia can satisfy these cravings—has increased to such an extent in our society that there is no end today to the public display of such merchandise. An aversion to moderation is characteristic of women everywhere—and by their own doing. Even if some women avoid a more obvious show of their wealth, others only pretend to live modestly.

But to return to the subject of my work—it is a shawl for a woman, and displayed in the middle of it is a savage leopard with a vast array of spots.[37] A writhing, crested dragon dominates the left side of the shawl, its quivering forked tongue, its fiery eyes, and its painted scales ennobling the creature and suggesting its cruelty. Opposite these beasts, a lion with flowing mane and savage aspect stretches wide its gaping jaws toward the left; it is as though all the creatures on the earth were menacing and growling at one another, one by one. Higher up, an eagle swoops down through the air to attack a hawk; the eagle's wings cast a shadow over the smaller bird, while he, bent backwards, fights back with his beak and talons. Golden Phoebus, high above all, illuminates a silvery, crescent moon with his streaming beams of

---

31. Note the imagery of the commodification of time: *parsimonia, divisum, impensum, furatrix* in the Latin text (respectively: scarcity; parceling out or rationing; spending; thieving).

32. "Sed furatrix horarum vigilantia divisum die toto spatium invenit": literally, "But the all-night vigil, a thief of hours, finds some space to sector off from the whole day." The personification of her night watch as a "thief of time" is Cereta's own.

33. Cf. Cereta's description of her needlework *vigiliae* (night watches) in letter I.

34. Since the words she uses for her tools are generic (*acus*, needle; *tela*, cloth, loom, or canvas; *filum*, thread), it's impossible to know whether she is describing embroidery or needlepoint.

35. She alludes to Virgil, *Eclogue* 3, where the poet describes in lavish detail the elaborate scene the artist Alchimedon had carved on a wooden drinking cup.

36. The riveting image of time as a necklace (which adorns while it constrains) is Cereta's own.

37. Cereta describes her work as a "oblongulus cohoperturae panniculus," literally, "a rather longish piece of cloth for a woman to cover herself with."

light. Beyond the beasts, the lofty face of a mountain with twin peaks rises in the distance, and from it a river flows down in the opposite direction, coursing down through the valley that lies in between. Basketweave stitching encloses the equal areas where the two mountain ridges lie, and joins the two in a curving place between them. Bare overhanging rocks frame the plain on one side, and some of these rocks are piled one over another; from the rugged summit of this promontory, smoke and flames erupt in fiery billows. Meadows blooming with flowers and every herb, on hillock after hillock, clothe the plain on the other side. A wooded glade with shadebearing cover shelters both sides of the mountain, where first edible fruits ripen in their boughs, and then olive trees droop under the gentle burden of their berries. A field surrounds them; and vines are stretched and linked to one another all around, curling upwards and downwards with gracefulness. Among these, the creeping tendrils of the vine contain in their leaves darkening grapes. The farthest bordered extremity rings a certain small amount of space, in which the color purple, growing white in patches with gold runs forward, from one place to another, pierced with pinpricks. Then, from the slanting summit of a tiny spike, a hairlike mane of tangled thread of silver sprouts.

But I cannot include here a lengthy discussion of how the down used to make yarn is knitted together after being stretched thin and twisted. Nor need I mention that the Arabian silkworm is imported for the smooth and consistent quality of its thread. And lest I be said to be the Greek weaver Pamphile resurrected, or Arachne of Colophon,[38] who, when Athene became angered at her talent, challenged the goddess to a contest, I'll talk another time about how hemp must be carded for a long while with a comb with sharp points and how carefully and gently the expensive cloth out of which linen is made must be stretched.

But, ah, these are the meaningless concerns of women. What is it about our desires and our era that has caused us to reject the Oppian law, in which garments embellished with this kind of artfulness were characterized as "wantonly painted," as though those garments might, in, all their proliferation of color—their golds, silver, and blazing purples—run amuck under the

---

38. The lives of both these ancient female inventors and artists of spinning, weaving, and cloth production are in Giovanni Boccasccio's *De claris mulieribus*, chaps. 17, 42: in translation see *Concerning Famous Women*, trans. with an introduction by Guido A. Guarino (New Brunswick, N.J.: Rutgers University Press, 1963). The *De mulieribus* was a formative work for Cereta (and one to which she constantly alludes) as it had been for Christine de Pizan, whose *Cité des dames* was based on the *De mulieribus*; Boccaccio's source for Pamphile (Pliny, *Nat.* 11.26) was certainly well known to Cereta. Another Pamphile (of Epidaurus) who lived in the time of Nero was a scholar and historian of literature whose no longer extant works were summarized in Favorinus (in C. Muller, *Fragmenta Historicorum Graecorum* [1841–70], 3.520).

weight of so much useless erudition.[39] Scipio Africanus castigated Sulpicius Gaulus for this, and Lucius Torquatus denigrated Hortensius as a mere actor for this. But so be it: the decadent manners of this age of ours may well demand such laws.

These then are the things I have made with my own hands before the first rays of the dawning day. This grand volume of epistles, for which the final draft is now being copied out, bears witness, letter by letter, to whatever muses I have managed to muster in the dead of night. I have placed all my hope in my love of literature. Others may cross the seas in pursuit of worldly riches, but I, who am more cowardly, will molder away at home for the sake of a possession that is immortal, with the example of a diligent parent before me. For the possession of virtue fires great minds to pursue the fruits of fame, which are everlasting, though the labor itself is ephemeral.[40] January 1, 1486.

III
HER MOTHER

Cereta's letter to her mother, Veronica di Leno, the only one in the collection, stands out as singular for its period and genre since the figure of the mother remains largely absent from Renaissance humanist letters.[41] This letter—a small memoir of a perfect day she and her mother enjoyed in the countryside some months after Cereta's marriage—is also revealing in relation to other reminiscences of her early childhood in her letters, all of which concern her mother's abandonment of and separation from her.

The letter evokes fantasies of return to a utopian, womblike enclosure very like the imaginary space Julia Kristeva refers to as the *chora*, a place of sensations, sounds, pulsions, and musical rhythms in which mother and infant continue to constitute a unity even after birth.[42] There is in Cereta's valley a similar sense of engulfment; mother and daughter are enclosed in a sheltered valley bounded by mountains. Images of full udders, blooming

39. The *Oppia lex* was a wartime sumptuary law instituted by the tribune Gaius Oppius in 215 B.C.; it forbade women to own more than a half an ounce of gold or to wear multicolored dresses; it was repealed in 195; cf. Livy 33 and 34.1; Cicero, *Orat.;* Tacitus A. 3.33.

40. For the most famous model for the conceit she uses here ("Others may engage in commerce, etc. . . but I," etc.) see Horace, *Carm.* 1.1, which she clearly knew well.

41. Vat. 20 (fols. 20–20v); Ven. (fols. 42–42v); Tom. 11 (pp. 27–28); Rabil 14 (his date: September 5, 1485).

42. On Kristeva's *chora,* see *Desire and Language. A Semiotic Approach to Literature and Art,* trans. Thomas Gora, Alice Jardine, and Leon S. Roudiez (New York: Columbia University Press, 1980), p. 133.

meadows, ears filled with melodies and pleasurable sights and smells convey a sense of utopic plenitude and bliss. Only sensory, nonverbal signs are recalled from their day together: the smell of cattle and wildflowers, the lingering phrases of a child's song, the rhythms of the dance, the feel of deep shade in the copse.

In the middle of the day, as Cereta and her mother approach a garden, they encounter some peasants singing and dancing. Among them is a humpbacked girl who sings songs in which traditional folktales—stories her father told her—are set to the music of the lyre. Cereta's positioning of the story of the crippled female poet at the center of her letter suggests a relationship between herself and the child, between poetry and lack, and between writing and wounding. The connection Cereta makes here between loss and creativity foreshadows her treatment of her own mourning after her husband's death, the theme that dominates and colors the second half of her book. A constant tension is also set up here between the themes of human loss and lack, on the one hand, and the repeated evocations of the bounty of nature, on the other. This letter and its utopic landscape suggest a longing that cannot be fulfilled and a fulfillment—as in the Demeter myth—that can only signify the recurrence of loss.

To Veronica di Leno

The day we spent at the property boundary was so happy that it ought to be commemorated with a special token.[43] We gazed at meadows blooming with flowers and glistening with small stones and winding streams, and we felt full of contentment. Noisy birds were singing in the morning sun and as soon as we got out of the wagon, some rural folk came to meet us, and, garlanded with chains of wicker, they sang songs and made music with oaten pipes and flutes of reed. Some were herding flocks while others pressed milk from the swollen udders of sheep, and now and again the fields resounded with the lowing of approaching cattle.

In the middle of a garden stood a makeshift tent where a humpbacked girl sang, sweetening old tales she learned at her father's knee with her own melodies. And when she made the strings of her lyre answer the rhythms of her song, her fingers beat out harmonies with a Thracian quill. And then that little peasant girl with the dancing feet stepped aside, and a band of dancers

43. On the ancient commemorating of good days with a white pebble and bad days with a black one see the Roman satirists whose work Cereta surely knew well: Persius 2.1; Martial 9.52.5, whose vocabulary Cereta appears to be imitating here.

took her place, whirling and leaping to the pulsing sounds of the tambou-rines and the boxwood pipes.[44]

There was a pleasant grove of white willows, whose leafy boughs offered us coolness, and there was a bower for Idalian Venus, so that the lovely nymphs—the Dryads, the Nyads, and the Napaeae—could enjoy the plea-sures of the shade.[45] For greenness, my dear one, surrounded us on all sides. Thus, with charm and freshness, the sensations aroused by the land filled our citybred minds. It would have filled them still more elegantly, though, if you had come during the time of the Saturnalia, when your presence was re-quested and sought so many times.[46] September 5, 1485.

IV–V
IN PURSUIT OF FAME

IV
A PROLOGUE

Cardinal Ascanio Maria Sforza, son of Duke Francesco Sforza and Duchess Maria Bianca Visconti of Milan, was born into one of the most powerful fami-lies in fifteenth-century Italy.[47] A cardinal under three successive popes (Sixtus IV, Alexander VI, and Julius II) and a brother of the reigning duke of Milan in 1488, when this letter was probably written, Ascanio seemed an ideal patron for Cereta or any serious writer. Positioning her two letters to him at either end of her book, as the prologue and epilogue to the collection, Cereta follows the humanist tradition of dedicating a book of her personal correspondence to a well-known patron of the arts.

Cereta's letter to Ascanio contains more information than most others about her early development as both a humanist and a maverick woman writer, and consequently the letter displays themes that are commonplaces in humanist letters as well as ones in which she consciously marks her work as antihumanist, "female," and "other." The stock (male) humanist themes in this

44. Cereta represents the local inhabitants in terms that make it very clear that they are of a very different social class from her own: above, she calls the local inhabitants who meet them "agrestes" (rustics, rural folk); the little girl singer she calls "plebeculae" (little plebeian girl, little girl of the lower classes).

45. The wood nymphs, water nymphs, and dell nymphs, respectively; the nymphs in Greek and Roman mythology from Hesiod to Virgil are minor female deities who personify aspects of na-ture such as rivers, mountains, trees, etc.

46. The Saturnalia, a Roman religious fesival usually celebrated around the 16th, 17th, or 18th of December; so Cereta may be referring to the previous Christmas. The Roman Saturnalia re-sembled not Christmas but the pre-Lenten bacchanalia still celebrated in many Roman Catholic countries, known variously as Mardi Gras, Fasching, or Carnival.

47. Vat. 1 (fols. 1–4); Ven. (missing); Tom. (Prologus, pp. 1–10); Rabil 84.

letter include the following: her alternation between self-abasement and self-promotion; her insistence that her rhetorical showpieces are ordinary letters written in everyday speech; her depiction of her pursuit of learning as a journey; her complaints about the envy of rival scholars; and her flowery praise of the patron whose protection she seeks.

The dominant theme in this letter is the importance of Cereta's *ingenium*—the humanist term for an individual's inborn gifts and talents—in her intellectual formation as a scholar and writer. Since Cereta argues throughout her book of letters that she is not an exception but the exemplification of what women are capable of, her foregrounding of *ingenium* here in the prologue functions as a means to refute male humanists' claims of women's "natural" inferiority to men, both physically and intellectually.

The other group of themes with which Cereta represents herself as female and other are those that emphasize not only her status as an outsider but her anomalousness among male scholars: her exclusion from the "forum and senate" of (male) literati; her fear of being labeled a "crazy woman" and thus dismissed as an intellectual; and her concern over the rejection of some of her best work. Using animal imagery, she articulates her feelings that as a woman she belongs to a race different form that of men: she is a "small chattering woodpecker among poetic swans"; and she is a "little lamb among wolves." She also writes about her body in ways that male humanists never do: she worries about blushing, talks about her physical exhaustion from having to doing her writing in the middle of the night, describes her body as shaking from fear, and compares the pleasures of reading to eating.

To Cardinal Ascanio Maria Sforza

Though I was untrained and scarcely exposed to literature, through my own intelligence and natural talents I was able to acquire the beginnings of an education. While my pleasure in embarking on such a journey of the mind and my love of study were strong at the outset, the weak seeds of my small talent have grown to such a degree that I have written speeches for public occasions, and these I embellished grandly, painting pictures with words in order to influence people and stimulate their minds.[48] My love of reading caused me to sample different kinds of subjects, and only in study did I feel a sense of inner contentment. And, although I remained ill-

48. Cereta's theme *ingenium* (mind, native intelligence, nature, talent, genius) is an important one in her self-fashioning; her use of this image always underscores her natural gifts and her intellectual and artistic independence from her father, brothers, and would-be tutors. All her achievements have come from her own *ingenium*—however "tiny a seedling" it was in the beginning.

equipped for the task despite my passion for learning, I reached a decision that awakened in me a desire for fame and honor, as though my mind were challenging itself to scale new heights.[49]

As my eagerness for knowledge grew, so did the capacity of my mind, and in the course of this growth, the fruitfulness and the fertility of my pen caused me to prefer philosophy over all other studies, just as fruit would have given me more pleasure than leaves.[50] (But here a blush of modesty would expose the fact that I am only writing with such painstaking elegance—and taking so much time to do so—to beguile a patron!)[51]

To get back to my story then, at the end of my childhood, when I was approaching adolescence and was becoming more mature in my understanding of literature, a nobler thought came to me. Accordingly, I devoted myself to other kinds of books, giving myself over to insomniac nights and study, like someone who has a passion for mathematics. If my intellect did not reveal to me the things I longed for at that time, at least I had been allowed to cross the fourfold threshold to knowledge.

Still, this was not the home of happiness or pleasure that I sought, though it was adorned with a beautiful understanding of things.[52] For I was ignorant of the causes that would lead me to virtue; moreover, too great a diversity of studies disturbed my natural abilities.[53] Yet the decision I had made remained more firmly entrenched than before, and I was more unwaveringly committed than ever to proceeding with the study of sacred literature so that I might see if such writings had more nobility in them. This inward-looking path to knowledge played so important a role in my life that I devoted whole nights to this study without stopping to rest, and all other desire for relaxation eluded me like a thief and vanished.[54] For truly, there is a simpler truth in sacred literature that is useful both in its infinite subtlety and

49. Note the Cereta's articulation of the most *de rigueur* of humanist topoi here: the striving for honor and recognition among one's peers despite one's self-avowed intellectual shortcomings. See nn. 6, 8.

50. Since *stilus* (Cereta's pen) can be either a writing implement or the stem of an (edible) plant, the metaphor of eating is appropriate.

51. The word Cereta uses in this passage for "patron": is the generic term, *emptor*, "buyer."

52. The word "domus" (one's home or final destination) evokes Cereta's opening metaphor of the journey to knowledge; "beatae voluptatis" (literally, blessed pleasure) is a loaded pairing since *voluptas* (spiritual pleasure in Lucretius and later in Cicero) is such a key term for the Epicureans and *beatitudo* (happiness or blessedness) suggests in later Latin philosophical and religious texts a profound contentment of the spirit.

53. Again Cereta uses the term *ingenia* to refer to her natural intellectual and artistic endowments.

54. It's interesting that Cereta associates her nocturnal study of even sacred literature with "thievish" or subversive activity ("relaxamenti omnis alia respiratio subduxerit se . . . ab animo furtim"), as she did in letters I and II.

the pleasure it conveys through its beauty. On the road I have taken, I have found contentment in contemplation.

Now that I have availed myself of the counsel of religious texts, wherein writings about morality combine profundity with utility, I have found satisfaction in literature that would give me not smoke and darkness but something perfect, secure, and lasting. Since men receive an education in literature and other studies, however, so that they may benefit from the example of their forebears, the most elect men of diverse orders have said publicly that education has been wasted on me because it has benefited only me and not others.

I am happy to have the opportunity to express my opinion about something that may exonerate me from criticism. I preferred to please the crowd rather than myself. Stimulated by the desire for fame, I was drawn into a prodigious error in the course of my writing. Namely, the first thing I wrote was a funeral oration composed to be read over the corpse of a donkey.[55] This one humble oration stirred up the envy of a number of men, who cruelly sharpened the teeth of their spite against me, and as though their mouths had been swords, I was left trembling like a lamb among wolves. Full of their mockery of me, these men did not hesitate to dishonor me with their spittle, while I was hard-pressed by my wounds.

For a long time I bore all these attacks patiently in order that no one would be able to accuse me of writing about the consolation of philosophy while I indulged the whims of an unstable mind: thus a stern excellence of mind taught me to disdain those slanderers so that threats would not seem to be vying with counterthreats as though in a sword fight, or mutual blows parrying with one another.[56] For a self-restraint that is free from earthly passion will triumph in its own simplicity: patience, not turbulence, ought to be exhibited in the face of our troubles. Otherwise, our lives could constantly be wasted in vendettas. For even if injury can indeed be bought, vengeance should still not be sold.[57]

But since I became justifiably concerned about protecting my reputation, I could not imagine myself being worth so little that I would not respond in writing—whether I was provoked once or many times. And when I

---

55. See chapter 6 for a translation and critical analysis of Cereta's dialogue on the death of an ass, contained in both the Vatican and Venice manuscripts though not in the Tomasini edition. The dialogue raised hackles even after Cereta's death.

56. Cereta is concerned, as no male humanist would be, not to appear too angry and thus to run the risk of being dismissed as a "crazy woman" or "hysteric." Note in the second part of this sentence Cereta's unusually confident self-appraisal of her intelligence.

57. Note here the imagery of commerce and business: to "buy injury" and "sell vengeance" are typical coordinates in the humanists' language games involving getting and giving.

had written back, soon a great crowd of harassers wrote to me. I responded at greater length, and more eloquently than I would have believed. Nonetheless, after persevering for days, during which time a great deal of costly labor was wasted, I managed to extract from the business of writing to those men some residue at least that was suited to my work; for that which is bought at the cost of time is too costly. And so my epistolary commerce grew in both ways.

There is, however, one humble style that can give pleasure in all letters: this style should not astonish, even if it is adorned with very few, though living, colors. For what profit can there be in a brilliant oration framed by curving vine tendrils entwined with an elaborate foliage of words? Those works which cannot be dismissed as lacking in restraint are always better considered in a class of their own, and certainly educated readers respect a modestly written oration more than one that is not so: superfluous effort is exerted for superfluous elegance.

No one should expect me to possess a rarefied way of speaking that has come down to me from the age of Phoenix.[58] This native literature of ours will be enough for everyone, though here no Greek Amphion has ever burst into harmonious song, and no Demosthenes, no Theophrastus have made speeches; nor do these pages of mine, which are illuminated with pictures, represent Aesop as more esteemed than Virgil.[59] From all the maxims of antiquity, my mind distills figures that are alive and fresh.[60] Because of this, I may not express the opinion that the vulture is a more noble creature than the silvery little sparrow. For virtue does not inhabit the first living seeds of things—but what precious thing in the ancient maxims could be more precious than virtue?

And so I, who have hardly acquired even the first rudiments of learning, am a small chattering woodpecker among poetic swans. Each person should display her own particular gifts for study. For no one is safe who strives beyond her abilities; and thus it is safer to trust in reason than in men's opinions. The road to fame that is everlasting runs along the precipices and is difficult and narrow. I can boast, I admit, about the intellectual gifts the omnipotent lord has given me since rare is the girl in any age who writes books with

58. From Petrarch to Filelfo and Poliziano, it is a humanist commonplace to claim that one's collected correspondence (prepared for publication) is written in the style of ordinary everyday speech.

59. Amphion was a mythological harp player of such skill that he could move stones; Theophrastus and Demosthenes were fourth century B.C. Greek writers and masters of rhetoric.

60. Cereta's emphasis is on the live, fresh quality of her own rhetoric.

painstaking grace and brilliance.[61] I have spent on the liberal arts whatever the river of time has allotted me; yet all my strength of mind has composed only these few cold and lifeless letters with a short and inadequate pen.

Because my deficiencies as a writer have caused me to be fearful, I did not dare to trust myself to the criticism of readers without your consent. Your protection and kindness towards all men, however, have persuaded me to aspire to better things. Reason, supported by live evidence, urges me to take heart, since all those who rely on your support reach the goal they hoped for, aided above and beyond their due. I know you will take care for my safety, for you are accustomed to aiding those who are afflicted, with compassion and even when your assistance is not sought. Your piety does not wait for the requests of those who are in pain, and it causes you to help your friends before your pardon them.

I should beware more how I walk among the brambles and thorns. Those who are experienced know how much envy, which is full of nettles, burns the bare feet. Nor does envy ignore the learned, many of whom are writers, unprotected by a patron, who are barred from the senate and the meeting places of the most upright men. Odium makes a shambles of everything. The harm done by distorted interpretation besmirches everything. And although truth is the final judge in all matters, envy, the censurer of all men, bites even this judge. Envy, furtive and anxious, like a thief in hiding, ransacks letters and books until she catches the scent of an enemy.

Now that I have finally explained the purpose of my little work to you, who are the other general of the church militant and its firmest bastion, I beg and supplicate your majesty to allow me, a writer, to serve you as your protegée.[62] For, insofar as it befits my lowly station, in hopes of your favor—my father, lord, and judge—I have put myself in your charge. For if you, being human, are not a god, still you have risen to a place worthy of a god because of your virtue: so widely renowned is your name among peoples everywhere and so wholly do the faithful in Rome turn to you in religious awe.

The superb constancy of your faith and your mind, which is ruled by the most just laws, has rendered inviolate your most excellent office. For you have taken up the apostolic insignia of Peter, the fisherman, and you have governed the cities as a holy man should, with clemency and civility, like a peaceful shepherd whom both military kudos and civil authority have made

61. Instances of Cereta's boasting are much less frequent than those of self-denigration in her letters.

62. Cereta's request to be admitted into the Cardinal's stable of clients is so clearly couched in the terms of patronage and protection; she asks the Cardinal to allow "her writings" to enter into a role appropriate for a protegée: "Mea scripta in partes tutelares admittas."

eminent. You have most excellently executed your duties, and you appraise all events with the measuring rod of reason, while you look with great fore-sight toward the future. And with a firm yet generous mind, how often you have engaged in victorious battle with fortune on your side.

The fame of your extraordinary magnanimity, so forgiving of wrongs, will be handed down to posterity. All men come to you with entreaties and beg for your counsel, as though they were consulting a living oracle or one believed to be a divine authority. Your radiant virtue is worthy of Augustus, who won the love, esteem, and loyal service of both the fathers of the city and the plebs, so much so that the golden age breathes quietly and gently beneath your silver sceptre.[63] You foster the maintenance of peace in your holy consistory with a treaty between brothers. You deflect the ancient ha-tred of kings from the storm winds of war and bend them towards the blessed peace of concord. And you, sage and diligent governor of the empire, recoup for Rome, with the help of providence, whatever the embattled church lost in war.

And with all the honors of the ancients and your great magnanimity, you hold in awe those who would gladly endure all the good fortune and every disaster that came their way following your example, or those who, should it be necessary, would lay down their lives to save you from death or exile. On account of this, I, your servant, have liberated my study from all this in order to devote myself to your glory—not for the purpose of embellishing a throne as famous as yours with my small glory—but to be a participant in that glory myself, which would be the greatest honor. For just as the Par-thians paid homage to their kings with gifts, so the Latins do the same by dedicating the fruits of their work to their Atticuses and Maecenases, so as therein to make them famous.

While the former is not mine to do and while I have acquired too little of the world's learning, still the obligation rests with me now to commit to memory the things that have been entrusted to me, if polished eloquence can untangle the complicated impediments of language. As long as I am deserv-ing of these things, you will not be dishonored in any way, most clement of all men. I hope to offer a supplement to this great penury, this work, barren of words and rich ornament. Therefore this your little book, on which I have spent sleepless nights and long labors, although it is sterile in itself, will grow nonetheless more fertile in your hands. It will germinate, bear fruit, and flow

63. The rule of Augustus was referred to as the "golden age"; similarly, Rome under the humanist popes would come to be called the second golden age. Cereta's image of gold seeming actually to breathe is indebted to Virgil's image in *Aeneid* 6 of sculptors working proleptically in "breath-ing bronze" (847).

with juices. For who would not live secure from every slander if he entrusted himself to the integrity of a man who regards all things with the objectivity of an excellent mind, and who sees all and knows all things? Both future generations and men of the current age will know you as a man most highly educated in the whole of literature, and they will sing this torn invention of mine which will exalt and venerate your memory honorably and for a long time to come. March 1488.

V
AN EPILOGUE

Like the prologue, Cereta's epilogue, addressed again to Ascanio Maria Sforza, foregrounds both her resemblance to and difference from other humanists.[64] In a move absolutely stock in humanist letters, she proposes a trade: she will immortalize the cardinal through her published writings about his life in return for his patronage and public sponsorship of her work. But unlike her male colleagues, she makes a point of her gender: she is only a girl, she confesses, and she blushes like one. Also unlike the typical humanist in search of a patron, Cereta promotes the strangeness of her style and her lack of conventional training. Instead of humanist eloquence, it is her strangeness—her "viriditas" (greenness)—that imbues her work with a power and lushness that will ensure its recognition and acclaim at some future time. While the typical humanist of the period might boast that his work is superior to Virgil and Cicero, Cereta denies all connection to the famous writers of antiquity. She disavows having either imitated or borrowed themes from their work. Instead, she depicts herself as shrinking back in fear from the Latin language and doing violence to it.

She suggests that because her writing is foreign, uncultivated, and wild, it ought to be traded for other exotic imports. Nude of ornament (*nuda*), her work may appeal, if not to Italians, to savage tribes who themselves go naked or cover their bodies only with war paint. The prominence in the epilogue, as elsewhere in her letters, of agricultural metaphors is also unusual in the context of humanist letters: her references to her literary offering to the cardinal as the crops from her field (*primitiae*) and her critical assessment of her own writing in terms of its (lack of) ripeness (*cruditas, viriditas*) make clear, in an unusual way, her location outside the city and far from the *res publica litterarum*.

64. Vat. 83 (fols. 72v–73); Ven. 74 (fols. 153–54v); Tom. 72 (pp 227–30); Rabil 83.

To Cardinal Ascanio Maria Sforza

*Y*ou, who have been so very kind, will now receive the first fruits of my immature and intemperate pen, which I once was rash enough to promise you from the safe distance of a letter.[65] But then, you are accustomed to examining not the gifts but the minds of your donors, though you are deserving of a greater gift than this.

I delayed in sending my gift; I did not forget. But my face was so red with shame which came from deep in my heart that at first I was afraid to send it.[66] I worried that the lengthiness of my letters would be repugnant both to read and to address, and that the shabbiness of my style would disgrace my work and, really, me, since I am one who shrinks back in fear of the Latin language. While my mind, uncertain in its deliberations, vacillated between different solutions, it grasped at the following remedy for shame: the hope of your pardon, of which I was assured, since you refuse neither the simplicity of those who are ignorant nor the sins of those who err by choice. And so I, in my innocence, have dared to send you these letters, though they are bare of every ornament and are informed by neither any erudition nor literary polish at all.

The vigilance of a mind greater than mine will, I hope, give me fresh inspiration, once I learn your opinion of my work, which has—owing to my youth—been so often spared the interrogations and imprecations of the wise. Nor have I stolen material from other writers—even that which is worthy of the famous ones. A simpler road awaits me—the road to lofty doctrine—and the light of my increasing ardor, so very near, will raise me up. Only the precedent of your approval remains for me in my journey; for with your public sanction even things that are utterly bare may be clothed. But when I am better armored, I will not be afraid. And even if people from the envious plebs should stare at me, giving each other quizzical looks, I would dare—feeling secure even amid their noisy mockery—to send this book across the ocean to distant nations around the world.

No wonder. For the rugged Cyclades, prophetic Delos, fierce Crete, and faraway Thule have now awaited this book of mine long enough.[67] With

---

65. The "first fruits" (*primitiae*) is an agricultural term referring to the first crops harvested in a season, which were offered in Roman times to a deity: Virgil, *Aen.* 11.156; Statius, *Theb.* 6.146; Apuleius, *Met.* 10.29. The adjective she uses to describe her pen is *rudis* (crude, raw, or unripe as with fruit), which expands on her agricultural theme.

66. "Suffudit adeo ex alto corde rubor ora pudentia": Cereta's explicitness about her bodily reactions violates the norm in humanist letters, where the body and its functions are barred from the premises of the text.

67. What follows is a standard list of peoples around the world—Greeks, Africans, Central

you as my patron, the wandering Numidians, the fierce Hyrcanians, the Scythians with their painted bodies, and naked Garamantes will soon request my book. Both Mede and Arab will send me the incense from their forests. The Tagians and Hermians will offer me gold from their shores; the Mauritians will present me with their monkeys; the Ethiopians, their rhinoceros and cinnamon; the Orient and the North, their gems, and Judaea will send a tribute of rich balsam. Such is the fame of your wisdom in every nation, such the glory of your works, and so great the majesty of your name and authority. The excellence of your mind and your erudition, worthy of the Athenian Stoa, is astounding. Through your lips, Socrates and Plato utter their oracles and the virginal Muses of the Helicon speak, making themselves known to us even without thunderbolts.

Therefore, this book of ours will reach the world's peoples so enhanced by your glory and so graced by your wit that no earthly honors, prizes, or riches will elude it. Truly, even if I, a girl still unknown, should not yet have either tasted the honey of Mt. Hymettus or possessed Polycrates' ring, Pyrrhus's agate, Nero's emerald, or the pearls brought from India and Persia,[68] which I would give you as my gifts, still, in return for whatever kindness I might receive, I would bring forth small (though I hope adequate) gifts from the secret places of my mind—a greater discovery, which, under your auspices, will cause new amazement to draw many people throughout the world to the greenness of my glory for centuries to come.[69] February 28, 1488.

VI
HER CIVIC PERSONA

Cereta's letter to the Venetian patrician and humanist Paolo Zane is almost an antipatronage letter.[70] As a key piece in the mosaic of Cereta's self-portrait, it offers an antidote to her cloyingly sweet letters to her wished-for patron, the cardinal, and shows a different side of her personality. In this let-

---

Asians, and Middle Easterners—that would have been familiar to any humanist reader of Herodotus, Pliny the Elder, or Cicero.

68. Cereta refers to legendary jewels that were associated with the kings of Samos and Epirus (Polycrates and Pyrrhus respectively) and the emperor Nero: see Pliny, *Nat.* 37.3–5; 37.62.

69. The image *viriditas* which I've translated as "greenness" is hard to render in a single word; in Latin it captures the essence of Cereta's claims for herself—her freshness, immaturity, greenness, rawness, luxuriance, vividness, a taste perhaps still too tart, etc.; this quality *is* her drawing card. The phrase "from the secret places of my mind" conjures up not only an exotic geography but secret treasures that will match any foreign traders' finds.

70. Vat. 2 (fols. 4–5); Ven. 2 (fols. 25–27); missing from Tom.; Rabil 19. The text of this letter has been published in Agostino Zanelli, "Laura Cereta al Vescovo Zane," *Brixia Sacra,* XIV, 1923, pp. 173–78.

ter to Paolo, who succeeded his uncle Lorenzo Zane as the bishop of Brescia, Cereta proffers not praise but outrage at the way he has conducted his office, since ultimately the responsibility for the maintenance of the cathedral in Brescia is his.[71] She shows that she is a woman writer not merely worthy of a socially prominent cardinal's support, but also one courageous enough to launch a public attack on a man who is both a public figure in Brescia and a papal appointee. Since Zane appears, however, more to represent the Venetian patriarchy than he does the Roman church, Cereta's criticism of his neglect of the cathedral may be simply a bid for popularity among her fellow Brescians.

To Paolo Zane, bishop of Brescia

*T*he Roman Catholic Church possesses a decree concerning the worship and relics of the saints which was formally sanctioned by the celebrated consistory of the Church. How well our ancestors observed this decree is shown by their preservation of the tablets of the commandments, the chest holding the scriptures, and the figure of the serpent of Moses. In Rome, in fact, various images are displayed at various entrances to the city's churches that foreign pilgrims have venerated and treated as their own. Veronica's hankerchief, in which the shadowy outlines of the face of Christ can be seen, bears witness to this.[72] The crowded shrine to the virgin mother in Rome, whose threshold no woman may cross since it is among the holiest of the holies, is further proof of this veneration.

It is no wonder that our countrymen had the names of local deities in their official tablets—men they revered no less in death than life; the men of Athens, impious in their errors, worshiped images of Apollo which were engraved in living bronze.[73] The Roman fathers also kept ancient relics from the Greeks, a statue of Jupiter the thunderer, one of the mother of the Gods, and the Sibylline books on the Capitolium and treated them with the highest respect;[74] for there the ever wakeful Vestal virgins guard the living flame of

---

71. On Paolo Zane (1460–1531), elected bishop of Brescia in 1480, see *Storia di Brescia: II, La dominazione Veneta (1426–1575)*, ed. Giovanni Reccani degli Alfieri, (Brescia: Morcelliana, 1961), pp. 418–20; Rabil, *Laura Cereta*, pp. 61–62. On Lorenzo Zane and other members of the Zane family in Venice see Margaret King, *Venetian Humanism in an Age of Patrician Dominance* (Princeton: Princeton University Press, 1986), pp. 446–47.

72. St. Veronica was a woman of Jerusalem who wiped the brow of Christ as he carried the cross to Calvary.

73. On the image "living bronze" (*spirantia aera*) see n. 63.

74. The Capitoline Hill (Capitolium), one of Rome's seven hills, was the city's religious center

Vesta's shrine and tend their perpetual watchfires.[75] In Macedonia, however, it was the fragrant perfume of Darius that Alexander conserved in a box covered with gold and jewels and protected with a guard.[76]

Many poets sing of the golden fleece at Colchis and the apples gleaming with gold in the garden of the Hesperides at the palace of the daughters of Atlas, which was guarded by a scaly dragon.[77] In more recent times, while the venerable Saracens a thousand miles away, rumor has it, did not stand guard over Mohammed's tomb, Severus Alexander, when he became emperor of Rome, ordered the statues of Virgil and Cicero to be placed in a shrine under guard.[78] We know that the Spanish, among their religious donations, memorialized the imperial head of Julius Caesar at Cadiz with a marble bust. Yet still more devout, the Christians honor, venerate, and preserve the wood of Christ's cross, his thorns and nails in sacred reliquaries. Now churches everywhere are renowned because they contain the bones of the martyrs and apostles and the bodies of the innocents.

God alone—the omnipotent, the god of such great majesty, the king of men—is not considered as important by the priests of the law as are the inane superstitious of the pagans I have described; nor is he thought even as important as the inanimate gold and silver kept in a foundry where coins are struck.[79] Consider for example the treasury of the Venetians; your eminence knows with what guards, what grand surrounding wall, what great iron works, how many locks and bolts, and with what a mighty gateway it has customarily been protected. But let rest in peace those things that are held to be of such great value.

Who is so crazy or so wasteful of money that he would leave his cash or clothes or pearls lying around in a public place? Look at how our church,

in antiquity and on it the Romans built temples to Jupiter and Juno. The legendary Sibylline books contained prophecies purportedly written by the Roman seer Sibylla.

75. Six female virgins between the ages of six and ten were chosen, each of them serving for five years, to tend the sacred fire of Vesta, goddess of the hearth.

76. Darius III (380–330 B.C.), an Achaemenid king of Persia, was defeated by Alexander the Great in 330.

77. Cereta refers to perhaps the most famous thefts of gold in Greek mythology, both involving the slaying of a dragon by the hero: Jason's theft of the golden fleece at Colchis, which was the goal of the Argonauts' expedition, and Heracles' theft of the golden apples from the garden of the Hesperides, which was one of his twelve labors.

78. Note how Cereta unfavorably compares the impiety of the Saracens, nomadic peoples from the east, with the piety of the "civilized" peoples of the west. Marcus Aurelius Severus Alexander was emperor of Rome 222–35 A.D.

79. "Sub flatura signatae pecuniae": the noun *flatura* (foundry, mint) is hardly found in classical Latin except in Cereta's favorite author, the encyclopaedist Pliny, *Nat.* 7.197.

which is half in ruins, languishes under a crumbling roof. No one need call out the guard, for none was commissioned; no one knows that this place is a shrine. No one batters on doors already open, for the entrances lie free and accessible to one and all. The host is protected by no bolt, no barrier, and never by any lock. Today when the holy relics were brought forth from their small hiding place, they cried out: "We pardon you, ungrateful believers. But God does not pardon you, since you take up the son from such a lowly and undeserved place: the son, coeternal with the father, whose flesh and blood any thieving, irreligious member of the human race can steal, sell, violate, and trample. Thus the most divine body of the son of God is now left at the disposal of everyone; thus the sacred preparations of the altar, where the services for the dead are sanctified through expiation, are now the property of magicians and night-wandering stages."

Although these may not be suitable professions for an unlearned girl who for the most part agrees with what the popes' decrees have sanctified, still her mind does not accede to the notion that the great only-born son of the virgin of Judaea should be left in an open shrine both night and day, freely accessible to the impious. However, if my audacious criticisms are in any way untrue, I beg you, most perfect and honorable proconsul and one most learned in all law, to decide either what I should think on this subject or what I, your little daughter in Christ, should unlearn. September 22, 1485.

VII–VIII
GENEALOGY

VII

In this letter to her maternal uncle, Lodovico di Leno, Cereta presents the Leno claims to a noble lineage in a somewhat facetious light, linking her vocation as an amateur astronomer and scholar to her supposed descent on her mother's side from either of two mythological characters, Atlas or Endymion.[80] Especially interesting in this autobiographical letter, and unlike anything in the memoirs of her male humanist contemporaries, are Cereta's purely sensual recollections of her education. Her intellectual awakening is remembered as a fiery fluttering inside her body. In recalling her schooling, she compares her feelings to those of peasants trampling grapes with their bare feet to make wine. Yet, in the end, it is ambition alone that drives her. To be judged a successful writer by the Brescian literati is an overridingly impor-

80. Vat. 14 (fols. 18v–19); Ven. 13 (37v–38); Tom. 5 (pp. 19–21). Rabil 2.

tant goal for Cereta and one that, for the most part, she feels she has received, though immortality in the eyes of posterity is her ultimate goal.

To her uncle, Lodovico di Leno

My earliest ancestor on my mother's side was either Endymion or Atlas, of whom the former—so say the poets—was madly in love with Luna, while the latter carried the stars on his shoulders. Whichever of the two he was, the result is the same, since each one of them is considered remarkable for his knowledge of and relationship with the stars. What is more, the escutcheoned coat of arms in your house, in which a man's head is displayed with a star and the moon, adds honor to your lineage.

This was the live spark that first set my mind afire with a burning desire to know the courses of the heavens and the spheres of the planets. This fire was like a sense of purpose that stood over me sentinel-like in the night.[81] This being my guide, my schooling first opened up new doors to me so that I could trample the leisure I had reaped.[82] Nor should you think that, in return for such sweet labor, I promised myself the rewards for literary studies of an Augustus or a Maecenas.[83] I knew well what greedy desire, that torturer of kings, would bring. I took on all this work myself so that the name of Laura, so wondrously celebrated by Petrarch, might be preserved in a second and quite new immortality—in me.[84]

However, at this point I believe that public acclaim has built a solid enough foundation for my immortality, and in this way an initial reservoir for my glory has been established: I, for example, who was a young girl to the wonderment and perturbation of everyone until now, may perhaps emerge as an exceptional woman. Indeed, the glitter of eloquence, which feeds the hunger and dryness located deep within discordant lips, is faint. Nonetheless, some attention still is paid to the acquiring of mental powers and the most penetrating minds are seasoned with the fiery food of virtue. A public

81. For precedents for Cereta's night watchman metaphor see Cicero, *Phil.* 7.20.

82. "Quo duce and calcandum pedibus ocium primos schola mihi fores aperuit" (Tom.: "aperiunt"): this striking Ceretan figure alludes to the rural custom of the trampling of newly harvested grapes with the bare feet to make wine, recalling Cereta's description of how the peasants tread the grapes at her friend's farm in the letter that immediately precedes this one (Vat. 13, Ven. 12, Tom. 4).

83. The names Maecenas and Augustus, the patrons of Horace and Virgil, are almost metonymic for literary patronage.

84. Cereta's concern that she be publicly recognized and acclaimed is certainly one of the major themes in her letters.

acknowledgment of one's fame is, in the order of things, quite important. But it is for the mind to struggle, so that with an effort equal to its reputation, it will measure the courses of those stars dispersed by Atlas and Endymion throughout the eternal convexity of heaven. July 16, 1485.

VIII

Cereta's letter to her maternal cousin Bernardino di Leno is autobiographical in two ways.[85] It reiterates the family's pretensions to nobility on her mother's side. Her uncle Lodovico di Leno has written to her about the antiquity of the Leno name and has described a fresco in his house displaying the family coat of arms: the foreground of the shield contains a man's head, while in the background, the portals of a temple and a sculpture of three lions can be seen, one of them being bitten by a serpent. Cereta's implication is that she, like her leonine ancestors, is a noble warrior locked in combat with opponents who are unworthy of her. The letter also represents a rare moment, when she writes candidly of her determination to win recognition as an important writer whose works will be read not only by future generations but by men and women of other cultures.

To her cousin, Bernardino di Leno

*M*y letter to Uncle Lodovico—in whose house a face painted on the wall between a fixed star and a wandering one adds to the family's ancestral grandeur—was apparently adequate.[86] Now tangible proof will ennoble the origins of our family name: a marble inscription indicates that "Leno" originally came from "lion-born."[87] Even now, two lions can still be seen, portrayed at full-length.[88] Standing erect, they support the en-

---

85. Vat. 41 (fols. 30–30v); Ven. 36 (fols. 59v–60); Tom. 34 (pp. 72–74); Rabil 33.

86. The parenthetical relative clause "Lodovicum, unde nam splendor avitus pictum parieti vultum inter fixam atque erraticam stellam acquisiit" (literally, Lodovico, from whom our ancestral splendor acquired the face painted on the wall . . .) is deliberately vague without her letter to Lodovico (letter VII above), which explains the connection between him, the painted face, and the "family splendor."

87. "Ab leonibus": in this second paragraph Cereta intimates that she has recently received from her uncle Lodovico the detailed description of the painting in the family crest she spoke of in her letter to Lodovico (letter VII).

88. "Vel longo prospectu visuntur": note the painterly language here; otherwise we would have no clue other than the context of letter VII that her ekphrasis describes a wall painting, which I presume is part of the crest Cereta referred to earlier.

tranceway to a temple with a column-bearing arch, their manes flowing over their shoulders and their mouths open as if to sniff the sky.[89] In a more prominent position and obviously roaring, an equally large third lion sits on the temple roof. The savagery of each one of these animals is terrible to see, but worst of all to behold is the lion around whose legs a writhing, hissing serpent coils. Whatever ignoble aspect of these beasts this work portrays, its antiquity assures its imperviousness to criticism. It is after all a monument worthy of royal expense. So defined, the temple is royal, the street is royal, and of course your family is royal because it has discovered its origins in the king of the beasts.[90]

And so, because my mother bore me to be a sister to you, my heart chafes and swells with a burning desire for fame; in this way my noble hopes of becoming an exemplum for posterity are fed. Since the Amazons' name is now extinct, and those women who bore arms have returned their weapons and bows to the temple of Bellona, I have completely transferred my passion for feminine things to the love of literature.[91] And this love has caused the rigor and acuity of my erudition (what little I may have) to thrive and grow, as though nourished by a milky breast and as if my journey to glory could not be ensured in any other way—even though I was only a delicate and vulnerable young girl up to that point and at a child's stage of learning. But as I began to mature, greater interest in learning also grew in me, and little by little it became so important to me that the desire for learning and cultivation left me thirsting for more. For certainly the work of study comes very easily to minds naturally suited to it. I spent seven years so that I would be able to purchase this priceless dowry for myself, for who would not go into debt to buy this most luxurious jewel?

Time is not something that belongs to us; it depends instead on the nature of the sun's journey. Thus, after the fruits of my study ripened and the golden grain fell from the stalk, I began to gather the harvest with my rustic pen, so that it could safely and quickly be transported to faraway peoples of the world. And although this ordinary knowledge that I have (whatever it is) may amount to nothing since I have not yet mastered, for example, the more obscure and knotty examples, still, I shall write an elegant enough work about the things that I do know. And, with you as my judge, this work can

89. See Pliny, *Nat.* 18.364, for this strange expression "olfactare caelum," in which cows are "sniffing the sky."
90. "Regium igitur templum . . .": this must refer to the cityscape portrayed in the wall painting.
91. Just as Boccaccio's Amazons in *De claris mulieribus,* a text Cereta often cites, traded in their feminine cloth making utensils for arms, so does she for literature.

win a place for me, a woman writer, among the most highly praised of our ancestors.[92] February 26, 1486.

IX–XVI

HER FATHER

Letters IX–XVI reveal several different sides of Cereta's relationship with her father. In 1485, the year that Cereta was married, her father Silvestro, a lawyer and magistrate in Brescia, was banished from office and left the city. In her letters dated to this year, Cereta, fifteen at the time, represents herself as assuming certain legal, familial, and personal roles and responsibilities of her father's which he, owing to either physical illness or depression, had delegated to her.

Letters IX and X, addressed to her younger brothers and the master of their boarding school, show Cereta playing the unusual role of surrogate father to her brothers. Speaking in a voice both paternal and patronal, she gives her brothers' teacher, Giovanni Olivieri, whose humanist school was well reputed in the region, instructions and advice: it is Olivieri's duty to care for, feed, and protect her brothers as well as to teach them, their learning in turn will stand as a testimony to his work (letter IX). In the companion letter to her brothers, Cereta warns them against falling in with the wrong crowd at Olivieri's school and urges the boys to apply themselves to their studies and to live up to the standards of their father (letter X). A subsequent letter to Olivieri, dated to 1487, shows Cereta assuming a different role towards her brothers' teacher, one that is deferential and even filial (letter XI). Soliciting his comments on her own literary work and expressing respect for his judgment, this and several of her subsequent letters to Olivieri suggest that intellectual relationships between older men and younger women still, by the end of the fifteenth century, grow out of social and familial ties and not the other way around as is typically the case in male humanist patronage.

In letters XII–XV, Cereta plays a role of a kind of father to her own father. In a series of letters that suggest faltering friendships and broken bonds between Silvestro Cereta and his former friends and colleagues at the bar, Laura acts as a broker or intercessor, in some cases making excuses for her father and in others pointing a blaming finger at friends for their harshness or lack of patience with him. In a letter dated August 5, 1485, to Bonifacio Bembo, a humanist teacher from Cremona and longtime friend of Silvestro's, Cereta explains that her father, who is no longer living in the city, is unable to assist Bembo in the painful court case that has brought him to Brescia; she

---

92. Cereta uses the rare feminine form *scriptrix* to indicate that she is talking about herself as a female writer.

assures him nonetheless of her father's continuing affection for him and his commitment to the friendship (letter XII). The circumstances of Cereta's letter to Felicio Tadino, a physician and former friend of Silvestro's, are quite different (letter XIII; dated December 31, 1486). Here the tables are turned: Tadino, portrayed as hostile and implacable, refuses to see her father or answer his letters despite Silvestro's repeated pleas. Cereta begs Tadino, for her father's sake, to relent. Cereta's letter to Alberto degli Alberti, a Brescian attorney, judge, and longtime associate of her father's, written on February 3, 1486, in the second year of Silvestro's exile from the city, again represents her own attempt to smooth out the relationship between an estranged friend and her father (letter XIV). Writing from a primitive house in the small village where she and her husband are living at the time, Cereta blames herself for not having written sooner and describes her father as too despondent and tearful to write to Alberti. She begs the judge to take the first step. The last of Cereta's brokering letters between her father and the outside world, dated to September 1485, reflects happier times for the family. Cereta here plays her father's learned alter ego; she answers invitations he receives from the local gentry and relays his greetings to them in graceful, Ciceronian cadences (letter XV).

The last in the group of what I call Cereta's fathering letters is the only letter in the collection addressed to her father (letter XVI). In this piece, dated to February 6, 1486, she demonstrates that she can and will defend herself against a certain local group of male writers who, motivated by jealousy, are doing everything they can to tarnish her reputation as a writer. Considering that this is the only letter to her father, the piece is more telling for its omissions than for what it actually says. In this letter, there is no suggestion that she attributes her education or literary accomplishments to her father, and there is nothing that would lead us to believe she expected him to do something on her behalf.

IX

To Giovanni Olivieri, professor of grammar and rhetoric [93]

I can never forget the kindness and generosity, both of brow and hand, that your wife Elena has shown us so many times. And you should not

---

93. Vat. 46 (fol. 33); Ven. 41 (fols. 66–67); Tom. 39 (pp. 85–87); Rabil 7. This is the first of five

think that your great work[94] has been forgotten, whose worth, in view of your dedication and humanity, is valued more as each day goes by.

Every day I think, however, of my two brothers Ippolito and Basilio. If you compare them to precious stones, one is like coal, the other like an emerald—and I don't know whether reason or the heat of sisterly love[95] is responsible for my coming to this conclusion. It's enough to say what I have been predicting—and this is worth writing—namely, that the mind is sometimes capable, as though by divine agency, of foretelling the future. I know therefore that, given your virtue, your admiring students will not lack the attributes that are both necessary and appropriate in a teacher. These include the feeding of those in your household and the protection of your pupils. For my part, I have not the slightest doubt that you will dispatch your duties with the greatest care, especially since I am committed to immortalizing your name and I shall always honor this commitment.

You yourself should also think about the merit you will acquire in our eyes or the honor that will be judged yours if you look upon their learning as a testimony to your work and your effort. My father hopes with me, and so do we all, that the end result will be that, with you as their guide, Ippolito and Basilio will prefer virtue to pleasure. And mind you, there is nothing that will bind my father more tightly to you in his enduring appreciation and mindfulness of your service to him than if you have instilled in his sons moral integrity, a knowledge of letters, and the conviction that the love of one's fellowmen must always in the most just of worlds be valued above all other things.

But besides, these brothers of mine will not only obtain great advantage for themselves in the course of their studies, but they will also weave a garland of glory for you, as the best of all teachers. My father, now banished from the city,[96] looks after his fields and lives the rustic life. His intention was to come to you, or at least to write often to you, and not just to send you a

---

letters in Cereta's letterbook addressed to Giovanni Olivieri (born c. 1444 in Chiari near Brescia), one of the best-known humanist teachers in the Veneto; see also Ludovico Ricci, "Notizie di Giovanni Olivieri," *Nuova raccolta d'opuscoli scientifici e filologici* (Venezia: Simone Occhi, 1770), vol. 20, opis 6, pp. 3–18.

94. Ricci (see above, n. 93) knows of no "monument" or "great work" left by Olivieri. I assume that by "monimentum" Cereta refers simply to the contribution Olivieri has made as proprietor of a fine humanist boarding school.

95. "Charitatis ardor": here translated as "the heat of sisterly love" as opposed to other forms of love (*amor, eros, amicitia*).

96. We have no information on why he may have been removed from his civic post and banished from the city.

letter now and then. But while he strove, while he pressed on persistently, soon recurrent difficulties, of the sort that clutter this earthly life of ours, prevented him from doing so. August 1, 1485.

X

To her brothers Ippolito and Basilio [97]

Although I had to tell your teacher many things about you by letter, still I knew it was only right and fitting for me to send these letters on to you, lest it should later seem that it was through my doing that your natural talents, which, we hope, will enable you to arrive at the culmination of your studies in the liberal arts with outstanding results, were prevented from coming to the fore.

For this reason, while some of your schoolmates are fussing with their hair, and others are spending their time grooming themselves—whether they dodge school to play in places where they won't be found, or sit around taking their leisure—while some of your friends waste their nights sleeping and others squander their days babbling and telling idle tales, I urge and implore the two of you to press on with your studies and to be diligent and remain alert. In this way your native intellectual gifts will enable you to obtain knowledge, which is a more lasting possession. In addition to his being of assistance to you, Olivieri is a man of authority and distinction who has taught students in his home, in the fields, and in the streets, just as he has taught in academies. If you obtain his counsel, you will acquire a great deal of knowledge.

But at your tender age, I'd like you to pay attention to the direction in which my warnings could lead you. You, who live in the best city,[98] have as a father a man who is renowned; he has endowed you with the finest values and an excellent name.[99] See to it that people don't say of you that you sank into a life of licentiousness, in a retrograde path from where your ancestors began, or that you were tempted to give up your trust in a great teacher. Since nature has made it possible for you to surpass intellectually the endowments of many men, light now the torches of the better part of your soul for the sake of

97. Vat. 47 (fol. 33v); Ven. 42 (fols. 67–68); Tom. 40 (pp. 87–88); Rabil 9.

98. She refers of course to Brescia.

99. These colorless, standard, and completely impersonal statements about her father are about the closest Cereta ever comes to praising him; nowhere in her letters does she explicitly express gratitude towards him.

learning. This effort is of crucial importance, since either pleasure will separate you from the great men of this city or virtue will distinguish you from the
dregs of the populace. The choice between these two roads is, however,
yours. Take care lest the precipitous plain of desire should cause you to be
afflicted with a still greater wound—that of regret. The quiet serenity of virtue inhabits the loftiest places in the hills. August 3, 1485.

XI

To Giovanni Olivieri, professor of grammar and rhetoric [100]

Although I have neither consulted the divination of Tages nor the
Sybilline books in order to know the future,[101] nor have I been
possessed by the god, or guided by auguries, still I had a suspicion that had
already caused me to write on another occasion that I thought you'd be
rightly amazed that I'd have enough courage—mere woman though I was,
untutored in literature, and utterly ignorant—to send you a little epistolary
oration, however crude and in need of editing with a scythe it might be.

Anyway, look how conveniently it has worked out that a more prescient
mind than mine has provided inspiration from higher places. Your wife has
approached me in a friendly manner—and she is very charming and addresses everyone in the right way and at the right time. It seemed she
wouldn't leave me alone until she asked me to write something on the spur of
the moment to you even though I had nothing in the least worthwhile to say.
I don't know if she came over, in the role of a scout or deserter herself, to have
a look at the modest education I've had. In any case, I do see the nature of
these attempts of hers: and they are—if you'll permit me the liberty of saying
so—underhanded missions under the guise of which you expect me to get
tangled up in the net of my own inexperience, just as you tend to imagine me
wandering around on unknown roads, blind and without a father's guidance.[102]

---

100. Vat. 45 (fols. 32v–33); Ven. 40 (fols. 65–66); Tom. 38 (pp. 63–65); Rabil 70.

101. Tages, a grandson of Jupiter, taught the Etruscans the science of augury and divination
(Cicero, *De div.* 2.23; Ovid, *Met.* 15.558). The Sibylline books contained compilations of prophecies. Guarded by a college of priests, these books were religiously consulted by the Romans in
times of danger to the state until the time of Sulla, when they were destroyed by fire.

102. "Tanquam is qui me putes absque baculo patris . . .": literally, she wandered without her

Education is a thing highly esteemed—and this is something learned men certainly know well enough. I've obtained whatever plumage I do have from strong wings—this I don't deny. But finally I progressed beyond the stage of being a chick and my skill at flying has became so good that the great forest of Mt. Ida might find me worthy of adopting. Perhaps in a short time the radiant realm of the sun will receive me, to which, in our own era, the rare phoenix flew.[103]

And now let me refine my argument so that the things I've said in all seriousness won't be taken as merely an attempt to show off my talent—since this could make it seem as though I was starting a war between the lovers of wisdom and philosophy, though surely the truth is that I, your most obedient servant, esteem you for your virtue best of all. This is all for now. October 31, 1487.

XII

To Bonifacio Bembo, professor of grammar and rhetoric[104]

*Y*ou take offense at titles, Bembo, and you oppose—if you will allow me to say so—the order of things; yet you call yourself the "little client" of a patron to whom you have always been both a comrade and a guide on moral issues.[105] My father has read your letters, which are certainly no less dear to his heart than they are distant from his own thoughts and hopes. From these letters, he knows with whom you are engaged in dispute,

---

father's staff. Note the rusticity of the image; a *baculum* suggests a shepherd's crook. The whole gist of this group of letters is that indeed a father's guidance is precisely what she seems to lack.

103. The phoenix, according to Pliny, was an ancient Egyptian bird sacred to the sun which resurrected itself from its own ashes 540 years after its death and flew to the sun: *Nat.* 10.3.

104. Vat. 12 (fol. 18); Ven. 11 (fols. 36–37); tom. 3 (pp. 17–18); Rabil 10. Bembo (?–1495), also a correspondent and friend of Cassandra Fedele, was born in Cremona, studied at Padua, and opened a humanist school in Paisola in 1487; he was appointed professor of rhetoric at the University of Pavia in 1489, and professor at the Studio Romano in 1493. He left biographies of Trajan and Nerva; his other poetry and prose did not survive. See *Dizionario biographico degli Italiani* (Roma: Istituto della Enciclopedia Italiana), 8 (1966), pp. 111–12.

105. Cereta uses the words *clientulus* and *patronus*, suggesting an unequal relationship between Bembo and her father. In Renaissance letters, the patronage relationship is usually referred to via the euphemistic vocabulary of Ciceronian *amicitia* (friendship); such terms as "patron" and "client," because they suggest dependency and exploitation instead of reciprocity and intellectual bonding, tend to be avoided (on the language of patronage see Diana Robin, *Filelfo in Milan. Writings, 1451–1477* (Princeton: Princeton University Press, 1991).

and he also knows in whose interest the court is likely to decide the case. It was he who put you in the hands of this man, and he did so punctiliously, just as he had been used to putting himself and his wealth in this man's hands.[106] Such acts, not pledges, are the marks of friendship. For whatever fortune or nature gave to my father, you hold in your own hands. Certainly he is pained terribly that you who have been disturbed for so long by your own countrymen seem now to have arrived either by desire or necessity under the aegis of the rights protecting returning exiles, at the house of a friend who is absent.[107]

Besides, that court case of yours need not seem painful to you, since my father would gladly oblige his native city and do his duty by coming here to see justice done, just as he did recently.[108] For my father, who has always appeared to be here for you, though absent, remains the same in his feelings for you. But as to the kind of man he has shown himself to be, no one knows better than you. August 5, 1485.

XIII

To Felicio Tadino, physician[109]

*S*oon after Pyrrha and Deucalion survived the universal flood and disaster in their ocean-borne craft, those sowers of human beings replenished the lands that met them with rocks they scattered as seed. After this, the human republic began to be born, began to be restored, whose stony first fruits lay the foundations for city walls from the hard rock born of Mars. Afterwards, nature gave you your ancestors and great-grandfathers, who were born of rugged stones; and you, who are tougher than iron or oak, do not differ from them.

These are not things I sought to learn through palmistry or blasphemous soothsaying. They became clear to me through the stony and obstinate si-

---

106. For the legal jargon *litem contestere* and *rem discernere* see Cicero, *Q. Rosc.* 53 and Virgil, *Aen.* 12.898, respectively.

107. "Ex postliminio": according to the right to return home after being exiled: see Apuleius, *Met.* 3.25; Cicero, *Orat.* 1.182.

108. More legal jargon: "Quod patriae gerat et functus munere civitatis, huc pro iure dicundo quasi nuper accesserit"; on *ius dicere* (to decide a case in court, to administer justice or act as a magistrate) see Cicero, *Tul.* 8; Livy, 45.12.13; Seneca, *Ben.* 4.28.5; Suetonius, *Jul.* 7.1.

109. Vat. 4 (14v); Ven. 3 (fol. 27r–28r); not in tom.; Rabil 28. There are two other letters in Cereta's letterbook to Tadino; other than these, there is no other information about him.

lence with which you abuse a friend who, of all your friends, misses you more and is more loyal than any other. Surely this man, who is my father by blood, is equally your son's father in spirit, and the doors to his friendship are always open to you at your command as well as at your pleasure. This man, your Silvestro, who so many times assuaged the raging anger of the Santa Chiarians and soothed their harsh opinions with humble orations, has been banished by you for a long time now. From that man you, who are more brutal than the savage beasts, more cruel than the bloodsucking Scythians, and more unmovable than the Acheron, now flee. Who would believe that, after he had begged you with so many letters and pleas, you could not be wrenched from your oath to remain silent, not by any art or pleading, as though, having shaken off your humanity, you could establish a reputation for yourself by showing contempt for a friend?

Therefore, if things go otherwise than I augur, and if you are ever moved, by sweet compassion for the children who supplicate you, to enter into this sort of letter writing, then I entreat you to do so with these prayers and in the name of the divine spirit of supplication that allowed the Thracian prophet and poet Orpheus to carry Eurydice all the way to the open jaws of Hades with the help of the gentle modes of his lyre. December 31, 1486.

XIV

To Alberto degli Alberti, attorney [110]

Though I wander among these rural houses at my leisure, the pure memory of my loyalty toward you rusticates and travels right along with me. Nor does this stand in the way of my being the diary of wrongs done to my father and a friendship that was violated. Nor do I think it is an easy thing to excuse that I previously sent you no letters. Really, I am a little angry with myself and I am already ashamed at my long and hateful silence.

110. Vat. 29 (fols. 23v–24); not in Ven.; Tom. 22 (pp. 43–45); Rabil 31. There are nine letters in all addressed to Alberti in the collection: Vat. 23, 28, 34, 36, 39, 48, 52, 68. On Alberti, a Brescian attorney, judge, and humanist scholar, see Vincenzo Peroni, *Biblioteca Bresciana* (Brescia, 1816), 1.20; Mazzuchelli, *Gli Scrittori d'Italia*, 1.1.297. Alberti was clearly a longtime friend and associate of her father's (also a lawyer in Brescia). The letter describes a kind of rural exile in which the Cereta family (or at least she and her father) are living and a breach in relations between her father and Alberti.

But I cannot be exonerated on this account; instead I would hope to be able to expiate this error of mine, if I willingly serve a summons on myself[111] to appear in your court of law, which is more merciful and more humane than any other among just men, especially if this slothful hand will not be afraid to take on the onerous task of writing.

The divine spirit of friendship must instead be given to undoing the wrong that has been cultivated with intense efforts on both your parts— yours, father Alberti, and that of my parent. For when he strives on a daily basis to write to you, tears suddenly flow down from his eyes in great drops. Thus, he often took up the pen he dropped, and then dropped the pen he had taken back up, groaning and sighing to himself as he did so, as though he were a man who envied you, desperately and self-destructively. Your mutual tenderness, deeply engraved in his heart, grew so much. Thus did I myself freely, and that man violently, wreak our damage.

Therefore I beg you to want to absolve both my father of the wrong he did you through his silence and his daughter of her sympathy for the wrong, particularly since, once a case has been reviewed, it lies within the jurisdiction of the judge to revoke the penalty, whether in the case of a criminal or civil proceeding.[112] But if you have weighed the case itself clearly and simply, you will become a greater judge in proportion to how forgiving you are. Nor will you be welcoming me back into a friendship from which I never withdrew, but instead you will be pardoning me for the sin of rusticity here in my rustic peasant's hut,[113] even if I have already begun to be sated with the common folk in this village,[114] where every street and narrow alley is filled with trash and piles of dung.

For here the rush mats next door to us can be seen in plain view. Here are the little houses of shepherds with their wooden shingles, and here some rough farmers herd flocks of sheep while others drive cattle. A cart is being pulled out from this very place; a groom is shouting at the horses. His clothes are caked with dirt, and he stiffens, worn-out and disheveled from toil. Many of the folk here practice rural habits;[115] most use degenerate slang.[116] Our

111. Note the legalese use here of the Latin *mihi diem dicere*, to serve a summons on myself.

112. Legal language dominates this sentence: "Quom praesertim ad potestatem iudicis a mulcta [Tom. reads in error "multa"] fit revocatio . . ."

113. The word Cereta uses to describe her dwelling. *Tugurium* (hovel, hut, shack) is probably an exaggeration.

114. Highly class-conscious like most of her humanist compatriots, Cereta doesn't hesitate to use the pejorative Latin *plebs* (*plebe* in Italian) to lump together the uneducated lower classes.

115. What Cereta means by "rurestres mores" may refer to both sanitation and sexual practices.

116. The humanist trope of flies, gnats, and fleas creating discomfort in the supposed paradise

sole means of rest and relaxation in the heat has been the fly-swatter.[116] February 3, 1486.

X V

To Domenico Patussi, attorney[117]

I recently received one of your letters which, flowing from your Pierian pen, displays emblems of our close kinship that have not been forgotten. And indeed, I think just as highly of you and your family as you do of my most precious husband, Pietro. Therefore, since I consider you to be among those who are thought to be experts at the law, the promise of our affinity is not such that it should be so quickly destroyed by forgetfulness.

Since you have graciously invited me to visit your country estate, your suggestion has pleased me very much and I thank you because your heart is so disposed towards us. Therefore, so that every excuse not to come may be brushed aside, I promise that all of us will come to the Feast of the Cross the day before to enjoy your company, so that there may be at the least an occasion for merriment among your vineyard workers, while they crush the harvested grapes with the traditional treading of the fruit with their feet.

My parents send greetings back to you, your brothers, and mother. With this note then, I place their well-being in your hands, relying on your concern. Nor should you expect, in addition, that the little ships of my halting talents will keep up with your verses, swimming as they are in the midst of an Ovidian sea.[118] Instead, I prefer to send you this letter in the form of a petition for your indulgent perusal, be it dry and slow in its subject matter. For this everyday, this pedestrian, quotidian type of writing of mine has always poured out coldly, aridly, and insubstantially.[119] September 10, 1485.

---

of the countryside comes first from Horace's widely imitated *Satires* 1.5; for an early adaptation of the trope see Francesco Filelfo's letter to Matteo da Pesaro (September 17, 1451) in Filelfo, *Epistolae familiares* (Venice: Gregorii, 1502), p. 67. For the unusual vocabulary word *muscarium* (fly-swatter) see Pliny, *Nat.* 12.127.

117. Vat 13 (fols. 18–18v); Ven. 12 (fol. 37–37v); Tom. 4; Rabil 16. This is the only letter in the collection from Patussi; nothing else is known about this humanist attorney from Brescia, who no doubt was an associate of her father's.

118. The strained quality of her imagery in this letter—"little ships . . . in an Ovidian sea," etc. (*navicula . . . in medio mari Nasonis*), an unusual metaphor for letters in any case—may reflect the fact that she's addressing someone who has sent her poetry rather than just a letter.

119. Cereta's description of her elaborately crafted rhetorical style as an "everyday, quotidian style of writing" is a *topos* straight from Petrarch's *Epistolae familiares* 1.1.

XVI

To her father, Silvestro Cereta[120]

T had only just recently moved to Chiari because the ignorant public and other certain men who had suddenly got learning of some sort or other came to me, since they were stricken with the sickness of jealousy of my literary knowledge (and how slight that knowledge really is). Although their sputtering bile sometimes made me so angry that I was sick, I am not such a country bumpkin that I believed I should reject them as opponents in a literary exchange, even though they had challenged me—disadvantaged though I was by an unsteady hand—to an epistolary contest.

I know they are jealous, since, having received, in addition to my pledge, something greater and more hallowed by time from me, they have no more challenging a game than to boast about their quickness of mind, by which these cowards could preempt my letters quickly with their own epistles to me, as though they believed that an error composed in haste would have more authority than a well-conceived correctness.

These men, just as certain others, find fault with the slowness that immortalized the mature verses of Euripides' *Alcestis*. They extol the speediness of their talent because it is faster than everything else, while their own writings, being scattered here and there, also vanish here and there, and are neglected in a senseless and futile manner. Moreover, these empty little teachers of rhetoric are irked because it shames them that their motivation for speaking comes from me, with the result that they rightly consider that their own empty hostility cannot be compared with the thought of the orators. Accordingly, puffed up with tumorous swelling they wallow in a succession of excuses, and like firebrands they proclaim their poisonous maledictions. But the ignorant ones who are more careful secretly withdraw in unseen treachery.

Nor is it characteristic of my nature to hide in meadows that have been mown down with a sickle. You yourself have seen most of the writings they've sent. Consider, in your role as judge, this two-day epistle which you yourself might compare, in response to their bragging, to the epistle I wrote in an hour, so that literary moderation can more clearly assert itself in opposition to these ignoramuses. Thus it will be obvious to you that both sides are responding with the same material and the same argument. February 1, 1486.

120. Vat. 27 (fols. 23–23v); Ven. 26 (fols. 49v–50v); Tom. 18 (pp. 40–42); Rabil 30. This is the only letter in the collection addressed to Cereta's father. Curiously, the letter is relatively impersonal in comparison to her letters to other friends, acquaintances, and family members.

II

WOMEN AND SOCIETY

Letters XVII and XVIII are companion pieces that represent Cereta's most feminist and polemical work. Each is a formal essay dealing with the role of women in society as a class and with women's supposed nature. Both essays represent revisions of Boccaccio's misogynistic catalogue of famous women's lives, *De claris mulieribus;* and in both, Cereta borrows extensively yet selectively from Boccaccio's catalogue, rejecting and revising the material in his lives, much as Christine de Pizan does in her catalogue of women's lives, *The Book of the City of Ladies.* As such, both essays belong very much to the *querelle des femmes,* the literary debate about women which begins with Christine's *City of Ladies* (1405) and continues into the eighteenth century. The subject of the first essay is women and marriage; the second, women and education. Both essays have a three-part structure: each begins with a prologue introducing the subject and argument; each has a lengthy middle section consisting of exempla that support the argument; and each has a short epilogue that wraps up the argument.

The first of these orations, on marriage, begins with a prologue on the position of the planets and constellations indicating that this is a propitious moment for her correspondent, Pietro Zecchi, to marry. To persuade Zecchi that the loving commitment of a woman in marriage is a good thing for a man, Cereta presents a series of famous exempla of virtuous wives from the ancient world.

The dominant image of woman in this essay is that of the nurturing mother, a role Cereta's exemplary women play out vis-à-vis their sons, husbands, parents, and even the state. Whereas Boccaccio's *De claris mulieribus* represents loyal wives as exceptions to the rule of women's mutability and weakness, Cereta's history of women foregrounds the maternal as an emblem of women's natural loyalty and strength. "Great is the power of maternal authority," she writes (*Ingentes maternae auctoritatis vires sunt*). Indeed, mothers such as Veturia, Agrippina, Zenobia, and Vitellia are all powerful in Cereta; when their son's realms are threatened they take up arms and become warriors to protect the territories of their heirs.

Cereta suppresses the negative representations of these women in Ovid, Tacitus, Valerius Maximus, and other ancient authors, though her readers would have been familiar with these texts anyway. While Boccaccio and his classical sources portray Nero's mother, Agrippina, and Semiramis, queen of the Assyrians as sexually voracious and power-hungry seducers of their sons, Cereta, like Christine de Pizan in the *Cité*, does not allude to the incest tradition in either of their histories. She also treats the familiar rape narratives of her models differently, suppressing the rapes rather than focusing on them and their aftermath, as Boccaccio does when he lingers over the way a woman from Galatia carries the severed head of her rapist back to her husband, hiding it in the bosom of her dress as she flees the enemy. While Boccaccio's narrative builds toward the act of rape as the climactic moment in his stories of Lucretia and other chaste mothers, Cereta's bypasses the act of rape.

The breast, the emblem of feminine authority in Cereta's depictions of famous women, is perhaps the most striking image in this work. The maternal breast not only feeds and nourishes; it provides both emotional and actual shelter from danger. It can also serve as an instrument of revenge and purgation. Curia hid her husband, Cereta writes, after he was proscribed, in her bosom ("in sinu"). In a characteristically Ceretan revision of Boccaccio's tale in *De claris mulieribus* of a newly delivered young mother who breast-feeds her own mother in prison to rescue her from starvation, the focus is on the young woman herself and her conflicting roles as daughter and mother. Boccaccio's emphasis is on the abstraction—the daughter's exceptional *pietas* (loyalty to parents, family, kin)—and the governor's pardon of her owing to her *pietas*. He also differs from Cereta in his failure to mention the young woman's feeding of her baby as well as omitting what for Cereta is an important thematic detail: that the woman's baby is a little boy (*filiolum*); thus while keeping a dying matriarchy alive, though barely so, Cereta's woman nurtures and feeds the future patriarchy. Cereta's point is not that this woman is loyal. It is that woman, the figure for the maternal, is forever torn between loyalties and between loved ones.

The story of Lucretia's rape by the successor to the Roman throne, Tarquinius Sextus, and the demise of the Tarquin monarchy as the consequence of that rape, is a key narrative in Renaissance humanism. Cereta's narrative, in contrast to that of Boccaccio and his classical sources, privileges the power of

Lucretia's purity (*castitas*) over the king's "crime" (*flagitium*, an image that usually suggests sexual transgression in Latin literature). In a refiguration of Lucretia's rape and suicide that is entirely her own, Cereta makes Lucretia's breast and its dripping blood (*cruentum pectus . . . stillansque cruor*) the agents that cleanse the state (*delavit*) by causing the king's expulsion. Thus in Cereta's alteration of the paradigm of Lucretia, it is the nurturing female breast and not male vengeance that washes away monarchy and enables the birth of the republic.

In the epilogue to the letter, Cereta moves away from historical examples of the loyalty and devotion of women in marriage to an attack on the institution of marriage and its destructive effects on modern women. In a general indictment of marriage, Cereta describes how, between the sanctions of the Church and the dictates of nature, women are caught in a vise. Nature inclines women to choose marriage and children, but they must endure years of "wailing and all night vigils" as the consequence of this choice. In a much more pessimistic figuration of the maternal imaginary, Cereta, alluding to a passage in Pliny where a mother panther rolls over on her back and strikes a begging posture to persuade a passerby in the desert that she will not harm him if he helps save her cubs, describes wives as metaphorically rolling over like dogs (*circumvolutat se, blandienti [cani] similis*), in hopes that their husbands will show them some mercy. The advantages of matrimony are all on the male side, Cereta advises Zecchi: women debase themselves like animals in marriage, and the end they meet is widowhood, poverty, and grief. Yet in Cereta's tiger woman, a classically ambivalent figuration of the mother emerges: catlike, she is alternatively perceived by the men in her life as dangerous and cuddly, treacherous and nurturing, needy and giving, longing for satisfaction yet demanding punishment.

XVII
ON ENTERING INTO THE BONDS OF MATRIMONY

To Pietro Zecchi[1]

The ascent of the planet Venus on your birthday is connected with the second appearance of Pisces, while the power of Venus rising in

---

1. Vat. 76 (fols. 63–65v); Ven. 66 (fols. 121–26v); Tom. 64 (pp. 178–87); Rabil 32. [See Introduction, note 1, for full citations] Vat. and Ven. name Cereta's correspondent as "Petrum Zeccum" (Pietro Zecchi); Tom. has "Petrum Zenum Patavinum" (Pietro Zeno da Padua). This is the only letter Cereta addressed to Zecchi.

the house of good fortune is a benefit to your marriage bonds;[2] for it is Venus and Pisces who control the process of procreation. But a fortunate wife will be given to you as a bride when Jupiter appears, and by her you will receive a grandson from a happy son. The discordant Great Bear moves toward the influences of these heavenly bodies, whose eightfold pairs of rays had begun to rise with you at the first darkness of the night. And although Chance might cause you to be deceived in a prior promise of marriage, still you will be consoled: in opposition to Fortune, you will soon evade the enemy and two hearts joined together under the law of chastity will enjoy themselves in an indissoluble knot of love for a long time to come.

In the case of such happy auspices, who would not put aside second thoughts? Who would fail to obtain favorable omens with a sacrificial offering of a turtledove of noble purity for the god? Who from Cyprus would not give grain for a sacrificial offering to Isis of Phasis? You will prepare the cracking of nuts of Hymenaeus, who lies in ambush at virtuous weddings. You will repeat the fortunate name of Telamon; Picumnus and Pilumnus will receive the dowry gifts for the bride in their hands;[3] and you will say pious prayers for peace to your god, Sleep. But if you do not believe in the friendship of favoring fate, if you accord very little weight to the oblique positions of the gliding constellations and the planets that wander in and out of various places among themselves, or if the migrations of the stars, which are perpetually in motion, do not impress you because you are someone who has a naturally suspicious mind that oscillates like a pendulum between skeptical deliberations, then I will point the way to love—to the extent that I can in a mere letter—by using examples in which the dignity and purity of women have caught fire with the flames of chaste love and a noble heart.

Historians have handed down as a faithful record of the past the story that Dido Elissa, that unmovable rock of constancy, courageously chose to commit suicide because of her resolve to preserve the purity of her widowhood, and on that account she threw herself on her knife; and, as she lay on her funeral pyre while the Africans pressed around her menacingly, she repeatedly called out in an imploring tone the name Sychaeus, the husband she had longed for most.[4] Who could oppose the well-earned praise of Penelope

2. The opening of this letter, though intact in Vat. and Ven., is missing in Tom.; Rabil, *Laura Cereta*, p. 50," provides the missing text.

3. Picumnus and Pilumnus: two early Italian deities who were associated as a pair originally with Mars (see Fabius Pictor, *Iur. 5*; Pliny, *Nat.* 18.10; Festus, p. 205M).

4. Cereta takes this and her other exempla in this letter directly from Boccaccio's *De claris mulieribus* (*Concerning Famous Women*, trans. with an introduction by Guido A. Guarino [New Brunswick, N.J.: Rutgers University Press, 1963], chap. 38, pp. 81–83, hereafter referred to as

when, after her conduct had remained pure and unbending in the face of a thousand proposals of marriage, she anxiously received her beloved Ulysses in Ithaca, home from Phaeacia, having waited for him twenty years?[5] Did not Hypsicratea, a woman of unflagging loyalty, always stand beside her husband Mithridates, wondrously enduring tribulation on land and on sea through every battle, though he was as often vanquished as he was victorious.[6] In the same way, when Lentulus was destitute, toiling, and proscribed, Sulpicia, his faithful companion, did not fear her husband's long exile in the interior of Sicily, though it meant the abandoning of her mother Julia and willfully turning her back on the many delights of her family's ancestral splendor.[7] Curia among other women is also worthy of mention. She protected Quintus Lucretius, who was condemned to exile in the lists of the triumvirs; and, while keeping him safe in the inner recesses of her house and other most secret hiding places, she was just as good at masking her emotions as she was in carrying out her task with great cunning.[8]

The fervid love of an only daughter, Claudia, was shown towards her father, whom she rescued and set free from the violent hands of a tribune,

---

CFW). In focusing on Dido's chastity and devotion to her dead husband, Cereta follows here Boccaccio and not Virgil. On the *donne famose* tradition (catalogue of famous women) in humanist literature see Pamela Joseph Benson, *The Invention of Renaissance Woman* (University Park, Pa.: Pennsylvania State University Press, 1992); my "Space, Woman, and Renaissance Discourse," in *Sex and Gender in Medieval and Renaissance Texts: The Latin Tradition,* eds. Barbara K. Gold, Paul Allen Miller, Charles Platter (Albany: State University of New York Press, forthcoming), and my Introduction to this volume.

5. See Boccaccio, *CFW,* chap. 38, pp. 81–83, on the most famous example in Greek myth of the faithful wife, Penelope, queen of Ithaca and wife of Homer's hero Odysseus.

6. See Boccaccio, *CFW,* chap. 76, pp. 170–72, on Hypsicratea, famed for having fought in battle by her husband's side dressed in a man's armor. Her husband, King Mithridates VII of Pontus (d. 63 B.C.), who engaged in battle with Sulla, Lucullus, and Pompey, was famous for his cruelty. He murdered Hypsicratea and their children; and according to Plutarch, he massacred 150,000 Romans living in his dominions.

7. See Boccaccio, *CFW,* chap. 83, pp. 186–87, on the noble Roman Lentulus Cruscellio, who, after being proscribed by the triumvirs, hid in the wilds of Sicily; disguised as a slave, Sulpicia followed her husband to Sicily, where she lived with him in poverty.

8. See Boccaccio, *CFW,* chap. 81, pp. 183–84, on Quintus Lucretius, who was proscribed by the triumvirs, and his wife Turia (Curia in Vat., Ven. and Tom.), who hid him for years in her own bedroom. Cereta is vague on the details; she says "in sinu servavit incolumnem," which can mean that Curia (Turia) kept her husband safe in her bosom, in a sheltered place, or possibly under the folds of her skirt. Boccaccio says Turia hid her husband "between the walls of the house." (p. 183) In Christine de Pizan's version of Boccaccio's history of women *The Book of the City of Ladies* [published in 1405 under the title *Cité des dames*], trans. Earl Jeffrey Richards (New York: Persea Books, 1982), 2.26.1, Turia hides her husband "in her arms." On Christine's feminization of Boccaccio's *CFW* see Maureen Quilligan, *The Allegory of Female Authority: Christine de Pizan's* Cité des Dames (Ithaca: Cornell University Press, 1991).

when he was celebrating his victory on the Capitoline Hill.[9] At the highest summit of spotless purity, shone Hippo, who was a Greek girl and the daughter of Tetyos and Oceanus.[10] Realizing she was about to be raped by sailors, Hippo became so despondent and embittered that she threw herself into the bitter sea to preserve her chastity, and thus drank a death more bitter than bitterness. Not hope for better things, however, but the strength of her conjugal fidelity spurred on Argia, the daughter of Argive Adrastus; true loyalty made her heart steadfast.[11] Because of this, defying Creon's order, she dared to search among the sightless bodies of the dead for her husband Polynices' corpse, unburied and despoiled by carrion, and when she had commended his body to the flames, she had the courage to save his ashes and entomb them in a covered urn.

The powers of maternal authority are great.[12] For when Coriolanus' mother approached him, these powers softened her obdurate son's anger when he was laying siege to Rome; for Roman plebs had not been able to appease this anger of his with entreaties, and neither had they been able to do so with the pleas of their envoys nor their priests swathed in veils.[13] Nero should give equal thanks to his mother Agrippina for the empire he controlled because she poisoned Claudius with mushrooms she daubed with a deadly drug.[14] Similarly the warrior Zenobia, with arms and determination, restored the reign usurped by Odenatus to her sons, Hermonianus and Timolaus.[15] The Roman empire would have fallen to alien tribes, had not the Athenian Irene, who was with child, given birth by her husband Leo to Constantine, the scion of a great royal line.[16] Who would have sat on the throne in the Teutonic court if King William of Sicily had not had a daughter, Constance, who in her later years bore a son and heir of unusual fame to the emperor Henry?[17]

9. See Boccaccio, *CFW,* chap. 60, pp. 135–36, for the story of this aristocratic daughter's violent attack on a tribune of the plebs who dared to assault her father in a public place.

10. See Boccaccio, *CFW,* chap. 51, p. 116, for the story of the suicide of Hippo, a Greek girl whose parents, Oceanus and Tetyos, were sea gods.

11. Her source is Boccaccio, *CFW,* chap. 25, pp. 58–59, on Argia.

12. Cereta's articulation of a key theme in Latin literature—that of "maternal authority"—is also a major theme in her own work.

13. Her source is Boccaccio, *CFW,* chap. 53, pp. 118–21, on Veturia, Coriolanus's mother.

14. Cf. her source, Boccaccio, *CFW,* chap. 90, pp. 205–8, on Agrippina, mother of Nero, renowned in Tacitus and Suetonius for her incestuous behavior in public towards her son Nero and her involvement in palace intrigue. All this is characteristically suppressed in Cereta.

15. Cf. her source, Boccaccio, *CFW,* chap. 98, pp. 226–30 on Zenobia.

16. Cf. Boccaccio, *CFW,* chap. 100, pp. 234–36, on Irene, empress of Constantinople and mother of Constantine.

17. Cf. Boccaccio, *CFW,* chap. 102, pp. 239–41, on Constance, empress of Rome and queen of Sicily. According to Boccaccio, the son that Constance bore at the age of fifty-five.

Next come Marpessa and Lampedo,[18] warrior widows, truly two lionesses among the Amazons, who, thirsting for the slaughter of men to avenge their Cappadocian blood, armed their unvanquished hearts with such intransigent animosity that they preferred to perish in a formidable blaze of vengeance rather than live under a barbarian sword. It is said by many that when Vespasian's soldiers marched on Terracina it would have been to challenge Lucius Vitellius, had not Vitellia, girded that night with arms and proud cruelty and wearing a regal crown, shown herself the victor.[19]

Portia made famous the story of her life by emulating the constancy of her father Cato, when she, because of her love, though more truly her sorrow for Decius Brutus after his death at Philippi, drank burning wood with a greedy throat.[20] It is right to remember how Fortune, the perpetrator, fittingly found for Pyramus and Thisbe the ill-fated sword, how this young girl stabbed herself with it, and how, wounded and anxiously gasping for her last breath, she groaned as she called out Pyramus's name.[21] Paulina Pompeia exemplified the splendor of her name when, intrepid and contemptuous of life, she opened her veins as she entered the warm bath with Seneca.[22] Caesar's daughter Julia's sudden death, however, bows to no example among her ancestors; for she loved Pompey so ardently that when she saw his robes bloodied from the sacrifice of an animal, suspecting that her husband had been slain, she collapsed and died.[23] Antonia the younger also stands out as no ordinary example; for when Drusus was murdered, grieving miserably in her woman's heart, she devoted the rest of her life to weeping and took refuge in eternal mourning.[24] The Minyans among Jason's celebrated Argonauts, sentenced for their conspiracy against the Lacedemonian republic, were de-

18. See Boccaccio, *CFW,* chap. 11, pp. 23–24, on Marpessa and Lampedo, who are coupled in one chapter.

19. The story of Triaria, wife of the consul Lucius Vitellius and mother of the future emperor Aulus Vitellius, and her capture of Terracina is told in Tacitus, *Hist.* ii.53, iii. 76, and Boccaccio, *CFW,* chap. 94, pp. 217–18.

20. On Portia (married to Marcus Junius Brutus in 45 B.C., confused in Boccaccio and Cereta with Decius Brutus) Cereta follows Boccaccio, *CFW,* chap. 80, pp. 181–82. According to Boccaccio, Portia committed suicide by swallowing lumps of burning coals.

21. Boccaccio, *CFW,* chap. 12, pp. 25–27, is the source for Cereta's rendition of the Pyramus and Thisbe story, including the responsibility of Fortune for the tragedy and Thisbe's calling out of Pyramus's name at the climactic moment of death, a detail not in Ovid, *Met.* 4.

22. See Boccaccio, *CFW,* chap. 92, pp. 212–13, Cereta's source for Seneca's wife, Paulina Pompeia; Boccaccio differs from Cereta by adding that Paulina was saved from death by her servants and survived her husband.

23. See Boccaccio, *CFW,* chap. 79, pp. 179–80, on Julia. Cereta does not vary the story.

24. See Boccaccio, *CFW,* chap. 87, pp. 198–99, on Antonia. Cereta's story differs: Boccaccio says Antonia simply withdrew from society since she didn't wish to remarry; Cereta's mention of mourning and grief is her own invention.

spondently awaiting their execution when their wives, veiled and dressed in filthy rags, were admitted to the prison compound to see their husbands who were soon to die, for a last farewell. The wives exchanged their mourning clothes for their husbands' garments, and sent the condemned men out of the prison, while they themselves remained inside the compound, fearless in their contempt for death.[25]

The unheard-of loyalty of a daughter who herself had just given birth was shown to the rest of the Romans when one succeeded in feeding with her own breasts not only her baby son who was crying at home, but also— thanks to the carelessness of the prison guard—her mother, who, having been condemned to die, was starving to death in prison.[26] Artemisia, the daughter of Lydamus, erected a grave of precious marble for her dead husband, Mausolus, and gathered the ashes of her husband's heart and entombed them in an urn.[27] Ah, how great a glory, how great a piety did the steadfast constancy and the desperate chastity of the Cimbrian women attain, when they, all of them, hanged themselves in a single night after their husbands were murdered by Gaius Marius.[28] The courageous severity of the avenging of chastity and matronly splendor, firmly and vigilantly defended by an avenging sword, must be remembered, when that Galatian woman, full of courage and gleaming with glory, and Judith, most loyal among the Jews, shone, each because of the rare nature of her chaste example. For while Judith delivered up to her people the drunken neck of Holofernes, the woman of Galatia, returning unscathed from the bosom of the enemy, brought back to her kinsmen the severed head of the centurion Manlius Torquatus.[29] However, an example of unviolated chastity burned with a bright flame when Lucretia cut her bleeding breast with a sword and her innocent blood washed

25. See Boccaccio, *CFW*, chap. 29, pp. 62–64, on the wives of the Minyans (Meniae in Cereta). Whereas Boccaccio ends the story with the fate of the women unsettled, Cereta emphasizes the women's self-sacrifice.

26. See Boccaccio, *CFW*, chap. 63, pp. 142–43, for the story of the woman who breastfed her own mother. See Christine's version of the tale in her *City*, 2.11.1; see also Quilligan, *Allegory*, pp. 118–21.

27. See Boccaccio, *CFW*, chap. 55, pp. 123–27, on Artemisia, queen of Caria, and her memorial for her king, Mausolus. Cereta doesn't follow her more gruesome model, Boccaccio, who says that Artemisia drank her husband's ashes so that she could retain them inside her own body.

28. See Boccaccio, *CFW*, chap. 55, pp. 176–78, on the wives of the Cimbrians. Cereta omits two significant parts of Boccaccio's story, first that they asked to be permitted to be Vestal virgins in Rome and, second, that they dashed their own children to death before hanging themselves.

29. Cereta's tale of a Galatian woman's beheading of a Roman centurion suppresses the narrative of her rape by the soldier and other grisly details in Boccaccio, *CFW*, chap. 71, pp. 160–62; instead she makes her story analogous to the Old Testament heroine Judith's murder of her attempted seducer Holofernes, one of the most popular subjects in Renaissance painting.

away the outrageous crime of Sextus Superbus, causing his everlasting exile.[30]

Aemilia, a victor over wrongdoing, conquered her own heart, for she was certainly no inferior to Africanus the elder in the value she accorded to patience.[31] So that no hint of dishonor should tar the unblemished reputation of her deceased husband, she took to her grave the long list of his violations of their marital bond, concealing these in the secrecy of her breast. This learned teacher of tolerance had women who were docile and willing as her pupils, and some of these sent female pupils of their own down to posterity, while other docile women, born later, have filled an entire lineage full of their descendants who are dispersed throughout the world.

If you ponder these things in your mind, and consider them with a keen eye, manfully and with foresight, you will conceive of a surer plan for entering into marriage and you will prepare the kinds of torches you should be lighting at the altar of holy matrimony. Surely the great and unshakable faith of wives in their husbands is excessive; for they, remaining constant through all fortune's changes, enter into your dangers, while their own desires may be rebuffed.[32]

Birds have learned to build nests for the purpose of laying eggs for their offspring. Nature inclines toward the propagation of its species. She teaches us to hope for heirs to perpetuate our name and our deeds. The church, moreover, has instituted a sacrament that allows us to enter joyously into a sweet oath to beget children. The unbroken probity of conjugal love beckons us to fulfill this oath, and it is this probity, content[33] with toil and duty, that enables us to rear up children amid wailing and all night vigils.

These are women who have pledged themselves to you under oath in a court of law, and who guard your treasures and offices with solicitous love for the long duration of your life. And while they preserve the always flourishing

---

30. On Lucretia see Boccaccio, *CFW,* chap. 46, pp. 101–3 and Christine, *City* 2.44.1. Again Cereta did not hesitate to suppress the tale of her heroine's rape—an act over which Livy, Ovid, Boccaccio, and others lingered respectfully. This was a rape that, for the humanists, or so Stephanie Jed has argued (see her *Chaste Thinking* [Bloomington: Indiana University Press, 1989]), represented the founding moment or republicanism in Italy.

31. On Tertia Aemilia, wife of Scipio Africanus, see Boccaccio, *CFW,* chap. 72, pp. 163–64. Cereta follows the main lines of Boccaccio's story, though she omits the tale of how Aemilia rewarded Scipio's concubine after his death. But note again here the prominence of the woman's breast in Cereta.

32. Note also that while Boccaccio praises to the skies Aemelia's docility, Cereta looks with dismay on Aemelia' behavior as a bad example that modern women have too often viewed as a model of feminine virtue.

33. Vat., Ven.: "contenta"; Tom.: "contempta."

and much-cherished unity of holy matrimony, these women govern themselves by obeying their ancestors and they smoothe over all the pain when
there is dissension in the household with their own good sense. They mount
unheard-of plans in the face of inescapable events; they keep the din of war
far from their borders and towns; and, relying both on arms and the bonds of
kinship, they protect kings and they pacify realms. And if ever they are summoned to resolve the injuries of their husbands, these women immediately
wash the animosity away from the heart that has been bruised, having first
dissolved it with their little tears. And, soothing egos with compliments to
promote a happy mood, they extinguish noisy shouting when tempers flare.

You have no need of little sparrows who are accustomed to come to your
hand. Wives come to their husbands just to receive their nods of perfect approval, like little girls who depend on their nurse's opinion. Why do you men
hold noisy pet dogs in your arms? A woman rolls herself over like a dog begging and, while she longs for a word of praise, she talks about whips.[34] But
when old women become poor and pitiable, they go fearlessly to their down-
fall for the sake of the protection of a home. They instruct daughters-in-law
and granddaughters with examples, and they show them kindness when they
are weak and sick. Women at the end of their lives accept the solace of a quiet
bed for themselves: when their husbands are stolen from them by death after
a lifetime of fidelity, these women, in an anxious daze, bury their own living
hearts with the bodies of their men. They disrupt everything with their cries
of mourning, nor does any hour go by when they are free from memories of
the dead. But in old age, devoid of sight and toiling at the tedium of their
lives, they take such pity on their dead that they make public their sighing
lamentations of surrender to death with the half-eaten sorrow of a heart that
has burst. Vale. February 3, 1486.

XVIII
IN DEFENSE OF A LIBERAL EDUCATION FOR WOMEN

In letter XVIII, to Bibolo Semproni, Cereta expresses her ideas about the intellectual capabilities of women as a class more fully than anywhere else in
her correspondence. The essay begins with her main thesis: learned and intellectually gifted women like herself are not exceptions to the rule among
women, as Boccaccio claims. Instead, a long history of brilliant women
thinkers, philosophers, writers, and prophets precedes her. Learned women,

---

34. "Circumvolutat se, blandienti similis, mulier: et gestiens gratiam de verberibus refert": here
Cereta's language is clearly modeled on Pliny, *Nat.* 8.59, where a female panther pleads with a
man to rescue her cubs by rolling on her back and putting her paws in the air in a begging
posture.

she asserts, have had a long and noble lineage: a *generositas*. Much as Christine de Pizan uses the metaphor of the city, its walls, and buildings to suggest that gifted women have had a tradition of their own, Cereta employs the image of a family tree of women geniuses. Her focus throughout the essay is on women as a class rather than as individuals. She begins the letter by expressing her own feelings of outrage at her correspondent, not so much for calling her an anomaly among her sex as for denigrating women as a species.

The central portion, and bulk of the letter, leads the reader through a series of exempla of famous learned women, which Cereta for the most part has borrowed from *De claris mulieribus*. But again she radically alters Boccaccio's reception of these women's lives, as she did in her essay on marriage, omitting certain of his details and adding new information of her own. She presents the famous female prophets of antiquity together as a subcategory of learned women, for example, grouping together the Egyptian Sabba, the Italian Sibyl Amalthea, Evander's mother Nicostrata, and Tiresias's daughter Manto. Linking prophecy to scholarship and erudition, and thus connecting the irrational to the rational—as Boccacio does not do in any systematic or consistent way—Cereta makes all of her female prophets women of learning as well. Far from the typical humanistic separation of thinking and writing from feeling and emoting, the oral culture of divination is consistently bound up in Cereta with the culture of literacy and book learning. In the same vein, Cereta transforms and domesticates the Neoplatonic ideal that the true philosopher's first task is the ascent to, and contemplation of, pure truth. She envisions the journey to truth as an activity that is not cerebral and abstract but takes place within a familiar, homely locus. She imagines the path to God as a walkway within the interior of a house and she figures reason as a window in that house. Her philosopher is a kind of architect or builder who fits the house out with the proper features for the work at hand.

While the intellectual and genital aspects of women's lives are always closely connected in Boccaccio, where thoughts of learning always trigger thoughts of sex and vice versa, in Cereta they do not. While Boccaccio follows his ancient sources (Ovid, Valerius Maximus, et al.) in having much to say on the subject of Queen Semiramis' incest with her son and Leontium's prostitution, Cereta does not allude to the sexual practices of her female exempla. Even chaste learned women's lives, such as Cornificia's and Proba's, serve Boccaccio as springboards for remarks about the "lasciviousness" of women in general. Cereta's negative generalizations about women, as is clear from this and several other letters, are reserved for their taste for luxury and fashion.

In an epilogue to the essay, Cereta summarizes her ideas about women and education. All human beings, women included, are born with the right to an education (*Naturam discendi aeque omnibus unam impartiri licentiam*), she writes—

a radical statement for a fifteenth-century humanist. The idea that the capacity or greatness of a man's mind is not necessarily tied to class or birth is a familiar enough one in Quattrocento humanist thought; the extension of this notion to include gender is not. On the other hand, the educated woman is neither a modern phenomenon nor one unknown in antiquity. There is, she argues, a historically documented and constituted "republic of women": *respublica mulierum*. This is Cereta's own variation on the humanist commonplace *respublica litterarum* (republic of letters), a metaphor for the notion that there is an imaginary city of men who share a commitment to the study of literature that transcends geopolitical boundaries. Thus there is not only a lineage (*generositas*) of learned women to be taken into account, but a women's *respublica*— an image with resonances different from the ones that Christine's "city of women" has, since the term "republic" is a politically loaded one in fifteenth- and sixteenth-century Italy, carrying clear overtones of antimonarchist, anti-signorial, and no doubt anti-imperialist sentiment, considering Cereta's position as a native of Brescia, a town long exploited by Venice.

Cereta's final argument is that whether women acquire an education or not is a matter of choice (*electio*). Women have the freedom (*licentia*) to choose to become educated, but they must also opt to commit themselves to the study and hard work it takes to become learned. Knowledge is not a god-given endowment; it is won by toil. She is more pessimistic about the choices she sees her contemporaries making. Most women, she fears, are too content with their condition as dependents to push for advancement. Thus in this letter, while she attacks the typical attitude of her male contemporaries in the person of her correspondent Bibolo Semproni, for his erroneous assumption of women's inferiority, she blames women's lack of schooling on women themselves rather than on either "nature" or society and its institutions.

Cereta's slash and burn tone throughout the essay marks the piece as a typical example of humanist invective. True to the dictates of the genre—the humanist ur-model for which is Cicero's *Philippics*—she characterizes her adversary, Bibolo, and other detractors as alternatively insane, bestial, plebeian, ignorant, and drunk, which even the name of her correspondent suggests.

To Bibolo Semproni [35]

*Y*our complaints are hurting my ears, for you say publicly and quite openly that you are not only surprised but pained that I am said to

35. Vat. 77 (fols. 65–67); Ven. 67 (fols. 126v–131v); Tom. 65 (pp. 187–95); Rabil 77. Cereta's correspondent might be either a real acquaintance whom she is addressing with a comical nickname—Bibolo might be translated "tippler"—or a fictional creation and vehicle for her polemic.

show this extraordinary intellect of the sort one would have thought nature would give to the most learned of men—as if you had reached the conclusion, on the facts of the case, that a similar girl had seldom been seen among the peoples of the world. You are wrong on both counts, Semproni, and now that you've abandoned the truth, you are going to spread information abroad that is clearly false.

I think you should be deeply pained—no, you should actually be blushing—you who are no longer now a man full of animus but instead a stone animated by the scorn you have for the studies that make us wise, while you grow weak with the sickness of debilitating leisure. And thus in your case, it is not nature that goes astray but the mind, for which the path from the appearance of virtue to villainy is a fairly easy one. In this manner, you appear to be flattering a susceptible young girl because of the glory that has accrued to her—my—name. But the snare of flattery is seductive, for you who have always set traps for the sex that has been revered all throughout history have been ensnared yourself. And duped by your own madness, you are trying, by running back and forth, to trample me underfoot and smash me to the ground with your fists. Sly mockery is concealed here, and it is typical of the lowborn, plebeian mind to think that one can blind Medusa with a few drops of olive oil.[36] You would have done better to have crept up on a mole than a wolf, since the former, being shrouded in darkness, would see nothing clearly, while the latter's eyes radiate light in the dark.

In case you don't know, the philosopher sees with her mind; she furnishes paths with a window of reason through which she can ascend to a state of awareness.[37] For Providence, the knower of the future, conquers marauding evil, trampling it with feet that have eyes. I would remain silent, believe me, if you, with your long-standing hostile and envious attitude towards me, had learned to attack me alone; after all, a ray of Phoebus' can't be shamed by being surrounded by mud. But I am angry and my disgust overflows. Why should the condition of our sex be shamed by your little attacks? Because of this, a mind thirsting for revenge is set afire; because of this, a sleeping pen is wakened for insomniac writing.[38] Because of this, red-hot anger lays bare a heart and mind long muzzled by silence.

My cause itself is worthy: I am impelled to show what great glory that

---

36. See Boccaccio, *CFW*, chap. 20, pp. 43–44; Boccaccio's version of the Perseus-Medusa myth involves the hero's seduction of Queen Medusa; Boccaccio downplays as a mere fiction of the poets the queen's famous ability to turn men into stone.

37. "Videt si nescis animo sapiens: et in subeundam animadvertentiam fenestrat sibi ratione vias."

38. "Chartas vigiles: another now familiar reference to her lucubration, her necessity for night writing, which she calls her *vigiliae*, her night watches.

noble lineage which I carry in my own breast has won for virtue and literature—a lineage that knowledge, the bearer of honors, has exalted in every age.[39] For the possession of this lineage is legitimate and sure, and it has come all the way down to me from the perpetual continuance of a more enduring race.[40]

We have read that the breast of Ethiopian Sabba, imbued with divinity, solved the prophetic riddles of the Egyptian king Solomon.[41] The first writers believed that Amalthea, a woman erudite in the knowledge of the future, sang responses near the banks that surround the Avernus, not far from Baiae. She, who as a Sybil was worthy of the gods of this lineage, sold books full of oracles to Priscus Tarquinius.[42] Thus the Babylonian prophetess Eriphila, looking into the future with her divine mind far removed, described the fall and the ashes of Troy, the fortunes of the Roman empire, and the mysteries of Christ, who would later be born.[43] Nicostrata, too, the mother of Evander and very learned in prophecy as well as literature, attained such genius that she was the first to show the alphabet to the first Latins in sixteen figures.[44] The enduring fame of Inachan Isis will flourish, for she alone of the Argive goddesses revealed to the Egyptians her own alphabet for reading.[45] But Zenobia, an Egyptian woman of noble erudition, became so learned not only in Egyptian but also in Latin and Greek literature that she wrote the histories of barbarian and foreign peoples.[46]

39. *Generositas* (noble lineage, lineage, birth, nobility of stock) is the key image in Cereta's letter; the term suggests the notion of a noble race of learned women from which she, Laura, is descended. Note again the prominence of the image of the female breast in Cereta; here her lineage itself is safeguarded "nostro pectore."

40. Here again Cereta expresses the notion of women as a collectivity, as a race, breed, or generation "more enduring" than that of males. Note also her use of terms common in property and inheritance law: *legitima, hereditatis, possessio,* here applied to the intellectual and cultural legacy of generations of learned women.

41. See Boccaccio, *CFW,* chap. 41, pp. 93–94, on Saba, Sabba, or Nicaula, queen of Ethiopia; in Boccaccio, however, it is Queen Saba who comes to Solomon to consult his wisdom and not the other way around. In *CFW* Saba has a royal lineage and great wealth but she is not a seer.

42. See Boccaccio, *CFW,* chap. 24, pp. 50–51, on the Sibyl Amalthea, who lived at Cumae near Naples and the Avernus. According to legend, the Sibyl sold King Tarquinius of Rome three books of prophecies, having originally offered him six others which he refused.

43. See Boccaccio, *CFW,* chap. 19, pp. 41–42, on Eriphila or Herophile, the Sibyl. Cereta is faithful to Boccaccio.

44. See Boccaccio, *CFW,* chap. 25, pp. 52–55: Cereta's description agrees with Boccaccio's: Nicostrata's literary training and her intellectual acumen is connected in Boccaccio to her prophesying ability.

45. See Boccaccio, *CFW,* chap. 8, pp. 18–19, on Isis. Cereta's story of Isis's gift of "her own alphabet" (*sua elementa*) to the Egyptians agrees with Boccaccio.

46. See Boccaccio, *CFW,* chap. 98, pp. 226–30, on Zenobia. Boccaccio says Zenobia was be-

Shall we attribute illiteracy to Theban Manto, the prophesying daughter of Tiresias, and to Pyromantia, too, who was full of those Chaldaean arts when she spoke with the shades of the dead and foretold events in the future through the movements of flames, the flight of birds, and livers and entrails of animals?[47] Where did all the great wisdom of Tritonian Pallas come from, which enabled her to educate so many Athenians in the arts, if it was not that she succeeded in unraveling the mysteries of the scriptures of Apollo, the physician, to the delight of everyone?[48] Those little Greek women Phyliasia and Lasthenia were wonderful sources of light in the world of letters and they filled me with new life because they ridiculed the students of Plato, who frequently tied themselves in knots over the snare-filled sophistries of their arguments.[49]

Lesbian Sappho serenaded the stony heart of her lover with tearful poems, sounds I might have thought came from Orpheus' lyre or the plectrum of Phoebus.[50] Soon the Greek tongue of Leontium, full of the Muses, emerged, and she, who had made herself agreeable with the liveliness of her writing, dared to make a bitter attack on the divine words of Theophrastus.[51] Nor would I omit here Proba, noted both for her exceptional tongue and her knowledge; for she wove together and composed histories of the Old Testament with fragments from Homer and Virgil.[52]

The majesty of the Roman state deemed worthy a little Greek woman, Semiramis, for she spoke her mind about the laws in a court of law and about kings in the senate.[53] Pregnant with virtue, Rome bore Sempronia, who,

---

lieved to have written summaries of certain ancient histories; Cereta carries Boccaccio a step further by asserting that Zenobia was so erudite that she herself wrote histories.

47. See Boccaccio, *CFW,* chap. 28, pp. 60–61, on Manto. Cereta's remarks on the seer come straight out of *CFW.*

48. See Boccaccio, *CFW,* chap. 6, pp. 14–15, on the goddess Athene. Boccaccio credits the goddess with having invented or practiced every art and craft except divination. Cereta calls Apollo "physici" (doctor, physician).

49. Students of Plato. See Diogenes Laertius, *Lives of the Philosophers.*

50. See Boccaccio, *CFW,* chap. 45, pp. 99–100, on Sappho. Cereta follows Boccaccio and makes her unresponsive lover an anonymous male.

51. See Boccaccio, *CFW,* chap. 58, pp. 132, on Leontium; Cereta is faithful to Boccaccio's text.

52. See Boccaccio, *CFW,* chap. 95, pp. 219–20, on Proba, about whom Cereta is fairly faithful to Boccaccio's portrait. Cereta makes her a speaker as well as a writer, but in Boccaccio there is no mention of Proba's oratory, and his emphasis is on Proba's exceptionality in comparison to most other women, whom he dismisses as idle and pleasure-seeking.

53. See Boccaccio, *CFW,* chap. 2, pp. 4–7, on Semiramis (Semiamira in Cereta). Cereta differs: Boccaccio says nothing about a connection between Rome and Semiramis, a queen who led her nation as its king and chief military leaders, according to Boccaccio. Her sexual relationships and her incest with her son with which she is associated with in most accounts of her life are suppressed in Cereta.

forceful in her eloquent poetry, spoke in public assemblies and filled the minds of her audiences with persuasive orations.[54] Hortensia, the daughter of Hortensius, and also an orator, was celebrated at a public meeting with equal elegance. Her grace of speech was so great that she persuaded the triumvirs, albeit with the tears of a loyal mother, to absolve the women of Rome from having to pay the debt levied against them.[55] Add also Cornificia, the sister of the poet Cornificius, whose devotion to literature bore such fruit that she was said to have been nurtured on the milk of the Castalian Muses and who wrote epigrams in which every phrase was graced with Heliconian flowers.[56] I will not mention here Cicero's daughter Tulliola or Terentia or Cornelia, Roman women who reached the pinnacle of fame for their learning; and accompanying them in the shimmering light of silence will be Nicolosa of Bologna, Isotta of Verona, and Cassandra of Venice.[57]

All history is full of such examples. My point is that your mouth has grown foul because you keep it sealed so that no arguments can come out of it that might enable you to admit that nature imparts one freedom to all human beings equally—to learn.[58] But the question of my exceptionality re-

54. See Boccaccio, *CFW*, chap. 77, pp. 173–75 on the "Roman Sempronia." Cereta's Sempronia resembles Boccaccio's in her eloquence, classical training, and poetic skill but the sexual side of Sempronia's life—the dissolute Sempronia of Sallust's *Bellum Catilinae*—is suppressed.

55. See Boccaccio, *CFW*, chap. 82, p. 185, on Hortensia. Cereta here follows Boccaccio but adds a detail of her own not in B.: namely, that she persuaded the triumvirs with her oratory and her "motherly tears." Again for Boccaccio the emphasis is on how exceptional Hortensia is for her sex: she seems, he remarks, to "be a man."

56. See Boccaccio, *CFW*, chap. 84, pp. 188, on Cornificia; Cereta's imagery and even diction come from Boccaccio. But as usual Boccaccio differs form Cereta by adding a passage at the end of his chapter on Cornificia in which he stresses the point that "most women" are really only good for sex and childbearing.

57. Cicero's daughter Tullia (Tulliola), Cicero's wife Terentia (later the wife of Sallust), and Cornelia (the mother of Tiberius and Gaius Gracchi, who was famous for her learning) are all Roman women who were legendary in the ancient world for their learning. Isotta Nogarola of Verona (b. 1418) and Cassandra Fedele of Venice (b. 1465) became legendary for their erudition during their own lifetimes. But what of the phrase "in the shimmering light of silence"? Cereta apparently didn't think modern Italian women scholars like Nogarola and Fedele got the press they deserved.

58. "Naturam discendi aeque omnibus unam impartiri licentiam": the idea that both women and men were born with the right to an education was a radical statement for any fifteenth-century thinker. On the controversy over women's intelligence and the exceptional-woman theory from Boccaccio, see Benson, *The Invention of the Renaissance Woman*; Constance Jordan, "Boccaccio's Infamous Women: Gender and Civic Virtue in the *De claris mulieribus*," in *Ambiguous Realities. Women in the Middle Ages and Renaissance*, eds. Carole Levin and Jeannie Watson (Detroit: Wayne State University Press, 1987), pp. 25–47; Constance Jordan, *Renaissance Feminism. Literary Texts and Political Models* ((Ithaca: Cornell University Press, 1990); Margaret King, *Women of the Renaissance* (Chicago: University of Chicago Press, 1991); Patricia H. Labalme, "Venetian Women on Women: Three Early Modern Feminists, *Archivio Veneto* 5.117 (1981): 81–109; and Valerie Wayne, "Zenobia in Medieval and Renaissance Literature," in *Ambiguous Realities*, pp. 48–65.

mains. And here choice alone, since it is the arbiter of character, is the distinguishing factor. For some women worry about the styling of their hair, the elegance of their clothes,[59] and the pearls and other jewelry they wear on their fingers. Others love to say cute little things, to hide their feelings behind a mask of tranquility, to indulge in dancing, and lead pet dogs around on a leash. For all I care, other women can long for parties with carefully appointed tables, for the peace of mind of sleep, or they can yearn to deface with paint the pretty face they see reflected in their mirrors. But those women for whom the quest for the good represents a higher value restrain their young spirits and ponder better plans. They harden their bodies with sobriety and toil, they control their tongues, they carefully monitor what they hear, they ready their minds for all-night vigils, and they rouse their minds for the contemplation of probity in the case of harmful literature. For knowledge is not given as a gift but by study. For a mind free, keen, and unyielding in the face of hard work always rises to the good, and the desire for learning grows in depth and breadth.

So be it therefore. May we women, then, not be endowed by God the grantor with any giftedness or rare talent through any sanctity of our own. Nature has granted to all enough of her bounty; she opens to all the gates of choice, and through these gates, reason sends legates to the will, for it is through reason that these legates can transmit their desires. I shall make a bold summary of the matter.[60] Yours is the authority, ours is the inborn ability.[61] But instead of manly strength, we women are naturally endowed with cunning; instead of a sense of security, we are suspicious. Down deep we women are content with our lot. But you, enraged and maddened by the anger of the dog from whom you flee, are like someone who has been frightened by the attack of a pack of wolves. The victor does not look for the fugitive; nor does she who desires a cease-fire with the enemy conceal herself. Nor does she set up camp with courage and arms when the conditions are hopeless. Nor does it give the strong any pleasure to pursue one who is already fleeing.

Look, do you tremble from fear alone of my name? I am savage neither in mind nor hand. What it is you fear? You run away and hide in vain, for the traps that await you around every corner have been more cunningly set. Is it thus that you, a deserter, leave this city and our sight? Is it thus that, regretful

---

59. Vat., Ven.: "amictus"; Tom., erroneously "amicus."

60. Vat.: "Rem audacisicula summaria decidam"; Ven.: "Rem audaciuncula summaria"; Tom. omits sentence.

61. "Vestra est auctoritas, nostrum ingenium." One of the Cereta's key feminist aphorisms, it suggests that the greatest source of tension between the sexes lies in an unjustifiable power differential: though men are born with the power to rule, women have superior intellectual gifts.

of what you have done, you rely on flight as the first road to safety for yourself? May your shame then stay with you. My goodness towards men isn't always rewarded, and you may imagine in your disdain for women that I alone marvel at the felicitousness of having talent—I, who in the light of the well-deserved fame of other women, am indeed only the smallest little mouse. Therefore when you hide your envy under a bogus example, you clothe yourself with defensive words in vain.

For truth which is dear to God always emerges when falsehoods are overthrown. That road is twisted where you walk under the black gaze of an envious mind—far from human beings, from duties, and from God. Who will be surprised, do you think, Bibolo, if the lacerated and wounded heart of a girl who is filled with indignation bitterly rears itself up against your sarcasm and satire from this day on, now that your trifling arrogance has wounded her with bitter injuries? Do not think, most despicable of men, that I might believe I have fallen out of favor with Jove. I am a scholar and a pupil who has been lulled to sleep by the meager fire of a mind too humble. I have been too much burned, and my injured mind has accumulated too much passion; for tormenting itself with the defending of our sex, my mind sighs, conscious of its obligation. For all things—those deeply rooted inside us as well as those outside us—are being laid at the door of our sex.

In addition, I, who have always held virtue in high esteem and considered private things as secondary in importance, shall wear down and exhaust my pen writing against those men who are garrulous and puffed up with false pride. I shall not fail to obstruct tenaciously their treacherous snares. And I shall strive in a war of vengeance against the notorious abuse of those who fill everything with noise, since armed with such abuse, certain insane and infamous men bark and bare their teeth in vicious wrath at the republic of women,[62] so worthy of veneration. January 13, 1488.

XIX
AGAINST WOMEN WHO DISPARAGE EDUCATED WOMEN

Letters XIX and XX represent expansions of themes touched on in the essays on marriage and education. Letter XIX, "Against women who disparage educated women," also reads like a formal oration or a standard humanist invective. Addressed to Lucilia Vernacula (perhaps a fictional correspondent), the

---

62. *Muliebris respublica* (womanly republic, republic of women) is an expression I have not seen elsewhere. While mine isn't a word for word translation, I did try to capture in English Cereta's prose rhythms, bombastic diction, and overstatement, and also the characterization of her opponents as viciously growling dogs ready to bite (*infestius mordaciusque delatrant*), which is so typical of the genre of invective.

tone of the letter is hostile and distant and its language exaggerated and violent. Meant to display her mastery of the genre of the invective, Cereta launches a counterattack on women who abuse other women, explaining that they are envious of women who are achievers because they are frustrated, because their lives are empty, and because they lack the self-confidence they would need to work at becoming educated themselves.

To Lucilia Vernacula[63]

I should think that the tongues should be cut to pieces and the hearts brutally lacerated of people whose minds are so wicked and whose envious rage is so incredible that they deny in their ignorant rantings the possibility that any woman might master the most elegant elements of Roman oratory. I would pardon the morally hopeless and even people destined for a life of crime, whom wagging tongues are accustomed to castigate with obvious fury. But I cannot tolerate the gabbing and babbling women who, burning with wine and drunkenness, harm with their petulant talk not only their sex but themselves. These mindless women—these female counselors who emerge victorious from the cookshop jar after a prodigious vote among their neighbors—hunt down with their bilious poison those women who rise to greater distinction than they. The bold and undisguised passion these women have for destruction and disgrace, this hunger of theirs for calamity, which strives to smear even those who are completely above reproach, deserves to bring a worse disgrace on itself. For the man who does not take care to have himself absolved of wrongdoing[64] wants his own moral lapses to be excused.

Besides, these women, being idle with time on their hands[65] and no interests of their own, occupy themselves with keeping watch over other people's business, and, like scarecrows hung up in the garden to get rid of sparrows, they shoot poison from the bows of their tongues[66] at those who cross their paths. What after all is the purpose of honor if I were to believe that the barking roars of these sharp-tongued women were worth tolerating, when decent and cultivated women always extol me with honorable words? I am not a woman who wants the shameful deeds of insolent people to slip

---

63. Vat. 67 (fols. 52–52v); Ven. 56 (fols.); Tom. 54 (pp. 122–25); Rabil 71.

64. Vat., Ven.: "turpitudinem"; Tom., erroneously "turpidinem."

65. Cereta's indictment of the women gossips as lazy about their leisure time (*otio desides*) is interesting: they neglect that which is all-important to her: *otium*, the time when a woman is free from housework to study, write, and think (see chapter 1, letter II).

66. Literally the "bow of their tongue" (*arcu linguae*), a strange metaphor, undoubtedly original with Cereta.

through under the pardon of silence, either so that in the end I'll be said to approve of what I'm silent about or so that the very women who lead their lives with shame will continue to entice a great many people into their licentiousness as accomplices. Nor would I want, because of my speaking out, someone to criticize me for intolerance; even dogs are allowed to protect themselves from more aggressive fleas by crushing them with their nails. An infected sheep must always be isolated from the healthy flock. For the greatest number are often harmed by the least. Who would believe that disease in trees is caused by ants?

Those insolent women are therefore silent about every law of honor who, burning with the fires of hatred, would silently gnaw away at themselves, if they didn't feast in their slanderous talk on others. Mildew of the mind afflicts certain demented mothers, who being veritable Megaeras can't stand to hear even the epithet "learned women."[67] Their faces are spongy-looking, and in the vehemence of their speech they sometimes produce the words of a very large louse form their wrinkled cheeks, and sometimes in the presence of onlookers whose eyes grow round with horror at their thundering idiocies.[68] Human error causes us to be ashamed and disgusted that those women who are themselves caught in a tangle of doubt have given up hope of attaining knowledge of the humane arts, when they could easily acquire such knowledge with skill and virtue. For an education is neither bequeathed to us as a legacy, nor does some fate or other give it to us as a gift. Virtue is something that we ourselves acquire; nor can those women who become dull-witted through laziness and the sludge of low pleasures ascend to the understanding of difficult things. But for those women who believe that study, hard work, and vigilance will bring them sure praise, the road to attaining knowledge is broad. Vale. November 1, 1487.

XX

AN ATTACK ON FEMININE CULTURE

Letter XX, entitled "An attack on feminine culture" and addressed to Agostino Emilio, is unlike any other letter in the letterbook in that it begins with a personal memoir of Cereta's last moments with her husband Pietro at his deathbed, and moves from there, rather abruptly, into a formal oration on the frivolousness of women's obsession with clothing and makeup. Heavily indebted to Juvenal's sixth satire against women, Cereta borrows from him even details about the customs of Roman women to describe the excesses of

---

67. Megaera: the name of one of the Furies in Greek mythology.
68. Vat., Ven.: "sub oculis rigentibus"; Tom., erroneously "sub oculis regentibus."

women in contemporary Brescia. In an unexpected conclusion, given that Cereta's criticisms have been directed at women and their choices, she lays the responsibility for women's obsession with fashion and luxuries at the door of the men of the ruling class (*Vos tantae auctoritatis supereminentissimi viri . . . videte cautius*). Although women are the weaker sex physically, they need not be so intellectually; women must choose to pursue the important things in life not the superficial ones. Thus if women are to pull themselves out of their present condition, the effort will have to be a joint one and the responsibility will have to be shared by both sexes.

To Agostino Emilio[69]

I was driving alone in the country, and in the restful serenity of the moment I was taking pleasure in thoughts of human events. But you meanwhile were worried about my arrival at my family's house, as though you were thinking of me as an important person whom you didn't know.

When I arrived at last, my husband was feverish. I, myself dying, watched over him, now nearly lifeless. I consoled him when he was a little better, wept over him when he was dead; I myself fell lifeless over his corpse, and the house that awaited me on the day of my wedding, now draped in mourning, received me for his funeral. Thus one unspeakable year saw me a girl, a bride, a widow, and bereft of all the goods of fortune.

These were not things that fate had in store for you; for the events that you in your kindness have asked about happened through Necessity and the purging agency of fate.[70] And so, because of these things, I thank you for thinking of me as a person of higher value and for holding me in greater honor, though I can scarcely be thought of as belonging to the same category as Sarah, Hester, Sephora, and Susanna, but am rather like a luminous glow-worm[71] compared to the brilliance of the stars in the firmament. And so, I do fear that my dignity in your eyes may come from somewhere other than your own opinion and estimate of it. Do be aware, though, that you are going to see a little woman who is humble in both her appearance and her dress, since I am more concerned with letters than with adornment, having committed myself to the care of virtue, which can indeed confer honor on me not only during my lifetime but when I am dead.

69. Vat. 38 (fols. 28v–29v); Ven. 33 (fols. 56–58); Tom. 31 (pp. 66–71); Rabil 54.

70. Vat., Ven.: "necessitate fati purgentis"; Tom. omits this phrase.

71. Cereta's comparison of herself to a glowworm (*lampyris*) exemplifies the uniqueness of her voice in humanist letters and her attempt to produce a different, feminine voice.

There are some people who are impressed by the attribute of beauty. I myself would rather see senatorial uncorruptibility[72] rewarded since, as with the physical beauty of youth, so often the stimuli for such attractions burst into flames themselves. But honor, the light of beauty, surpasses all the contrived arts of polishing and all the little flowers of softness. Mark Anthony might delight in the bejeweled Cleopatra; but I myself will imitate the integrity of Rebecca. Paris might seek the promenading Helen; but I have chosen to imitate the modesty of Rachel. Wives are too often led astray by ostentation; but the men who squander their patrimonies because of their appetite for such display err more profoundly.

Today our city has become a disciple in the passions of women; indeed the city has become a pillager of the orient.[73] In no age has there been a more wasteful tolerance for vanity. Those who don't believe me should visit the places of worship. There they should observe the wedding ceremonies full of married women sitting in the congregation. Let them have a good look at those women who, striding down the streets with superb arrogance, cut right through the midst of the crowd. Let them attend public spectacles and let them marvel, as they survey the little courtyards in the city and the narrow passageways of any atrium, at the various and diverse ornaments these women possess.[74] Some of these women sport a knot of somebody else's hair piled up like a tower; another woman's hair hangs down on her foreheaded in curls.[75] Another puts her blond hair up, tying it back with a soft gold clasp so that she bares her neck; still others wear necklaces on their shoulders or arms, or hanging down from their necks to their breasts.[76] Some wind strings of pearls around their throats, as though they were captives proud of being owned by free men; most of these display fingers sparkling with gems. One woman walks with a limping gait, her belt loosened from her attempts at popularity. Another woman's breasts become larger when she wears a tighter sash.[77] Some trail silken tunics from their shoulders. Still others, redolent with perfumes, swathe themselves in Arabian veils. Women who reveal slip-

72. "Honestas" (honor, purity, integrity, incorruptibility), is also linked in humanism with the ethos of civic service, of working for the commonweal and of acquiring a good name for oneself in doing so.

73. The passage is typical of humanist and classical attitudes toward the "decadent" culture of the "orient"; trade with the east is attacked because it devalues (according to humanist writers) the products manufactured at home.

74. This entire sentence, contained in Vat. and Ven., is omitted in Tom.

75. On women's coiffeurs Cereta is indebted to Juvenal 6.492–503.

76. See Juvenal 6.457–59; the rest of the paragraph is indebted to Juvenal 6.

77. Following this sentence Vat. contains a number of sentences I omit since they do not appear in Ven. and Tom.

pers turned into high-heeled footgear of leather are not poorly dressed, but it is common knowledge that other, more elegant women bind their legs more delicately with fine cloth wrappings.

Many women press bread on their faces to soften it,[78] and many erroneously polish skin that is full of wrinkles. Truly, there are few women who do not paint their bloodshot faces with a snow-white powder made from white lead. Some strive to seem more beautiful in their exquisite and exotic dress than the creator of beauty intended them to be. One is ashamed of the irreverence of certain women who redden their milk-white cheeks with purple dye, and who use their furtive little eyes and laughing mouths to pierce the hearts, already poisoned, of those who gaze on them.

Ah, how careworn one's brow grows at such a greedy consuming of honor. Alas, how crooked is the weakness of our sex in its delights. For what else have we that would enable us to imitate nobility other than earrings shimmering with rubies and emeralds dangling from our ears? For we weren't born to dote with corrupt devotion on the images of our own faces in the mirror, were we? Or have we Christian women refused ostentatiousness at our baptismal ceremonies so that we could make ourselves up like Jewish or pagan women? Our misguided ambition for this kind of superiority should make us blush. The lascivious nature of our madness should make us shrink back in fear from such arrogance; and mindful of the ashes from which we have come, let us put an end to sins reborn from our desires.

But how will there be a place for our lamentation, if anger and divine indignation grow hot against us miserable women? If those who rebel against a king prepare his neck for the ax, why should we women, who ourselves have been warriors and rebels against God, be surprised that a cloud of Turks should attack the Gauls in our defense?[79] Rome now weeps over the arrival of the Gauls? Conquered Italy now bewails the swords of the Goths. The Greeks are unhappy about the tyranny of Mohammed. But those are disasters that come from heaven, not from our women's arms. Let each woman take counsel; let each one heal the injury from which she, being wounded, now languishes. Let us pursue beautiful things, not the enticements of whores; and let us thus use and enjoy this life in such a way that we will remember that we are mortals.

For God the father decided that it was proper for the good to die well.

---

78. On the use of bread or dough to make the skin and face look more youthful see Juvenal 6.461–63 and 6.471–73.

79. Cereta's villainization of women (*they* are literally the enemy) as lovers of fashion is characteristic of her extreme ambivalence towards women as a group, which swings between pride and hostility.

Therefore, as many times as you, Agostino, have looked at me and have seen boasts devoid of great splendor, please pardon my age or at least my sex. For Nature, which produced our foremother[80] not from earth or stone but from the humanity of Adam, is complicit in our guilt. However, humanity always leans towards that which it can either assist or delight in. We are the more imperfect animal, and our few strengths are not effective in wars of courage. You, preeminent men of great authority, on whom the highest matters of state devolve, and who have amongst yourselves, by the right of assembly, so many Brutuses, Curii, Fabii, Catos, and Enylios, be careful to see that we women, being constituted as we are, are not taken in by the birdlime of this sort of elegance. For where there is greater deliberation in councils of state, there the greater blame should rest. February 12, 1487.

80. Cereta speaks of Eve as *genetrix nostra:* our foremother.

III

MARRIAGE AND MOURNING

These letters trace the further development of Cereta's persona as a writer from her erotic relationship with Pietro Serina, whom she marries, to her double bereavement: both of Serina, through his sudden death, and of her humanist studies, owing to her despair. The two groups of letters, representing her marriage and widowhood, are more similar in mood than they are contrasting; both groups are characterized by expressions of anger and disillusionment, loss and pain, and an extremity and excess of feeling. While her recondite vocabulary and imagery here reflect an ongoing immersion on her part in a more scientifically and philosophically oriented canon of later Latin writers, such as Pliny the Elder, Apuleius, Gellius, and Seneca, who only come to be cultivated by the humanists at the end of the fifteenth century, both the marriage and the mourning essays also suggest the lyric persona of the Roman elegiac poets, in her perpetual reaching, Orpheuslike, for that which is already lost.

XXI–XXV
HER LETTERS TO HER HUSBAND

XXI

Laura writes a teasing, coaxing letter to her husband in which she shows off her ability to sound like a lawyer, a skill she undoubtedly learned from her attorney father. Pietro, who is presumably tending his shop in Venice, has accused her of singling him out as the only one of her correspondents she thought she could ignore. Her response to him is aggressive and flirtatious: if he wants to make accusations, he will have to come back to Brescia to make them in person. And when she proposes that her innocence will be the "tin-der" (*fomes*) for his pardon (*venia*), her subtext is frankly sexual.

To Pietro Serina [1]

*Y*ou charge me with laziness and attack me for my long silence as though I were a defendant in court. You act as if I were the sort of person who would write to strangers and only neglect you, as though I were forgetful of you when in fact I accord you a place of honor above that of other learned men. And although I might boast that I have received whatever learning I have from you for the sake of your honor, still I won't offer further epistolary flattery in place of an excuse in any hope that there could be im-punity for one who has committed an offense: for the hunter of false friend-ships uses flattery to set up her nets. Consequently, my innocence alone will be the tinder for your forgiveness of me.

But really, the motive separates innocent from the guilty. And I should not be summoned to a court without a judge by a plaintiff who is absent, since the alleged offense seems to have been committed against him who is absent.[2] Otherwise you might as well blame the gods. And so, your accusa-tion requires the mounting of an indictment against the accused.[3] But no confirmation of witnesses or arguments of proof are necessary in this case. I am not going to deny the charge that I have been silent, provided that the one who accuses me, the plaintiff himself, appears.

This legal inquiry should not be protracted any longer. Some might well take the case from the benches to the highest tribunal; we ourselves will agree with the first verdict we receive, especially since the judge will be our common father. He, who is as just as the members of the Athenian

1. Vat. 17 (fol. 19v); Ven. 16 (fols. 40–40v); Tom. 8 (pp. 23–24); Rabil 3. [See Introduction, note 1, for full citations.] This is the first of four letters addressed by Cereta to her husband, Pietro Serina, whom she married sometime in either December 1484 or January 1485.

2. "Neque enim debeo absque iudice absente deferri": this is legal language; *deferre* is used here in the sense of "bring a case to court," accuse, or bring charges against. "Insimulatio suspecta" (the alleged crime, the supposed charges): again, legal jargon.

3. The rest of the letter is filled with more legalese. "Accusatio tua crimen accusati requirit": *crimen* here signifies not just a crime but a formal indictment or the mounting of charges by a plaintiff against an *accusati* (the accused). The ensuing sentences contain such typical forensic vocabulary as: "confirmatione testium" (confirmation of witnesses), "argumento probandi" (argu-ment of proof), "admissum . . . infic[i]" (to repudiate the charge), "auctor" (the plaintiff), "cog-nitio" (legal inquiry), "a subsellis ad rostra defer[ri]" (to take a court case from the lower court to the high tribunal), "iudicio" (verdict).

Aeropagus, will adjudicate the case not for his own family but for everyone.[4] You will come here, then, if your charges against me are just; nor will you ignore the time limit of two days, since the tolling of the bell in the middle of the town square will indicate the last day to you. Vale. July 14, 1485.

XXII

In this letter to Pietro, Laura reveals that she is experiencing serious difficulties in the marriage. She wants to respect her husband and even defers to him; yet she is repeatedly hurt by him. She tries to please him, but whether she enters into a conversation with him or says nothing, he ridicules and seems to enjoy taunting her. While he can always escape their frustrating domestic life by going off to his shop in Venice for months at a time, she is left to brood over the situation alone, feeling miserable and stuck in a marriage that is not working. Cereta's exotic imagery in the opening of this letter is reminiscent of a scene in Apuleius' novel *The Golden Ass*—a work she had studied carefully, as we shall see in chapter 6—in which the west wind carries the young heroine Psyche from the top of a mountain (*scopulus*, Cereta's word) to a valley below so that she can join her unpredictable and sometimes harsh lover, Cupid.[5] Cereta's letter bespeaks her longing, frustration, and sense of inadequacy in her relations with her husband. Nonetheless, the analogy she seems to draw between his manner with her and a gusting wind is anything but complimentary.

To Pietro Serina [6]

O ye more favorable gods, whose charge it is to protect innocence, for what times and what mores did this iron procession of ages preserve me to be born?[7] May I be endowed with both eloquence and reticence, so that I can either be silent or respond promptly to your reproach. I too seldom

---

4. Aeropagus was the hill in Athens where capital cases were tried; its members were the most distinguished citizens and jurists in Athens.

5. See Apuleius, *Met.* 4.35.

6. Vat. 19 (fol. 20); Ven. 18 (fols. 41–42); Tom. 10 (pp. 26–27); Rabil 5.

7. "O dii meliores . . . ad quos mores, ad quae tempora": a reference to Cicero's famous opening to the Catiline orations, "O tempora, O mores." Cereta's melodramatic complaint alludes to the classical view of history as a scene of progressively worsening conditions for the human race (Hesiod, Virgil, Horace, Ovid): after a legendary golden age when humans lived in happiness and harmony came the silver and bronze ages, which were followed by the iron age, a time of ceaseless war and toil.

reach the heights where that wind of yours gusts forth.[8] But still, if my silence is more boorish[9] than my conversation in your judgment, I have a compromise: and that is to whisper and to allow these lips to speak freely. For when you ordered me to speak, that virginal shame of mine caused me to refuse. You yourself urged me, though I was often trembling, to desire to free my heart from the fear in which it was drowning. Now, however, though uninhibited in my speech, I am not free from blame either. It is as though you pick arguments with me because either I'm silent when I'm angry or speak when I feel I'm impelled to, though apparently neither option is permitted.

Perhaps you invent these things on purpose so that I will row the unsteady seas under an unsteady sail between Scylla and Charybdis.[10] The situation deserves my tears and sadness; it consumes and gnaws at me. Thus I congratulate you, husband, dearer than life to me, because you have simply moved away from this place and have gone to Venice, while I still have cause for grief. But this is a beautiful and opportune thing for me since I, who gauge the outcome of things by the various stars, will be forced to resign myself to Time and Fortuna: her whom, unless the Catholic faith forbids it, I shall call the goddess all-powerful.[11] Vale. July 22, 1485.

XXIII

In her third letter to her husband, Cereta reveals the role she plays as wife to a greater extent than she does in any other letter in the collection. When she hears of the loss by fire of Pietro's business in Venice, she behaves like a business partner, offering him advice on the steps he should take to cut his losses. For his part, Pietro in his last letter has accused Laura of not loving him enough: a strategy that seems to set the stage for him to ask for some financial assistance from her or her family, to help him rebuild his business after the fire. Laura also paves the way for such a request when she refers to herself as a woman not only of virtue but also some means, and it is clear from this letter that she sees her role as both her husband's financial and moral supporter.

8. On the imagery of a gusting wind, etc., see my commentary above and n. 5.

9. For a humanist, there is no worse insult than to be criticized as "boorish" or "rustic" (here *rusticus*, countrified, oafish, rural); the suave Quattrocento humanist wants to be identified with the city, not the countryside.

10. Scylla and Charybdis: two famous perils for sailors off the coast of Sicily, both of them personified as she-monsters, part-beast and part-woman.

11. Her bow to the "goddess" Fortuna is a typical humanist gesture—a typical Christian humanist move, one could also say.

To my husband, Pietro Serina [12]

ith fear and trembling we have viewed, through your letters, the raging fires on the Rialto, and we have seen the sum total of your business all but thrown into the billowing inferno there.[13] And so, we can hope for nothing more than that you sell off piecemeal the tattered remains of your goods and household furnishings to other merchants at the open market, in such a way that the buyer who can offer you the appropriate silver for your goods will seek you out. But as to your writing me that I don't love you very much, I don't know whether you're saying this in earnest or whether I should realize that you're joking with me. Still, what you say disturbs me. You are measuring a very healthy expression of a wife's loyalty by the standard of the insincere flattery of well-worn phrases. But I shall love you, my husband. What does it mean to you that you reassure me with those trivial little compliments? Do you want me to believe that you expect me to comb my hair in a stylish fashion for your homecoming? Or to feign adoring looks with a painted face? Let women without means, who worry and have no confidence in their own virtue, flutter their eyelashes and play games to gain favor with their husbands. This is the adulation of a fox and the birdlime of deceitful birdhunting. I don't want to have to buy you at such a price. I'm not a person who lays more stock in words than duty. I am truly your Laura, whose soul is the same one you in turn had hoped for. Vale. August 13, 1485.

XXIV

In a foreshadowing of Cereta's inconsolable sorrow on her own husband's sudden death, which was to occur about two or three weeks after this letter was sent, in July or August of 1486, she watched her husband give himself over to weeping day in and day out after the death of his brother Nicolai. In this letter she reproaches her husband for his failure to come to terms with his brother's death, to get on with his life, and to put aside the unremitting grief that is causing him to turn his back even on her love.

As George McClure has recently shown, sorrow and mourning, with their rituals of breast-beating, disconsolate bouts of weeping, and consolatory letter writing, were all standard features of the Renaissance way of

---

12. Vat. 9 (fol. 16v); Ven. 8 (fols. 32–33); not in Tom.; Rabil 11; this is the third letter in the two manuscript editions of Cereta's letter collection addressed to her husband, Pietro Serina.

13. Cereta speaks of Serina's business in vague terms, *rerum tuarum*, here; we know nothing more about his business. I'm assuming that he had a small shop or office on or near the Rialto (which Cereta refers to as the "riv[us] alt[us]" in this letter) in Venice.

death.[14] Florid displays of grief on the death of a friend or family member were in fact expected. It was only when mourning lasted too long or kept the mourner from performing his or her obligations to family, friends, and community that it was pronounced excessive.

To Pietro Serina, my husband [15]

*Y*ou bear your bereavement over the untimely death of Nicolai with unending tears, as though you yourself had died, and in such a way that you seem to have banished all hope of living from your mind. Have you forgotten, most mindful and brave among men, that nature has so ordained dying for all men that only the good die well? And even if he had survived vile death, would you not be induced to tear your hair, cry out, and beat your breast at another man's funeral. Should I, poor thing, believe that you would lose sight of that magnanimity of mind that has enabled you to watch your own family struggling through years of death when it fell victim to the pestilent plague?

I myself would like you, and I do beg you now because it is time, to return to your former self, since you have a greater duty towards me than you do towards the dead: for a man and his wife must so mutually love one another that they will not turn aside from that love at any time. Get a hold of yourself, then, and control this weeping of yours that has affected you so bitterly and harshly, lest you seem either to be at war with yourself, or, by the Julian law, to have launched a campaign against the gods who steal men's souls.

You ought to remember that even if the fates were to give you to Nicolai, you would still be far more precious to me than to him, since we are now, and always will be, two souls belonging to a single being. Vale. July 17, 1486.

XXV

Everything about this letter addressed to a certain Pietro Stella suggests that the addressee may in fact be Cereta's husband. The intimacy of the scene she describes of the writing of another letter to Pietro—at 2 or 3 in the morning, presumably in her bedroom, in a private, dreamlike state of semiconsciousness—as well as her characterization of this Pietro as likely to be violent in

14. George McClure, *Sorrow and Consolation in Italian Humanism* (Princeton: Princeton University Press, 1991).

15. Vat. 15 (fol. 19); Ven. 14 (fols. 38–39v); Tom. (pp. 21–22); Rabil 44. Addressed to her husband (*Petro Serinae consorti*).

his reaction to her letters and her deferential attitude to him all suggest the tone and substance of Laura's previous letters to her husband.

To Pietro Stella[16]

*T*he moon had reached the middle of its journey in a night that was already fading, when swimming eyes, a drowsy mind, and my pen itself, as if in a dream, put into words the letter I recently sent you. And so, you shouldn't be amazed if the frequent blemishes caused by my sleepy meanderings have made a fool of me. Consequently you will pardon my drowsy haste, even if you don't pardon me.

Anyway, I urge you to make the effort of at least professing that this little letter is preferable to none at all, before you rip it bit by bit into a thousand pieces. But I know you'll think it worthwhile to grant me my wish, since kindness itself teaches you that it should be done of your own accord. Vale. September 23, 1484/5?[17]

XXVI–XXVIX
HER LETTERS OF MOURNING FOR PIETRO

XXVI
THE IMAGE OF DEATH

The subject of this letter, written within a week or so of her husband's death to the physician Felicio Tadino, is Cereta's own grieving, which she portrays as a gushing, flooding well gone out of control. In the midst of her despair, the image of death itself appears to Laura as in a dream, first in the form of a woman in a tattered cloak carrying a bow, and then as a snaky-haired Fury brandishing a scythe. At the close of the letter Laura's dread gives way to a desire for her own death.

16. Vat. 24 (fol. 22); Ven. 23; Tom 15 (pp. 36–37); Rabil 20. The addressee is one Pietro Stella. Given the intimate nature of the tone of this letter, I would like to argue that Stella (star) may have been what she called her husband as she stood at her window on those nights when he was away from home.

17. Since nothing explicit is said in this letter to indicate that the relationship is a conjugal one, it might also be conjectured that the letter could have been written to Pietro prior to their marriage in September 1484, not in 1485 as dated in Rabil.

To Felicio Tadino, physician [18]

Your letter has been a comfort to me, though I drenched it with tears before I read it: such is the tenderness of an embattled heart and so great the grief that wells up in an anxious breast. I had scarcely come to the middle of the letter in my short-lived reading of it when it prompted a fresh flow of tears for my mourning from eyes already bleary. Thus weeping evoked more weeping; and the floodgates were loosed in these two eyes of mine.

And so, in this overflow of mourning, winged death flooded my spirit deep within with monstrous horror.[19] For, swathed in the tattered cloak of death and carrying arrows spread out in her right hand and a menacing bow, she showed me her snarling, wan face, as she alternately ground and gnashed her teeth at me. I looked over at this underworld Fury, who barely clung to her filthy bones; and when the light caught her, garlanded with coils of snakes and brandishing a scythe and a grindstone, she hurled herself at me.[20] Frightened at the sudden attack of the approaching apparition, I was paralyzed with fear to the depths of my being. I marveled greatly that this little soul who appeared in the shape of a Cocytean figure shrank back into herself and fled. Once she was overwhelmed by the jaws and dark threshold of death, there could be nothing more I could hope for than that I should meet with death myself. For in the uncertain battle with death, what victor ever changes death's course, though she may retreat? For what dividends for one's life result from such a victory except that it increases the experience of the misery of dying with a hundredfold interest? August 10, 1486.

XXVII

This is one of four letters in Cereta's letterbook to the physician Michel Beto da Carrara, who has clearly been a literary mentor to her as well as a friend and supporter. Her imagery in this letter, in which the themes of eloquence and grieving form a delicate counterpoint, recalls earlier letters where noc-

18. Vat. 32 (fols. 26–26v); Ven. 27 (fols. 50–50v: Ven. lacks the first three sentences of this letter); Tom. 25 (pp. 55–56); Rabil 47. This is one of three letters in her letter collection addressed to the physician Felicio Tadino.

19. The images of excess, flooding, flying, and floating, are striking in this passage: "nimietate plorandi" (overflow a mourning), "perfudit" (flooded), "perspersi fontes" (streaming floodgates), "fletus fletum evocabat" (weeping evoked weeping), "mors volitans" (Tom.: flying or winged death; Vat.: "mos volitans").

20. It's not clear whether what she sees are two different figures or one that changes shape from death as an archer to a snake-infested Megaera, since she's obviously hallucinating.

turnal writing and study, writing and needlework as analogous activities of the mind, and the struggle for eloquence were key thematics. But here the work of mourning replaces that of writing; it becomes her "unus labor," and the desire for death her one preoccupation.

To Michel da Carrara, physician [21]

I have read your serious and eloquent letters, which have caused both goodwill and a fertile mind to flourish in me. You are in my thoughts and, if there is perhaps any part of this that I shall care about most, it is that I would not want you to be sorry suddenly that you had encouraged a girl to write letters that had nothing of the orator in them.[22] For although for a long time now my all-night bouts of writing have been less important to me, the one labor that remains for me is that of grieving, a thing which cruel fate has imposed on me because of my husband's death. Thus, struck by the incurable wound of mortality, I am so constantly moved by a desire for death that in the end I may at least become immortal in death, once no forgetting of the past can hold me back, since the vows of mortals are futile and the uncertainty of life brings unpredictable shifts and changes. Now, so much sorrow is left in me that every effort at eloquence runs clumsily aground among the reefs and at sea.[23] You, however, amid the copiousness of my style will not think ill of this letter, woven as it is of rather tiny pieces, and worn away for so long a time now by the corrosive sobbings of a young girl's pen.[24] Vale. August 13, 1486.

XXVIII
LAMENTATION FOR THE DEATH OF HER HUSBAND

In this letter of self-consolation, Cereta turns to Alberto degli Alberti, a friend whom she frequently portrays in the letterbook as a literary mentor of

21. Vat. 33 (fol. 26v); Ven. 28 (fols. 50v–51); Tom. 26 (pp. 56–57); Rabil 48. The letter is one of four letters in the collection addressed to Cereta's friend Michel Beto da Carrara, who, like Felicio Tadino, is a physician.

22. Cereta gives herself a backhanded compliment: although the humanist strives for eloquence, the professional orator always suggests insincerity and pretense; thus Cereta would want to show that she has something of the orator but not too much.

23. To write, for Cereta, is often to make a voyage; hence the images of shipwreck on the ocean and among rugged shoals.

24. Textile imagery is Cereta's particular trademark and can be seen throughout her letterbook, from letters I–III on. It is her constant resorting to figures of needlework and stitchery that distinguishes her writing from any male humanist I know of.

hers and a fellow attorney and longtime supporter of her father's. The prologue to the letter combines typical professions of humanist friendship with standard *topoi* in Renaissance mourning. Cereta bandies about such stock phrases as *officia et tuae letterae* (your services and your letters) and *tota imagine observantiae* (the total image of respectful regard), while baring her grief and despair to Alberti in a way more personal and private. In the central portion of the letter, she presents a series of exempla, most of which come from Ovid's *Metamorphoses*, of women in antiquity who lost their loves and were metamorphized—because of the gods' sympathy for them, according to Cereta—into other forms of life.

To Alberto degli Alberti, attorney [25]

*G*reat and remarkable things are being said publicly about your friendship with us; both your services and your letters to my father have strengthened what was already clear by implication on both sides. Your letters, flowing with milky liquor in the perfect image of loyalty and respect,[26] strive to comfort me with persuasion in my affliction; but the weakness of an injured mind has become so frozen inside me that I can no longer be restored by exhortations or advice; for my sorrow torments me and I am mute. Nor can I fail to be suffocated by a fortune without hope. I shall confess this, nor will shame stand in my way. Although many may call me a fool, I do not know whether life is dearer to me than death. How fortunate are those infants whose luck it is to die in a mother's lap. I myself have survived, but my weeping is reborn; and I have washed with unending tears the pale face of an adolescence soon to be gone.

I would surely consider the Atlantides more fortunate than I, for people believe that, after mourning for their mutilated brother Hyas, they were changed into a constellation.[27] No less fortunate is Halcyon, who on account of her weeping for Ceyx after he drowned, changed into a bird.[28] Like-

---

25. Vat. 34 (fols. 26v–27); Ven. 29 (fols. 51–52); Tom. 27 (pp. 57–59); Rabil 46 (p. 77). The letter is addressed to Alberto degli Alberti, an attorney in Brescia and an old friend and colleague of her father's: see chapter 1.

26. "Tota imagine observantiae": this is the vocabulary of humanist patronage; promised are service, respectful regard, loyalty, and attention to one's patron.

27. The Atlantides (also known as the Hyades) were the daughters of Atlas; they pined away until they died when their brother Hyas was killed in a boar hunt: Ovid, *Fast.* 5.165–82; Hyginus, *Fab.* 182.

28. See Ovid, *Met.* 11.384, for the story of Ceyx's drowning at sea and the metamorphoses into birds of both Ceyx and his lover Haylcon by the gods.

wise the grieving Heliades were able to relieve their sorrow, when, after Phaeton's fall, they grew into leafy poplars on the Po.[29] You too being scorned, Phyllis, were changed into an almond tree because of Demophoon's delay.[30] You, Scylla, saw well enough how passions dissolve, when you hid yourself from your lover Glaucus under the sharp Sicilian rocks.[31] Thus Cyane's tears disappeared from her eyes, when because of the rape of her friend Proserpina, she melted into a spring.[32] Thus Hecuba was metamorphosed into a dog to relieve her wretched weeping after losing her king and realm.[33] And thus Niobe was finally turned to stone, owing to the equal pity the gods took on her after her long period of mourning for her sons, whom Diana had impaled on a rock.[34]

Ah me, battered by disconsolate lamentation, for whom death, though hoped for, still waits in the wings: life, cruel and inexorable, does not withdraw. O that I might at least die a pagan, since it is not possible according to Christian dogma to elect not to live. Would that those changers of forms, the gods, now summoned so sorrowfully and humbly, might help me in my misfortune. August 5, 1486.

XXIX–XXX

In the letters of self-consolation to Felicio Tadino and Alberto degli Alberti, Cereta reveals a deep split between her public and private selves—between her bland smiles, dutiful letters to friends, and ritual gestures of mourning, on the one hand, and the interior world of pain, sighing, and soul sickness she experiences, on the other. Despite her acceptance of the classical division of the exterior from the interior self, Cereta confounds the classical and humanist separation of reason from emotion in her self-consolatory letters. "An uncertain confusion," she writes Tadino, "has developed in me between reason

29. See Ovid. *Met.*, 2.31–330, for the story of Phaeton and the daughters of the Sun, the Heliades. Phaeton lost control when he took Helios's chariot and horses off their usual course, but before the earth could be consumed in fire Jupiter hurled Phaeton out of the chariot to earth.

30. See Ovid, *Heroid.* 2; Hygin. *Fab.* 59 for the story Phyllis, daughter of the king of Thrace, and Demophoon, king of Athens, had an affair when Demophoon stopped in Thrace on his way home from the Trojan War; some say he never came back and Phyllis hanged herself; others say she was metamorphosed into an almond tree.

31. See Ovid, *Met.* 13.900ff.; 14.1–70. When Glaucus went to meet Scylla for a tryst, he found her bathing nude in her accustomed pool, but from the waist down her body had been changed into a pack of barking dogs.

32. See Ovid, *Met.* 5.112–485, on Cyane and Persephone (Proserpina).

33. Ovid, *Met.* 13.576–623, on Hecuba.

34. Ovid, *Met.* 6.160–312, on Niobe.

and feeling." Her mouthing, then, of the humanist commonplace that only reason can assuage sorrow must be read as deeply ironic. Mourning and lamentation are portrayed as more active agents in Cereta's letter to Alberti. For Cereta, life is a sown field from which the distillation of experience is harvested in writing; thus the sowing of death results for her in a ripened crop both of real mourning and its potential literary representation in letters. If it is all-consuming, however, mourning may extinguish eloquence. Cereta's lamentation is a crop that she "cultivates" as she once cultivated her writing and her mind. Though her tongue withers and dies from the cacophonous moans and sighs within, lamentation alone can lay siege to and bring down the "wall of bitterness" (*murum acerbitatis*) inside her.

XXIX

To Felicio Tadino, physician [35]

Linked together in inextricable knots, the stars and the occurrences of things shoot a deadly venom at us from on high, and we are either caught and sickened by it or else we are enveloped in the dire snares of death.[36] Ah, cruel fate, we are born, the years slip away, and the changing seasons deceive us. The power of disease finally seizes us, we are released in death, we are covered over by hollow marble, and our spirit flees to the shades. Thus the concerns of mortals, futile and incautious, are cheated by the fleeting dream of life. Why should we, wretched ones, fear death, which torments not the dead but the living? People should weep rather for those whose long day occurs amid the troubles of living. In the losing though death of the man I most longed for, death has taken everything from me. The pain draws tears to my eyes. Unconscious of bitterness, I have mourned my misfortune. I have spent a long time weeping, and even iron hearts have wept with me, but my wounded mind could not be healed with sobbing;[37] for reason, not lamentation, removes sorrow. Still, I have returned at last and I have

---

35. Vat. 35 (fols. 27–27v); Ven. 30 (fols. 52–53); Tom. 28 (pp. 59–60); Rabil 57. The letter is one of several in the collection addressed to the physician Felicio Tadino, and if dated correctly it would have been written about nine months after Pietro Serina's.

36. Tom. lacks the incipit contained in Vat. and Ven.

37. Note the repeated theme in her self-consolatory letters of her sorrow depicted as a wound and, more specifically, a pain located in the mind and spirit: "saucia mens" in this letter; "vulnerata mentis" in letter XXVIII.

striven, insofar as I could, to remove the sting of inner pain from the wound of a mind in turmoil.[38]

After a short time I put aside tears but not the deeper, inner sighing. And thus, the face smiled because it was restrained, while the spirit within was afflicted, so much so that an uncertain confusion developed in me between reason and feeling. For though the mutilated body of Hippolytus could be restored to life, the lacerated mind of Apollo could not be healed;[39] for the wound that love inflicts is more deadly than that of sorrow. But he who was designated for me in marriage was the one most desired; he was the one hoped for beyond all others who have lived, and when he loved me in return, all other desire in my heart lost its fire. Vale. May 1, 1487.

XXX

To Alberto degli Alberti[40]

*T*had most enthusiastically planned to take this strange and unpolished manner of speaking to the heights of Ciceronian brilliance and I set out not to neglect any distinguished scholar, even if, trembling with apprehension, I might not write him with the honor that was his due.

But misfortune occurred, alas, which was unexpected and hard to bear; and thus the seeds were sown that heaped up a harvest of funerary lamentation for me, in accord with the obligation of widowhood. For recently my beloved husband, whom I scarcely knew, perished under my very gaze, leaving my life though not my heart. My heart mourned this pitiable man with equally pitiable lamentation. An inner pain beset me; and I had no hope left in my heart, which, being unarmed and uncautious, was nearly pierced through and through by despair. I, like a sacrificial victim at a funeral service, seemed to die with the dead man, propelled toward death by the strange phenomenon of his dying. After this, a cry of grief, an attack of mournful weeping, launched by the siege engines of my mind, rose up suddenly and turned against the wall of bitterness inside me.

38. Cereta's rich imagery of a throbbing wound, an agitated mind, stinging pain, and inner grief and depression is hard to convey in English: "a commoti animi tanto percussu extinguere nitebar interni doloris acuelum."

39. See Ovid, *Met.* 15.520–41, on Hippolytus' mutilation after his denunciation of his step-mother, Phaedra, to his father, and Diana's rescue of him. On Apollo's unrequited love for Daphne, Coronis, Hyacinth, and others and the consequent suffering of the god, see Ovid, *Met.*, books 1 and 10.

40. Vat. 36 (fol. 27v); Ven. 31 (fols. 51–52); Tom. 29 (p. 61); Rabil 58. To Alberto degli Alberti.

And so, although I wrote to you tearfully on the occasion of your departure, and although filial obligation moves me to write you again, still I myself, because I have been distracted from my studies, am neither distinguishing myself among the Muses, nor am I pulled in a different direction by Apollo. Lamentation alone is left for me to cultivate. Thus my pen, cut down in the bloom of its eloquence, has dried up, and my accustomed thoughts have dissolved into tears.

Under these circumstances, it will not be a difficult thing to make the accusation that my poor little gift of an inept tongue has fallen victim to the confused groaning deep inside me. For who can involve a mind which is strained by a siege of sorrows in the pleasure of a polished oration? Since I must therefore occupy myself with reflection for the time being rather than with writing, I beg you, who are so steeped in the tropes of eloquence, to allow the thin ramblings of a letter sterile and discordant, which concerns the unhappiness of a wounded heart, to excuse me in your eyes. Vale. May 7, 1487.

XXXI

In this letter Cereta addresses Agostino Emilio as someone who has guided her in her humanist writings and studies. The theme of this letter is Cereta's double tragedy and double bereavement: once a loving wife and committed scholar, she has lost both her husband and her desire for knowledge. Her only interest since her husband's death is in exploring the theme of mourning in her life, psyche, and letters. In a prayer to the gods at the close of the letter, Cereta attempts to bargain with them: she proposes that the gods' protection of good men will result in their veneration and respect for the deities rather than in their fear. In the last analysis, however, mourning and the service of the Muses are not compatible. Despite her letters, she cannot, she confesses, deliver what Agostino wants. In characteristically Ceretan imagery, in which she suggests analogies between the cultivation of literary inspiration and talent and that of a sown field, she writes that her "well" (*fons*) has gone dry.

To Agostino Emilio [41]

I had devoted myself to the temple of Minerva and I had surrendered my whole mind to the Muses, so that I could observe the wandering, falling planets and those bodies which sometimes move in a retrograde posi-

---

41. Vat. 37 (fols. 28–28v); Ven. 32 (fols. 54–56); Tom. 30 (pp. 62–65); Rabil 53. To Agostino Emilio.

tion, sometimes in a descending course, and at other times with more velocity under the continual revolutions of the rising and sinking stars, since I was trying to find out, using rigorous proofs, whether the stars remained fixed while the heavens were descending, or whether they were propelled in a circular orbit away from us, equidistantly in a vast orbit. And I was as patient an observer as I could be, so that I might come to understand what higher causes, emanating from a lofty boundary, sprinkle the evil we experience with a certain celestial dew. Because of this, I dared to castigate those corrupt philosophical sects who predict the movements of the moon beneath the earth, the spreading of the sun's rays through the clouds, the gathering and dispelling of the rains, the wars and clashings of the winds, and the day on which these things will occur.

But O unhappy day, through the everlasting death of my husband, I have come to the road of mourning, common to all men, and on it I have left the glory of a wife's fidelity: my ululation and my torn hair. Ah, the uncertain lot of humans, ah, the unpredictability of things, and o mortality, unfriendly to greening minds. Shameless Fortune is jealous of a mind at peace. In her anger at me, she has hurled the darts of her own instability at the heart of an innocent girl. And with this wound of death, she has thrown the serenity of my study into confusion and she has redirected my investigations into the subtleties of heavenly things[42] to grim mourning—all so that she, who bore arms, could go to war against an unarmed girl. Thus, pained by this bitter laceration and this grievous blow to my mind, I abandoned every nourishment that I delighted in and that my love of active study used to relish. What wonder is it then, if I have abandoned my sweet night vigils of reading and my search for the causes of things, with the pressure I feel from my husband's dying?

For rain steals over the eyes and fills them—a rain that not only washes over a widow's face and her anxious heart, but that also purges her memory and her whole mind of the joy of speech. And so, may the gods of literature fight against the other gods for my poor sake.[43] Or if there is any bitterness among disputants, let them give over the judging of their cases to Mars and Saturn. For what victory can there be for a deity[44] if she mounts a secret campaign of arms, war, and anger against an unsuspecting girl? What should

42. "Coelestium vestigates subtilitates": literally, the subtleties that have been investigated of heavenly things. *Subtilitas* (subtlety, precision, fineness of workmanship, scholarship, or detail, intelligence, sophistication, and so on) is a loaded term in Cereta; it's one of her favorite words and highest compliments: it often denotes the standard of writing and thought to which she aspires.
43. Tom. adds "fictili illi" after "pro misella me."
44. Vat., Ven.: "ullo numini . . . victoriae"; Tom.: "ulli istorum."

always be the goal of war is glory, not blame. For just as God visits punishment on an enemy, so he should single out and embrace the innocent with compassion, so that his infinite majesty will be vested in an infinite capacity for piety. For it is a greater benefit to a prince to be respected than feared. The Romans demonstrated this clearly when they made the decision, after the Tarquins were expelled from the realm after the rape of Lucretia, to obey laws and not a king. Surely trust in a king is of higher value than fear of a tyrant.

Besides, instead of an example, in considering these concerns as they relate to the gods (and I shall speak calmly of the evil that oppresses me), if there are any gods in heaven who care about our troubles, I beg them at least to refrain from doing harm to those who are friends, lest decent men should sometimes howl at the gods for crushing them along with the wicked and lest they should despair, moreover, at the premature coming of death, since nature destines this to be the common fate of all living things.

But this is the turmoil and confusion of a mind that is roiling amid the tinder of my emotions. You yourself should consider what intellectual pleasure or delight in the pen there could possibly be for me now—whom blood exuding from a still beating heart has wet.[45] You have expected, I am sure, that my poor little letters would radiate with genius and the lamp of eloquence. Your opinion has deceived you in this and your trust was elicited under false pretenses—whether you were influenced by your love of me or my reputation. For while I have a lot of knowledge about desire, I know little about how to find a well for a pen that has gone dry. For it is not possible to do great things with small means. Vale. February 6, 1487.

XXXII–XXXIV

In modern terms, Cereta's three lengthy letters to Brother Thomas, a monk in Milan who plays a role similar to that of a psychotherapist to her, represent the recovery phase in her disconsolate grieving for her husband. After deluging her friends with pain and despair, Cereta's letters to Thomas mark the beginning of a reawakening of her longing to know, to write, and to live. To carry the analogy further between Cereta's self-consolatory correspondence with Thomas and the process of psychotherapy, her changing relationship to the monk represented in these letters resembles the psychotherapeutic phenomenon known as transference. Freud theorized that in the successful treat-

---

45. The still-beating heart she refers to seems to be her husband's; as she writes in the next letter in the Vatican and Venice manuscripts (Vat. 38; Ven. 33), she hovered over Pietro as his life ebbed away and was there to witness his end.

ment of emotional illness, the patient had to progress from the transference of negative to positive emotions onto her physician: she was supposed to move, that is, from hostile resistance toward, to collaboration with, her analyst.[46] Thus in the course of treatment, the analysand might see her physician, in turn, as an adviser, enemy, an object of her erotic desires, and ultimately—should a cure begin to take effect—as a benevolent ally. For Freud, both negative and positive transference arose from an erotic basis; at the same time he also saw the patient/therapist relationship as one inherently charged with hostility, not unlike Cereta's with Thomas:

> We have to conclude that all the feelings of sympathy, friendship, trust, and so forth . . . have developed out of purely sexual desires by an enfeebling of their sexual aim, however pure and non-sensual they may appear[47]. . . . [The patient] seeks to discharge his emotions [and] . . . the physician requires of him that he shall . . . subject them to rational consideration. . . . This struggle between physician and patient, between intellect and the forces of instinct, between recognition and the striving for discharge, is fought out almost entirely over the transference-manifestations.[48]

In Renaissance terms, Cereta's triptych of letters to Brother Thomas imitates, in its changing representation of Thomas' character, the form of a humanist dialogue in three books, like Valla's *De voluptate*, in which the ideal of *in utram-que partem*, the arguing of both sides of a question, is demonstrated. Cereta's first letter begins with a simple request for counsel and guidance; her second letter expresses her anger at and repudiation of her would-be mentor; and, in an about-face, her final letter embraces her correspondent with an impassioned appreciation of him as a friend and collaborator in her struggle to recover.

XXXII

Letter XXXII marks Cereta's first attempt to move her mourning into a new phase: toward action and change. Still in turmoil over the loss of her husband, she has begun to change her life by reading Augustine and Jerome. She will no longer pursue the world of learning and eloquence for its own sake: she will turn instead to God for true knowledge. Nor has she any intention of

46. Peter Gay, *Freud: A Life for Our Time* (New York: W. W. Norton, 1988), pp. 300–301.

47. Sigmund Freud, *Collected Papers*, trans. and ed. Joan Riviere (New York: Basic Books, Inc., 1959), 2.319.

48. Freud, *Papers*, 2.321–22.

taking the Platonic road to God through mere thought and contemplation. Her aim is to believe in God, not to intellectualize him. With this letter, she opens her heart to Brother Thomas' advice and instruction and she asks him to pray for her.

To Brother Thomas [49]

Whenever I read the most eloquent monarchs of the church militant, Augustine and Jerome, an awful, arid consciousness located in the interior of my mind makes me shudder at the pompous little formulations that have been the products of my small talent.[50] Such a sense of value, enjoyment, and utility wells up in me from readings of this sort, for I have not yet reached such a level of learning or art that I can be rightly called a pupil of those eminent men who have attained an enduring reputation as Catholic theologians. For I seem to sputter rather than to speak, and to fill pieces of paper with smoke, not orations: noise and meaningless sound is all the literature I make, which, after a faint sensation, dissolves into nothing—as though made of atoms.

Your letter seemed to reproach me because, although I have filled so many margins and now so many books with secular writing, I have neglected to write even a short commentary on a sacred topic, as though nothing to do with the subject of Christian nobility could be impassioned. Although you have criticized me with serious intent and knowledgeably too, still what you say seems hostile and hard for me to hear. But the argument is not equal to the subject at hand; nor is the basis for your accusation anything that would make me uncomfortable—as though I were a plaintiff in a case with no defense.

But really, if I were to oblige you, who are offering me the counsel I hoped for, not a sermon, I would try to begin again. In any case, to attempt an investigation into the causes of the occult in nature is no activity for a novice. It is certainly not a given that those men whose sole adornment is the glitter

49. Vat. 60 (fols. 40–41v); Ven. 54 (fols. 82v–84v); Tom. 52 (pp. 113–17); Rabil 49. Cereta to Brother Thomas, who is identified in the mss. as a Milanese priest and about whom we have no further information than that contained in her three letters to him (Vat. 60, 62, 64) and his three letters to her and another one to Cereta's father, Silvestro; Brother Thomas' letters appear only in the Vatican manuscript.

50. "Ingenioli mei sententiolas exsucca horridula interioris animi conscientia formidat": this string of self-deprecating diminutives (the -*olus*, -*ulus* endings) is unusual in Cereta; her sense of an "inner awareness," is, on the other hand, typical of her letters (see chapter 1, letter I). St. Augustine (354–430 A.D.) and St. Jerome (340–420 A.D.), both learned in classical literature, are foremost among the founding fathers of Christian theology.

of language in all its rhythmical and technical permutations will come to know God. The ability to speak in a polished and ornate manner is the mark of an orator, not a theologian.

Shall I—and I see myself as a girl who aspires to neither of these occupations—penetrate either with the eyes of my mind or the shining beacon of truth those eternal dwelling places, gazing up at which, as though under a prodigious weight, Thomas, Dionysius, and so many of our celebrated ancestors spent their days and nights?[51] I do not want to engage in the laborious task of contemplating God; I want simply to believe in him. Nor have I been entrusted with the task of approaching this more profound province of the mind.

The sea of knowledge about celestial things is vast, and its immensity surrounds the minds of humans, continuing on forever and disappearing in the distance. An eagle can fly above the clouds, soaring beyond the inaccessible tops of mountain crags. I, content with a lowlier path, shall follow the teaching of our Savior in the gospel. There is one law, one word of God, and one true virtue, which should be disseminated in the temple of our hearts in its purest form so that he may fill us with his love amid the vicissitudes of human fragility. Thus I pray that not I but God should be the object of my soul's desire, since I am subject to death. Surely if anything prevails in me that will cause me to ascend the mountain of the God of Jacob, this will be a gift given to me by God the father.

We miserable women, being nothing in ourselves as long as we are alive, are together overcoming the confused and turbulent passions of the mind by obedience to the law, to the extent that we can. There is one conversion of the will to God which surpasses all others, and this consists in the remembering of, and meditation on, the judgment and the resurrection. Therefore, since this mortal life of ours will live on after death, I have renounced—for it is holier to do so—that glory, transitory and slipping, which being full of the contrariness of earthly beings, separates us from the true religion of pious faith, and embroils us in hybristic displays of greater intelligence.

All posterity learns from the story which teaches that great is the heady power of knowing, which—like the sweet smell of imminent exaltation—enabled the serpent to fool Eve in spite of God's false hopes. Best of all the things that are knowable is the true knowledge of oneself. Therefore, my

---

51. "Mentis oculis" (eyes of the mind or soul): the reference is to Plato, *Repub.* 533d; see also *Phaedrus; Symp.* St. Thomas Aquinas (c. 1225–74) is the great scholastic Christian philosopher and Aristotelian; the Dionysius she refers to seems to be the early Christian theologian Dionysius the Areopagite (fl. 464 A.D.); both Aquinas and the Areopagite were known in the Middle Ages and Renaissance as synthesizers of Neoplatonism and Christian teaching.

commitment and devotion to learning will be one of these, with the result that I shall strive, relying on the right hand and help of God the celestial king, to examine those things more attentively that enable us to bear humbly the wretchedness of our condition. Because of this, torches of unextinguishable faith will be lit, the path that traverses this transitory life to heaven will be well limned by their brilliant beams, and there our withering mortality will be exchanged for blessed eternity. The snares of our age are higher things, which are set by our own perceptions in the darkness and error that leads us to strive for worldly honors. But you, who are a teacher to me more learned than all other men, who are restrained by the vows of the cloister, and who seek penitence in the silent eremite order in Christ, the bridegroom of your soul, come, I beg you, ponder in your speeches my case with my eyes: think about the sorrow and anguish of one who has no expectations of better things to come. For the premature death of my husband has brought me such grief that, crushed and in turmoil, my mind floats, storm-tossed amid the tears and depression of a heart in mourning. But alas, that thought, which my irrevocable loss reproves, is too late and surely too extreme: the solace of the convent, for which the recurring pain in my heart often longs, is no stranger to me. On this account, pray more constantly for me. For the Lord's mercies are manifold, and we can seek to walk in his paths. In the meantime I shall await whatever the unending compassion of God alone may grant to me. Vale. October 21, 1486; September 10, 1486.

XXXIII

Cereta's second letter to Brother Thomas is written in a different mood. Here she takes a hostile and competitive position toward the monk. She does so obliquely, always nesting her criticisms of him within a tapestry patterned with seeming compliments. Nonetheless, in a surprising reversal of roles, she counterposes her monastic Christian values to the monk's worldly ones. She pits her charity against his ill-will, her quiet receptiveness against his voluble contentiousness, her silence against his bustling debates, her "obedience to death" against his to public opinion, and her withdrawal to her own conventlike cell (*in cellula humiliore*) against his desire for fame and *auctoritas* in the public forum. But the most interesting part of the letter is Cereta's assertion, in contrast to the typical humanist mind-over-body dualism, that our minds and viscera cannot be separated from one another but are inextricably connected and that the emotions alone—and righteous anger in particular—are what empower the mind to be "free to exercise its own powers and strength."

To Brother Thomas [52]

Your thorny letter is an angry swarm of bees, whose numerous sharpened stings are hidden in so many honey-bearing knees. But this odious poison should touch minds more deserving of blame; I myself have not yet learned to walk the thorny paths of censure, nor do I purchase pens of such virulence that they drip with wormwood. If Plato rejects Parmenides, if Socrates does the same to Anaxagoras, if Philo of the Academy dismisses the Stoics and Diogenes does likewise to Euclid, and finally if Sallust reproves Cicero and Cicero does the same to Marcus Antonius, why should I be interested in those thinkers? [53] This amounts to a brawl and not a discussion among philosophers. The defending of a war of nasty insults held in the public arena is the task of a gladiator, not a critic.

I am happy rather than sad that the name Laura has become unpopular with everyone, because it is the truth contained in my writings that has caused them to offend the public. You don't believe, do you, that my words have emanated from my highest faculties? For the most part, these words were born in the lower, visceral regions of my being. For it is here that the mind, liberated from restraint, is free to exercise its own powers and strength. [54] Thus I am explicit with my friends about whatever it is that hurts my mind. My mind always causes me to hesitate, whenever I am persuaded that I should reproach friends to whom I have opened my whole heart. Because of this, through listening to my own counsel and conscience, I have established a life obedient not to other people's opinions but to my own death. I think it quite unjust that your own criticism, which is itself abrasive, should bemoan my abrasiveness, since you attack me—though I am innocent— in public.

---

52. Vat. 62 (fols. 43–43v); Ven. 58 (fols. 92–94); Tom. 56 (pp. 129–32); Rabil 73. To Brother Thomas.

53. Plato (b. 427 B.C.), founder of the Academy at Athens; Parmenides (b. 510 B.C. in Elea), founder of Eleatic school of philosophy; Socrates (469–399 B.C. in Athens), Greek philosopher; Anaxagoras (b. 500 B.C.), Ionian coast Greek philosopher; Philo Judaeus (flor. 39 A.D.), Judaic philosopher of Alexandria; Stoic school of philosophy, founded in 315 B.C. at Athens by Zeno, also a prominent school in Rome up until the time of the Emperor Marcus Aurelius (180 A.D.). Diogenes (4th century B.C.), Greek Cynic philosopher; Euclid (fl. 300 B.C.), Greek mathematician; Sallust (86–35 B.C.), Roman historian; Cicero (106–43 B.C.), Roman orator, statesman, philosopher; Marcus Antonius (c. 82–30 B.C.), Roman statesman and archenemy of Cicero's.

54. Contrary to the usual humanist Stoicism and exhortations to exercise moderation and decorum, Cereta tells us that her anger is part of the intellectual freedom that empowers her speech as well as her thought. Her view is that the brain, intellect, and genius for oratory, on the one hand, and the emotions (righteous anger in particular), on the other, are inextricably connected, not separated.

I respect you both as my instructor and as one well steeped in the readings of the philosophers, since the discipline of philosophy remains a venerable one among all men. But charity, not ill-will or enviousness, is the object of the well-ordered mind; nor can charity, whose hunger for the divine is always great, be fed on smoke. Aimless and empty are the paltry rewards for human glory. Our transitory journey through this fleeting life tells me to relinquish desire, trampling it underfoot. On account of this, I have renounced the world and set limits for myself within the law; and I shall want nothing beyond what is permissible within those limits.

As I prepare a mirror of my mind for death, I always hold up to my mind the teaching of our Savior. And though vain criticism may sometimes cause me to be distracted, still I rise up again from misfortune more determined than before with the help of God, and I think nothing of the usefulness of the body, for which the smallest plot of land will suffice. For my faith is contented in itself, and with it I am carried to God under the sail of humility.

But no one is a person of such integrity that he can attain sufficient happiness of the mind without humility. And so I felt the stinging nettles of your letter; this lethal potion caused even the hemlock that grows in brambles to tremble. But let the shining Catos make noise in the Senate, and let them commit those speeches to writing.[55] Let the clamorous academy of logicians entangle you in questions about definitions concerning the physical world.[56] Thus let the school of Porphyry introduce the first *isagogas* demonstrating the logical propositions, let the Peripatetics argue categorical pronouncements, and let Apuleius and Aristotle give birth to Perhiermenian subtleties from the virginity of their minds.[57] Since I, a mere female, inept at literary matters and deficient in talent, cannot cover myself with glory by making public my talent in the arenas of debate, I shall declaim my arguments against you in my small and humble cell, with Christ.[58]

May the various kinds of oppositions, hypothetical and paralogical, which differ among themselves, and may the many and varied kinds of defi-

---

55. She refers here to Marcus Porcius Cato the Censor (234–149 B.C.), famous for his advocacy in the Roman Senate of the strict morality of earlier times and for his repeated appeals to the Romans to destroy its archenemy Carthage ("Carthago delenda est").

56. Vat.: "diffinitionum naturalium quaestiones"; Ven.: "diffinitionum Ethicarum quaestiones"; Tom.: "definitionum naturalium quaestiones."

57. Prophyry (233–c. 301 A.D.), a Neoplatonist philosopher and a pupil of Plotinus; the Peripatetics, an Athenian school of philosophy founded by Aristotle (b. 382–322 B.C.); Apuleius (fl. 155 A.D.) novelist and Neoplatonist philosopher born in Madaura, Africa. The plural noun *isagogae*, meaning something like "first principles" or "basic paradigms," is not in Liddell-Scott and OLD has only one citation for the word: Gel.1.2.6.

58. "I, a mere female, etc.": this disclaimer is clearly ironic given the polished style of this letter.

nitions and arguments derived from rhetorical topics remain yours. The hallmark of my speech is not contentiousness but grace. Whatever your web
weaves too intricately will give me an excuse to maintain silence, and patience will be my beatitude. For more trustworthy are those ears which often
interrupt in an indirect manner.

Surely I am a person who can steer a ship safely past the bewitching
songs of the Sirens, with Ulysses unharmed.[59] For I have reason, which can
subvert passion, in my arsenal, and because virtue, not pleasure, is my main-
stay. Vale. November 11, 1487.

XXXIV

This is the third and final piece in Cereta's triptych of letters to Brother
Thomas. This last letter reflects her change in attitude towards her friend and
counselor from the anger and repudiation of her second letter to a mood of
trust and collaboration. She tells Thomas here that his letters have helped
her to begin to recover from the paralysis of her grief and mourning. Under
his tutelage, she has experienced an awakening of her desire to resume her
studies of the mysteries of the heavens. At the same time she praises his eloquence and the superiority of his learning: he is the best of the Aristotelians
but never a sophist; and he is the master of both literature and theology. He is
a model for her in his humility and his scorn for this life. While some monks
have chosen to lead a life of absurd and solitary asceticism, he has taken a
middle road, the austere yet communal life of the monastery.

The concluding passages of the letter recap the central autobiographical
themes and premises laid out in her letter to Nazaria Olympica: the turmoil
she experiences when Pietro dies, in which heart and mind (*animus*, the image
by which Cereta conveys the conflation and inseparability of mind and
body) are bound together in one grief; her naming of her pain of bereavement as "the wound of a broken adolescence" (*inuria fractae adolescentiae*); her
gradual sense of an inner awakening or awareness (*conscientia*), which she calls
"the most precious pearl of the wandering soul" (*animae peregrinae*); the personal relationship she strives to forge with the one she calls God and Savior
(*Deum, Salvator*); her long insomniac nights of study and writing (*vigiliae*); and
her debt to Thomas and others who have taught her about the emptiness of
the body and ephemerality of this world (*inane corpus hoc, volatilis vita*).
Thomas' life and its *regimen* are an example and an inspiration to her; his self-

59. On Odysseus' (Ulysses) return home to Ithaca after the Trojan War, one of the perils he and
his crew faced were the island-dwelling women called the Sirens, who lured men to their deaths
with their irresistible songs. Homer tells the story in the *Odyssey*.

discipline has helped her to conclude part 1 of her volume of letters (*clauditur familiarum litterarum prima pars*).

Her final questions to herself are: will she write, study and investigate, or will she remove herself from human affairs via the cloister or even death (*calamo deposito, stilo abducto*)? The letter ends with her acknowledgment that the desire to know is still alive in her and that the path of true virtue (the only road to God) requires hard work.

To Brother Thomas [60]

So I can respond to both of your letters now, I have postponed for a little while my late-night sessions of fairly rigorous study, which I had begun, patiently and because it was my desire to do so, to make measurements of the earth. For by proposing hypotheses, I have tried to pursue this subject more deeply, to investigate it, and to unravel the mystery of its causes. My curiosity has been heartened, and I am indebted to you, because by treating this subject at length in your letters, you have opened the doors to a mind whose light and energy, previously dulled by vertigo, lay inert in darkness.

I was at first stunned, admiring the sublimity of your eloquence, to which I could compare no one else's. For the primary virtue of your style is its polish and leanness, even when observed among the various flowers of orators throughout the world, whose speeches were redolent of a deity's and whose tongues were golden. Your prodigious and tenacious memory of all things supersedes their grace of style, and because of it you have gone beyond Simonides and Metrodorus with your quick mind and calm eye.[61]

Your inquiring mind[62] has added to your name kudos for your sublime intellect. For with the vigilant contemplation of your mind, you have unraveled enigmas and revealed the hidden causes of so many philosophical problems that are deeply and profoundly removed from our experience. For it is possible for us to come to know things other than those which have already been discovered. As long as we inhabit this body, the mind sleeps while the imagination remains in a state of contemplation; for this is the sleep that en-

60. Vat. 64 (fols. 47–48v); Ven. 73 (fols. 148v–52v); Tom. 71 (pp. 221–27); Rabil 78. Cereta to Brother Thomas.

61. Cereta's Metrodorus might be a conflation of two or more historical characters with the same name: one is cited by Plutarch for his retentive memory; another was both a philosopher and a painter from Stratonice, fl. 171 B.C. (Pliny, 35.11, Cicero, *De fin.* 5.1.). Simonides of Cos (fl. 538 B.C.), a famous poet who wrote elegies, epigrams, and epic poetry.

62. Vat. and Ven.: "intelligentiae vestigator"; Tom.: "intelligentiae indagans."

gulfs all men. Our descendants will teach things of which we were not aware, as even we know much that error-prone antiquity did not know. The vessels of our minds which serve as the receptacles for the innumerable ideas of things are very cramped.

You have, however, a clear affinity with Aristotle, after whom no one has come who is greater than you. You, who are the equal of the inventors of argumentation, have fully exposed the most specious ambiguities among sophistries, which the puzzling subtlety of the dialectic entangles even more confusingly. I would say confidently that to hold a discourse on the arcane divinity of the trinity without regard for the envy of the theologians is unique—and this is my guess—in you, who explain this most present and immediate plane by an investigation that relies not only on the seeing but also the feeling intellect.[63] Nor should you think on this account, I hope, that I believe that God is demonstrable matter—a machine made of clay. Rather, among the most preeminent of causes, he is the most powerful. This cause, as if the overseer and guardian over us, inhabits minds which have not been taken over by the passions in human ways.[64]

But you yourself know these things in a more profound way. And I would not want you to impute that which the most worthy form of truth demands to one who is silent. The proof is the multitude of thinkers who agree on your superiority over so many leading theologians and so many priests of many religions, men preeminent in literature of every genre; among these your influence continues. Never have you transferred your efforts from religion to literature; for you have served both, as though you were accustomed to using both hands equally.

In you, virtue always prospers. You pursue the road of righteousness and that alone, yet you consider yourself contemptible in the face of the true radiance of your humility. But nonetheless, the splendor of your virtue cannot be hidden in the darkness. The constancy of your mind, though flexible, is undiminished and inviolate. Thus your sublime mind always flies towards the celestial city, for you possess a soul in a human body infused with holiness. And still you hasten rapidly to God, having renounced all ambition, moving through the paces of a monk in a life that has been rectified; and to

63. Vat. and Ven.: "oculati intellectus . . . non minus quam . . . sensitivi." Note here Cereta's emphasis on what she sees as two complementary aspects of the intellect: the "oculati intellectus" and the "sensitivi," the seeing and feeling mind. Tom.: "oculata intellectus vestigatione, etc."

64. It is interesting that Cereta speaks of God as a feminine entity: she speaks of the Supreme Being as not only the impersonal "causa" but also the feminine "spectatrix" ("overseer," from the masculine noun "spectator").

accompany you on this journey, you have an image reborn and recreated for the remembering of death, which is always present and at hand.

For the superior, spiritual part of your mind rules you and, because of its counsel, you have such contempt for this world, since it is blind and ignorant of the hour of our death, that you may think that that inevitable hour awaits you in every place. Indeed, our homes in this life are inhospitable and brief, for the length of a life is so fleeting and short that today's footsteps press upon the heels of tomorrow with impatience.[65]

Therefore, the examples and evidence of your intelligence are impressive, but those of your religious exemplarity are no less so, since you did not crown yourself to increase your fame but to do greater service as a Dominican. You show yourself the equal of the depictions of the half-naked fathers for whom herbs and fountains provided delicious nourishment in remote regions of the desert. For while some monks sequester themselves, silent and alone, in private cells with beds of boards and pillows of rock, others bind their bare feet and empty stomachs with ropes full of knots, and others still, who come from wealthy lineages, are content to live in abstinence and contemplation. Some disseminate the teachings of the gospel in urban churches, however large or small the crowd of those assembled might be; and there are also bearded monks with a more ascetic way of life, who live in caves cut out from rocks or simple dwellings in the woods built of sod and mud mixed with straw. But you and your fathers, who exemplify a more moderate penitence in the community of the stern cloister, always rise to a vigorous fervor.[66]

Therefore when I learned from you that this body is empty, that the promises of the heart and mind are deceptive, and that the most precious pearl of the wandering souls of humans is the conscience, I abandoned my plan to seek fame through human letters, lest my mind, bereft, unhappy, and unaware of the future should seek happiness through diligence.[67] What is more, since too great a concern for knowledge raises the suspicion that one leads a prodigal life, our all-night sessions of study ought not to continue, as if we were born solely for the sake of literature.

We may, however, indulge our inclinations thus: orations must be deliv-

---

65. See Horace, *Odes* 1.4.13–14, for the image of death personified, pressing with his feet on powerless human beings.

66. Vat., Ven.: "tu . . . acrior"; Tom., erroneously: "tu . . . arctior."

67. Cereta's vocabulary in the succeeding paragraphs includes many key themes in the letterbook: *animus* (heart and mind), *animae peregrinae margaritam esse conscientiam* (conscience, the pearl of the wandering soul of humans), *vigiliae in studio* (all night sessions of study), *iniuria fractae adolescentiae* (the wound of a broken adolescence), *corpus inane* (the emptiness of the body), *volatilis vitae meae diecula* (the brief and fleeting day of my life).

ered about a topic, and God must be honored with the gift of service. For the innocent heart is thought to be a more acceptable sacrificial offering to God. Indeed, He who has no crown to adorn with our jewels wants our persons, not our possessions. For the Savior considers our wishes more important than all other things.

I, truly constituted under His eyes, am coming to know the brief and fleeting day of my life, and although I have scarcely completed a fifth part of it, still so many days have been removed from it by the wound of a broken adolescence that the expectation of death should be more certain than that of life.

Thus because of your example for a regimen of a life more free from anxiety, I have decided to reach out to take your hand. And so I owe you a debt of accumulated thanks, because you, who have taken pity on my numerous errors and have urged me on silently, have relieved me of this load of writing. Therefore, this first part of my "Familiar Letters" is concluded—arranged in a lame and faulty order summarily and by headings—and I have removed my pen. What remains for me now is to begin to make notes worthy of what I have written so that I may obtain without danger both lasting fame for this sinful and small soul of mine and also the reward of a higher good without illness.

I have opened the ears of my conscience to the precepts in your letters. And since she is always with me, I always am my own conscience, and thus I have one companion in temperance, and one simultaneous course that leads to God once human affairs are put aside.[68] On account of this, whether there will be a plan after this to feed the mind with more active studies that prepare those who are already knowledgeable for greater things, or whether, by putting away my pen, I will show myself to God after a period of recovery and tranquil rest, still, I shall not be able to keep myself from gathering together, at least mentally, information regarding hypotheses about the heavens. Nor does labor, the brother of virtue, allow the noble mind to be at rest. Vale. February 4, 1488; December 11, 1487.

68. Cereta's personification of *conscientia* is especially difficult to interpret and translate here.

IV

WOMAN TO WOMAN

There is nothing that distinguishes the ten letters to and about women in this chapter so much as their variety. Though all but one are written to women, all treat characteristically humanist themes, and none deal with topics that could be described as "domestic" or "feminine" in themselves. What marks these pieces as different from male humanist letters are the same personal, idiosyncratic, Ceretan touches that can be seen in all her correspondence, regardless of the gender of her addressee. Many of these "woman to woman" letters are surprisingly cold, remote, and less intimate than her letters to the men she knew. There is little warmth here, unless it is in the longer discursive, more autobiographical and philosophical essays that she addresses to Martha Marcella, the nun Deodata di Leno, and a woman she refers to as "Europa solitaria."

The letters in this chapter are organized in pairs. The first pair, addressed to Deodata and Europa, argue the Epicurean and Aristotelian sides of the question of whether it is preferable to engage in the life of the city or to withdraw from it and immerse oneself in nature. A pair of letters written to Barbara Alberti and Martha Marcella[2] look ostensibly at marriage from its opposite ends—that of the bride and the widow—though both letters are self-consolatory and focus on the inevitability, for women who marry, of loss, bereavement, and isolation. A third pair of letters, to Santa Pelegrina and Elena di Cesare, represent an oppositional, feminine approach to two stock humanist topics, the nature of friendship and the menace from the Turkish east. Another pair of letters reveal Cereta's complete about-face toward a woman whose friendship she had hoped to cultivate, Cassandra Fedele, the most noted woman scholar of her time. And a final set of two short pieces, to her sister Diana and the Abbess Veneranda, offer lessons on the necessity of humility at every stage of life. In this last pair of letters, Cereta addresses a

girl and a woman who might represent the threshold and apogee of the con-
stricted educational aspirations of women of their time. While the child
Diana idolizes her older sister, perhaps fantasizing about becoming a famous
scholar herself when she grows up and Veneranda has arrived at the pinnacle
of her career as the spiritual and intellectual leader of her convent, Cereta's
message to both "sisters" is essentially the same.

XXXV
A TOPOGRAPHY AND A DEFENSE OF EPICURUS

Taken together as a diptych, Cereta's letters to Deodata di Leno and Europa
solitaria exemplify—as though they were the speeches of two different interlocutors in a dialogue—the humanist ideal of *in utramque partem*, the arguing of
both sides of a question.

The letter to Deodata, entitled "A topography and a defense of Epicurus"
in all three editions of the *Epistolae*, is an imitation of Petrarch's famous letter
about his ascent of Mt. Ventoux.[1] In both Petrarch's and Cereta's letters, the
physical scaling of the mountain furnishes a pretext for a meditation on the
human quest for the divine; and the ascent of a mountain and the panoramas
viewed from the summit prompt both writers to reflect on the Epicurean concept of pleasure (*voluptas*) as one which is intellectual and enduring rather
than sensual and ephemeral, and, moreover, to consider the compatibility of
Epicurean with Christian doctrine on this subject. But there the similarity
between the two "ascents" ends. Less than half of Cereta's long letter is devoted to her ascent of Mt. Isola. The second half of the letter is a philosophical inquiry into the relationship between true pleasure, virtue, and the path
to God, whereas Petrarch's description of his climb continues from the beginning to the end of his letter, though he interrupts his own narrative at
various points to digress on the nature of true pleasure and other philosophical and religious issues, to be a quest for the good. Unlike Cereta's tableau,
which is full of sensual delights—the sound of rushing water, ripe fruit to
pick, animals and birds to watch—Petrarch's narrative neglects the landscape and emphasizes instead the sweat, fatigue, and unpleasantness of the
climb. There is no mention of food or drink during his ascent, nor are there
other pleasurable diversions on route.

Cereta, on the other hand, seems to wallow in pleasure in the first half of
the letter. While Petrarch's moment of ecstasy comes only when he reaches

1. Vat. 75 (fols. 61–63); Ven. 65 (fols. 114–120v); Tom. 63 (pp. 168–77); Rabil 76. [See Introduction note 1, for full citations.] See Francesco Petrarch, *Rerum familiarium libri. I-VIII*. Trans. and
ed. by Aldo S. Bernardo (Albany: SUNY Press, 1975), book 4, letter 1, pp. 172–80.

the highest point of the climb—alone, because his brother had gone on ahead—Cereta delights in sounds and tastes during every phase of the walk in the company of friends. She recalls the lowing of the cattle and the flutes of shepherds echoing in the valley. She remembers picking strawberries in the meadow and later gobbling by the handful the grapes that were ripening in the hillside vineyards; she basks in the shade of appletrees heavy with fruit, slakes her thirst with milk set out for travelers along the way, and soothes her tired feet in the cool water of the creek. At the very summit of Mt. Isola, she does not stop to contemplate the vistas and meditate on her life as Petrarch does. Instead, she and her friends begin to play; they lob rocks down into the valley from a precipice, rousing rabbits from their holes and the dogs from the shade.

The last half of her essay is clearly indebted not to Petrarch, but to Lorenzo Valla's two dialogues *On Pleasure* and *On Free Will*.[2] Like Valla, Cereta emphasizes the importance of the will (*voluntas*) in choosing the good. It is through the freedom of the will that emanates from a pure mind, according to Cereta, that true pleasure is constantly reborn in us. In a synthesis of the positions of Valla's Epicurean interlocutor Antoninus and his Christian character Nicolaus, Cereta argues that the greatest earthly good is the pleasure of the mind, which alone leads humans on the right path to God: "A pleasure that lives and endures is a thing not generally known; for disdaining that which belongs to this world, it purchases that which is immortal with the currency of virtue. . . . This one pleasure represents the highest fulfillment of the contented mind, the most tranquil satiety of our solace, by which we are led by the safe path of faith to God."

Since God alone is the proper object for the soul's desire, Cereta proposes a life of religious seclusion from the world for both Deodata and herself. She gives the Christian *contemptu mundi* (contempt for the world) theme a prominence it does not receive in Petrarch's "Ascent." And in a conflation of this theme with the classical *carpe diem* motif, she emphasizes the place of death as a fact more central to human existence than living, a state which she characterizes as being "so uncertain and aimless that time, speeding onward, tightly binds together the day of our birth to that of our death."[3]

What is different in Cereta's letter to Deodata from the urban epistolarity of Petrarch, Bruni, and Filelfo, or the dialogues of Valla, is her adaptation of a prose medium, the Latin letter, to portray nature in the sensuous terms traditionally associated with lyric poetry.

2. Paul Oskar Kristeller, *Eight Philosophers of the Italian Renaissance* (Stanford: Stanford University Press, 1964), pp. 1–36; Valla's dialogues were written in 1432 and 1443.

3. Tom., p. 176: "Est enim vagum adeo et instabile hoc vivere nostrum ut natalem extremumque diem velox hora perstringat."

To Sister Deodata di Leno

he subtlety of your question has opened my mind to more important roads to understanding.[4] But I am not the person to defend the
argument at hand, since empty air does not support wings that have no
feathers.[5] I have no desire to enter into an academic wrestling match with
you since I have acquired only a shadow of learning,[6] and this outside the
academy and without any study of the fine points of logic. You asked about
our departure point and the sequence of places on our itinerary.[7] The story
would be plain enough, but the difficulty lies wholly in our destinations, for
you tacitly impugn pleasure when you attack our delight in Epicurus. Still, I
would not so easily attribute pleasure to vice, since the philosopher locates
this pleasure not in the delights of the senses but in the sating of the mind.
But more on this later. Now to what you ask.

Our journey began at the town of Cereto. We arrived at Lake Iseo at
dawn with a company of men on horseback. Marco, who was waiting there,
brought us in no time up to the citadel, which is completely protected by a
natural formation of rock. When we had had a pleasant meal there, a crowd
of friends suddenly converged on us. After a short time they went off in different directions, and we withdrew to bed to rest, since the sun had set and
the stars were already beginning to shine.

As soon as Aurora's rays shone, we boarded a boat from which merchants were already hurrying up to the outskirts of the town. We left the
harbor and set sail, for light winds were gusting from the east. And so, the
sailors plowed the long furrows of the Sabine lake with a happy oar, trailing
their nets and songs. When we reached the other shore, messengers who had
come from the next village approached us. With these people showing us the
road through the adjacent mountains, we arrived at a settlement of farm
houses where the peak of the first hill could be seen rising up from its very
roots. The entire populace was out waiting for us there with great bustling
and excitement; the people's faces were full of friendship and yet kindly deference as well. At this level, the deep vales echoed with the resonant lowings

---

4. This opening sentence is packed with characteristic Ceretan themes and metaphors: "the
roads to understanding," the key positioning of her "ingenium" (mind, inborn talent, genius),
and the importance of training in rhetoric and dialectics (*subtilitas*, though such refinement always suggests the dangers of sophistry).

5. "Implumes alas," literally wings without feathers, is an unusual metaphor perhaps suggestive
of Icarus' flight.

6. "Litterarum umbram (literally shade of letters): this is a striking figure evocative of Plato's
cave in *Republic* 7 and his warning about the false knowledge of men of learning.

7. "Itineris . . . nostri": the language throughout the letter is allegorical; the journey described
will be metaphysical as well as physical.

of cattle; and from the highest crags, the pipes of shepherds could be heard, so that I might have thought Diana and Sylvanus inhabited these woods.

Thus the ascent was easy, but the path was rugged. We sat, caught our breath, and pushed on, peacefully picking strawberries and flowers in the lush meadow. We were led to other small gardens where climbing vines with knotty tendrils and trees heavy-laden with apples provided shade. Here freedom from care—and this is what helped us seize grapes by the handful and gobble them down, since hunger was definitely the architect of our tour—gave us the strength to continue, and laughingly we put aside all thought of turning back. We returned to the path, and embarked upon the alpine slopes. Uncertain of our way, we wandered about, arriving at deserted places without a path and mountain ridges steep and overgrown with brambles.

Finally, taking diverse routes, once we had reached the mountaintop and the highest point of its summit, we launched a cascade of rocks which rolled headlong down into the depths of the valley. Then, roused by the racket, rabbits flew down the slopes ahead of us. Dogs, keen-scented and well-trained for the hunt, accompanied us. Next, right in front of our eyes, a small, trembling goat began to grow agitated at the sound of their yelping, and while the dogs followed his scent and trail with aggressive intent, he, with the violent dogs at his heels, chose flight by leaping down from the jutting ridges.

Then seeking the way home again, we withdrew, since our path was obstructed, to the place where the dense forest rose to its highest level. Here we thirstily drank down great flagons of milk, for our cabins in the inn where we were staying were a long way away. Within sight of this side of the promontory was a lookout point with a prospect of the most charming farmhouses below us. After sliding down the breast of the mountain, we traversed narrow crags that faced one another, taking the unavoidable pass that lay between them. A roaring, rushing sound accompanied us as we walked, a sound which was met by an echo; and after this we sang about Pallas and the Muses, one after another in turn, under a rocky cave carved out within the promontory.

Then finally, walking on our tiptoes since we could scarcely put the soles of our feet on the ground, so severely had the fires of the hot sun burned them, we took hidden paths down to the river, slowly and unsteadily, where no traveler appeared to have gone previously. We washed, rubbed ourselves down, and, having spread out leaves beneath a sheltering tree, we decided to lie down where the land is watered by a winding stream. Soon, with the sound of falling water, a peaceful sleep easily stole over us, for the rushing creek and its curving banks foamed from the rapid current, while a skylark perched above us gently filled the air with song.

But Fortune, the mocker of us all, sent a cuckoo down to tease us repeatedly, waking us from our sleep.[8] We laughed and threatened the bird with birdlime and snares. And then the greedy bird fell into the tumbling, jutting rocks and the stream which inundated him in the roaring torrent from the cataract pounding down from above, and afterwards he was hidden and his path could not be seen. Not long after he disappeared, he met his end, whereupon, in a shallow part of the stream, he belched out a pebble.

After this episode, we dispersed to head for home, where we were greeted with heavy-laden tables set out in a narrow passageway that provided a supper worthy of Xenocrates.[9] The first course consisted of chestnuts, turnips, and polenta—a delicious snack for us. On a second table, individual loaves of barley bread were set out; and on a table in the middle stood one small jug of wine to be passed around. As for delicacies, hazelnuts and fruits were offered to us diners; and our hunger was adequately requited.

The sage is content with plain foods: he asks for that which nourishes rather than that which delights. For his frugal lifestyle and his moderation brought Socrates more glory than the enjoyment of luxury brought to Sardanapalus.[10] For one can compare the frugality in one's life to the life of the belly. While frugality and prudence raise up the contemplation of the mind to the heavens through the fire of love, the indulgence of the belly causes human life to resemble that of a greedy wolf. Magnanimity of the soul and the enslavement to pleasure cannot be contained in one and the same body; only the wretched flee from adversity and trial.

Let us awaken our souls from sleep, dear sister. Let those of us who are reclining and who are cowardly rise to greater illuminations of the faith. Let us put away the cares of this age from the threshold of anxiety and let us tear the slender threads of arrogance from falsehood and deception.[11] Enjoyment has to be considered the least important of human things and pleasures ignorant of constancy must be severed from the governance of the unreliable emotions. What does the serenity which comes from looking down on the fields from the tops of mountains do for the happiness of mind and soul?

8. Cereta's cuckoo is reminiscent of Pliny's in *Nat.* 10.25–27: *coccyx* in Pliny, *Nat.* 10; *cuculus* in Cereta and Pliny, *Nat.* 28.156, 18.249; see esp. Pliny's passage about a "greedy" bird in *Nat.* 10.27.

9. Xenocrates, an ancient philosopher famous for the elegant but simple supper he served Alexander's courtiers when they arrived unexpectedly; he was head of the Academy in Athens from 339–314 B.C.

10. Sardanapalus (d. circa 820 B.C.), the last king of Assyria, was celebrated for his extravagance.

11. Images of thread and needlework continue to be dominant in her work (see esp. letters I–III in chapter 1).

What has the quiet exuberance of a heart becalmed given us, although it allowed us to survey the far-flung mountains without noise or any mishap of fate? What help has this refuge, this prodigious and extended flight across steep crags and hilltops been, far from which the quickly passing year has now fled the most troublesome spaces of our days? Long enough have we wandered in all directions in an attempt to change places. But can this wandering through various pastures, this exchange of one forest for another, touch in any way the mind of one for whom the whole world is a hometown that feels too confining and small.[12] Surely what I thought was as follows, contrary to the precepts of the philosophers: I believed that I was crossing a threshold to greater tranquility by this running to and fro of mine.

Virtue alone finds the road to true peace of mind. False, sister, are the painted enticements that Epicurus was accustomed to scorn as ephemeral and transitory pleasures. For he, since he was a man of great moderation and temperance, spurned these casual diversions among the quieting forms of relaxation, and not rashly so. For just as the inclination of our emotions draws us toward those things which appear shining and beautiful on the surface, so the appetite becomes sated to the point of nausea once our desires have been requited. Epicurus thought that the pleasure which is born in us is constantly reborn in a more vigorous form through the agency of the freedom that comes from a pure heart and mind.[13] For the mind that emulates the gods in its pursuit of happiness is full and contented. All other joys, because they grow old, torment us cruelly, with a sense of burning.

The great blessedness of virtue ought to be admired. Thus that man Epicurus, full of moral fiber and wisdom, believed that all short-lived sweetness, all imaginary petty devices, all erroneous efforts to achieve true serenity would be punished. We, whom this foolish satiety in sweet things rightfully exhausts, should satisfy our hearts more delightfully with God's love and we should chart a course for a virtue unviolated in this fleeting life, with the sail of our hearts pulled taut.

In the meantime, let society women, whose counterfeit finery exposes their notorious lack of modesty, pet themselves and bask, to the extent that they can, in their own vanity. But we women, since we are the objects of contempt, should be conscious with the humility of our chastity that these fragile, small bodies of ours are chaff for fire and filth.[14] And although I am not yet called Laura in the place where you dwell, sister—that would be to

12. She's playing with the Stoic maxim popular among the humanists that the sage considers the whole world his home (*patria*).

13. Note the importance of the role free will (here *animi libertate*) plays in Cereta's thought.

14. The fragility and smallness of women's bodies is a repeated theme in Cereta and the writings of the humanists in general.

put a skylark next to a phoenix—still, out of the kindness of your heart, you will not cast me out of the purview of your love. For the magpie did not think the nightingale unworthy of her; nor did the peacock always show disdain for the hoopoe.[15] You will come up with a fair plan, I do not doubt, if you reflect how anxiety-ridden this time of ours is, for it draws all things born in this world, in an irrevocable course, to one end.

This end, however, has but one object for our soul: the one God; and he, so that we might enter Paradise, has placed us, since we are sojourners, in the exile of our fragile flesh. Let us devote ourselves, therefore, wholly to virtue and to the innocent and celibate life of our Savior and let our sinful life revert to him also. Let us imitate the many illustrious men in the Church who, detached from all desires, have yearned with full hearts for eternal life. Nature has taught us always to incline our hearts freely and deliberately towards the good,[16] so that it will finally come about for us that God will win us over as heavenly beings for all eternity.

This living of ours is so uncertain and aimless that time, speeding onward, tightly binds the day of our birth to that of our death. And so, no day should slip, for the sake of leisure, through our hands. Let us reclaim the nights with our speeches; let ordered thoughts alone give our minds respite. Let us believe each day that this is our last on earth; let us ponder that this life is a turbid well of grief, and that death is the parent of worms and decay. Look, the iniquity of raging Fortune carries us and all other things away, and all grounds for arrogance fly upwards when the spirit has fled the body. But surely our mind is too often bereft of judgment, clouded by blind hope and the false promise of flimsy pleasure.

To sum up, let us sweep away the seeds of the question here and now. A pleasure that lives and endures is a thing not generally known; for disdaining that which belongs to this world, it purchases that which is immortal with the currency of virtue.[17] This pleasure delights and cares for our minds in its nurturing bosom; it inhabits the fortress of respected religion. And it is protected, free from care, and blessed, even amid the Syrtes and the most diffi-

15. On birds and their lore Cereta clearly consulted her favorite author, Pliny, *Nat.*: 10.3 on the phoenix (*phoenix*); 10.45 on the peacock (*pavo*); 10.78; 10.98; 10.118–20 on the magpie (*pica*); 10.81 on the nightingale (*luscinia*): 10.86 on the hoopoe (*upupula*); 10.25–27 on the cuckoo (*cuculum, coccyx* in Pliny). See also *Nat.* 11.121 on the different crests of the phoenix, the peacock, and the skylark (*lauda*, in Cereta *laudula; lodola* in Italian). Cereta's habit is to mine a particular Latin text for new vocabulary and ideas and then to use that vocabulary up in a single letter (ex. her use of Boccaccio in chapter 2 and Apuleius in chapter 6).

16. Freedom of the will is for Cereta the key component in the Christian's yearning for, and striving toward, God.

17. "Viva voluptas" (pleasure that lives and endures): this is the image Cereta adopts to distinguish Epicurus' notion of *voluptas* of the mind from the short-lived pleasures of the senses.

cult terrain of our life. This one pleasure represents the highest fulfillment of the contented mind, the most tranquil satiety of our solace, by which we are led by the safe path of faith to God. For the right-thinking mind is the companion of the gods; and in this mind neither idleness, nor darkness, nor ghosts, nor any emotion shall hold dominion. All other murky allurements have been sucked into that ocean of evils which cause the voyaging human mind, whenever it is caught up in sudden storms, to drown in softness and false and empty consolation.

Write often, if you think of anything. Write even if you don't. Afterwards it will not be permitted to me to see you in that solitude of yours. Your letters raise my spirits so much that the wonderful memory of you brings you back to me as though you were here. Vale. December 12, 1487.

XXXVI
AN ADMONITION ABOUT THE FALSE PLEASURE
OF A LIFE IN SECLUSION

The philosophical distance between the two authorial voices in Cereta's letters to Deodata and Europa is also atypical within the genre of the humanist letterbook. Whereas in the letter to Deodata Cereta represents the *bonum*— the pleasures ⸂f the mind and pursuit of virtue, which enable humans to find the path to God—as an objective which the individual may pursue on a mountain peak or in a remote cave far from the city, one's family, friends, or community, in her letter to Europa she vehemently insists that such a life is morally unthinkable. While taking immediate issue with her own proposal to Deodata, Cereta's letter to "Europa solitaria" seems also to argue with Petrarch's treatise *De vita solitaria* (*On the solitary life*), which praises the virtues of life removed from the city for those who seek the good.[18] The new position Cereta takes in her letter to Europa closely resembles Coluccio Salutati's letter to Pellegrino Zambeccari, chancellor of Bologna (c. 1394), exhorting him not to retire from politics and urban life and not to enter a monastery.[19] Taking a posture both Aristotelian and Christian, Salutati urges Zambeccari to fulfill his responsibilities to his family, friends, city, and, above all, to minister to those in need. The paradox, as Salutati expresses it, is that in order to ascend to God, one must immerse oneself in the world, for by avoiding the

18. On Petrarch's *De vita solitaria* see Kristeller, *Eight Philosophers*, p. 14. Cereta's letter addressed to "Europa solitaria" and entitled "De falsa delectatione vitae privatae admonitio" in all three editions is in Vat. 82 (fols. 76r–77v): Ven. (fols. 143r–48v); Tom. 70 (pp. 214–20); Rabil 81.

19. George McClure, *Sorrow and Consolation in Italian Humanism* (Princeton: Princeton University Press, 1991), p. 89.

world one becomes mired in it. "Fleeing the world," writes Salutati, "can draw your heart from heavenly things to earth, and I, remaining in earthly affairs, will be, able to raise my heart to heaven."[20] Cereta's message to her friend is remarkably similar. She warns that the pleasure of taking refuge in nature is a false one: a rejection of the city in favor of the countryside will only result in an "uprooting" (*convellere*) of one's serenity, an image that ridicules Europa's seeming return to a kind of ur-home in the bosom of nature. Like Salutati, Cereta urges Europa to avoid Stoic *apateia*, to abandon the desolate wilds, and to involve herself with the poor and indigent in the city.

It has been suggested that this letter, addressed to an almost surely fictional figure whom Cereta calls simply "Europa" in the body of the text, should be read as a soliloquy.[21] Certainly the figure of the addressee in the text, who wanders disconsolate through the mountains and forests of Italy with torn hair and dress, resembles the persona of Cereta's letters of mourning. It seems appropriate to argue that, in the sense that all Cereta's letters are conversations or dialogues with herself and her friends—who represent little more than projections of her own ego—the entire letterbook is a soliloquy of sorts. The letter to Europa contains elements not only of an internal dialogue but, like Cereta's three letters to Brother Thomas, it participates in a dialogic that takes place across letters.

Cereta's choice of name for her straw woman, Europa, is significant. In Greek mythology, the story of Europa is essentially a variation on the myths of Persephone and Eurydice, who also lost their lives amid the bounty of nature. In Ovid's and Boccaccio's retelling of the myth, the god Jupiter, in order to seduce Europa, assumes the form of a bull so seemingly tranquil and gentle that Europa cannot resist him.[22] She unwittingly climbs on his back and he carries her into the ocean, far from all hope of return. Thus the name of Cereta's addressee also serves a cautionary function in this letter.

To Europa solitaria[23]

While vigilantly keeping watch, I have anxiously made inquiries and asked questions about what city you might be making your home, where you might be spending the winter, and what day you might

---

20. McClure, *Sorrow,* p. 89.

21. Rabil, *Laura Cereta,* p. 104.

22. A Renaissance version of the Europa tale was published by Boccaccio in his *De claris mulieribus* (*Concerning Famous Women,* trans. G. A. Guarino [New Brunswick, N.J.: Rutgers University Press], pp. 20–21), a book Cereta studied carefully, as we know from chapter 2.

23. See n. 18.

designate for your final return to us. Since no one has informed me, I have scoured all the churches with searching and thievish eyes to see whether you, since I had been looking for you, might arrive unexpectedly. And each time I lost the hope that I had, just when I had it in my hands. And so it often goes with a lover that his futile hope will mock his desire.

Finally, a peasant who lives in a simple hut here came to me, full of his lowly station and dirty feet, to deliver your letters in the crowded public square. A great number of onlookers can testify well enough as to how I went to the public square with as much yearning for a sister's love as I had honey-sweet anticipation of her kisses. My heart was exultant and my voice trembled with unrestrained desire. Suffused with joy, I went home at that moment, and then fled from the courtyard to my bedroom. But then I went outdoors and roused everyone as though I had been overcome by religious awe on hearing my fate from the oracle. For I consider your name so dear to my heart that you are as important to me as are my health and safety.

I have read your long-awaited letters, in the narratives of which you describe the enduring solace of the countryside. I congratulate you on behalf of all of us, and thank you on my own account because, by renouncing civic honors for the sake of your peace of mind, you have found—if rest is still to be had—recompense in your own private life. But I fear for your peace of mind, I have written, lest the sweet and gentle serenity of fleeting peace and quiet should elude you. For what tranquility can be vouchsafed in human affairs when as infants we howl, as children we are oblivious, as teenagers we are sluggish, and as old women we become withered and decrepit in our misery and boredom? We are all stricken by the onslaughts that come our way from the injustices of nature. Only the woman who does not give in to the power of Fortune is a sage.[24] But I also consider that woman wise who does not remove herself from participation in the commonwealth for the sake of the pleasures of solitude but who struggles for the reward of eternal life in the midst of cyclones of evil with a steadfastness that will prevail.

Therefore, whenever possible, you leave the city by the road that takes you to a place where there are small farms, and you wander alone, as though you were in a hermitage. There is the path to the mountains, and there you climb, crossing breezy hills full of shade. There from the highest lookout points in the Alps you seek the rough shelter of a cave, and now you look down on the steep inclines of the precipitous vale. And here, along the trackless solitude of a hilly path, you see the plane trees of the greening forest and its dense pines. You listen to the nightingale's modulated songs, which the

24. Vat.: "paret"; Ven., Tom., erroneously: "parit."

repetition of a garrulous call and response constantly varies, day and night. Your pleasure in this is derived from resting, in the bosom of the forest, on the banks of the curving Mella, which, pummeling the side of the mountain with its first springs, is carried gently into a sandy torrent, and here glides in a smooth journey over placid waves, and there runs down in streams enclosed by a winding mountain path through fertile fields. Exiting at some distance from here, the stream runs down a severe declivity onto rocks foaming with boiling white water. Then hurrying back again to the opposite peaks, now stagnant in a languid and wide-curving direction, finally it hurls rocks thrown forward onto the shoals of the Aglio.

The dense and untouched forest wilderness is very beautiful; here mountain goats leap and frightened hares flee. From this height, under the sheltering cover of leaves, you yourself stand gazing ardently at everything you see, stunned at the outcome; for in their precipitous descent down the mountain those goats may fall suddenly into snares laid for them. I will not mention now the pendulous grapes growing from wild vines nor will I describe the depths of the valleys, where so many wild strawberries, ripe green olives, and chestnuts covered with pungent rinds shade the densely wooded grove. It's worthwhile to see among so many sacred oaks the chestnut oaks, the mountain ashes, and the black junipers.[25] Why must I think back on the cornel trees and the shadbush trees, the hazelnuts, or the myrtles loved by Venus and the triumphal laurels? You have already discussed the flowering, grassy meadows, mown and dewy, where the serpent, relying on the toughness of its scales, comes out of the brambles to do battle with the storks.[26]

You are deceived, dearest Europa, by this empty restfulness; and while you live in tranquil seclusion, you are uprooting every bit of serenity from the good fortune that is yours. In this I will not imitate your plans which, following in the footsteps of noble men, emulate the stories of the past that are celebrated in schools. You believe, I think, that you, because of the nobility of your mind, are patterning yourself on Camillus and the Curii, Metellus, Publius Scipio, Quinctus Cincinnatus, and Sulla and, from among the Greeks, Pittacus, Anaxagoras, Euripides, Myson, Heraclitus, and Parmenides.[27] Some of these men, in order to pursue the quiet life, preferred clods of

25. Cereta's arboreal vocabulary is undoubtedly from Pliny, *Nat.* 16.11.

26. See Juvenal 14.314.

27. She names the standard emblems of the purported good old days of Roman history in the second and first centuries B.C.: Camillus, a Roman statesman and general who repeatedly drove the Gauls out of Rome; the Roman consul Manlius Dentatus Curius, noted for refusing bribes; the Roman general Metellus, who defeated the Numidian king Jugurtha; the Roman general Publius Cornelius Scipio, who defeated the Carthaginians in Africa and Spain; Quintus Cincin-

earth, rakes, and flocks of sheep to the heights of luxurious living. Others went to remote hermitages, steep overhanging ledges of mountains, and rocky seacoasts, in pursuit of solitary contemplation and study more removed from the world. Those men endured hardships with steadfast minds, nor did they refuse any sort of labor, to the end that the dignity of each man's name would be etched in the memory of posterity, even if they did not expect another life after this age. But when the sacrifices and sacred images of their clans were profaned, though they had no god, those men in their emptiness sought the deity.

I am afraid, however, that the brilliant shimmer of false goodness may suck such men into the dark abyss of the underworld. Still you, sister, being cleansed through baptism of the leprosy of this kind of infidelity, should find a more secure port for a shipwrecked soul. Yours is also a position different from those peoples whose strange paganism worshipped Pan, Sylvanus, the Napeads, and the Hamadryads in the mountain forests.

I do not condemn those who have ascetic houses on the highest mountain crags.[28] I condemn instead the antiquated thought of their time. For although Elizabeth made her home on a rural mountain with her companions, she never visited the dwellings on the wooded slopes alone.[29] You know that the angel Gabriel did not find Mary in a secluded glen of some forest. She was studying the teachings of the prophets alone by lamplight in her humble room. Jesus, however, who was the true messiah of the world, prayed and fasted, abstaining from food and drink for forty days in the steep mountain wilderness without the company of either friends or beasts. Therefore this private solitude of yours is not suitable at your age. Too much freedom from responsibility dishonors your womanly respect. It will be enough if you live in an urban cave and choose Antonius and Paul for your teachers about life, who never devoted their free time to idle repose or to any such pleasures either in the narrow confines of a cave or the bristling silence of a forest.[30] Nor did they rely for their happiness on the songs of the Philomena or Procne, or in servitude to untamed beasts, or in contemplating the stars in the

---

natus, who abandoned his plow to become dictator of Rome; and Sulla, Roman consul, military dictator, and reformer. Among the Greeks she cites Myson and Pittacus among the Seven Sages of Greece; the pre-Socratic philosophers Anaxagoras, Heraclitus, and Parmenides; and the tragedian Euripides.

28. The rest of this paragraph is missing in Tom.

29. The story of Elizabeth, Jesus' mother Mary, and the angel Gabriel is in *Luke*: 1.11–57.

30. St. Anthony and St. Paul were city dwellers.

middle of the night.[31] Instead they looked to God with this passion of the soul, with a ray of faith lighting their way even in the darkness.

In former times there were many philosophers whom antiquity judged as the one mouthpiece of God among all men because of the moderation in their counsel and virtue. Surely these are the incomparable qualities of a Christian mind that no noble deed in life or magnificent example of probity for posterity but the humble and pure integrity of an uncultivated mind can bring to the eternal hierarchies of the blessed. Too much happiness has always been dangerous for us humans. For the goodness in life which the teeth of pleasure chew with delight is false. Think more deeply therefore about what you must preserve in the choice of this solitary life so that, while you flee anxiety in your fortunate years, when you are an old woman you will not drown in the turbulent waves of a battered conscience.

If you hope for spiritual fulfillment, you are looking for soft nettles among the brambles. The lot of man has always been odious, and sorrow has always been mixed among the joys. But suppose you live as long as possible and under circumstances of one unviolated peace, will death come as a draught more bitter than any other cup of poison? All of us encounter evils in the course of our lives, for the relationship between joy and sorrow is that of brother and sister. Just as the entire span of our lives is wrapped up in inexplicable weavings, so the past days of our lives move together with the days still to come towards death.[32] But alas, for each one of us this life glides on, leaving behind days more precious.

Because of this, I wish you would quiet your wounded mind, regretful for the time lost. I wish above all that you would bring counsel and aid in response to the complaints of the suffering poor. I wish that you would feel the tears and sighs of widows and small orphans.[33] It is better for you, believe me, for the sake of Christ's bloody wounds, that you abandon the desolate wilds; it is better for you, I say, though your voice is broken, your clothing rent in sorrow, and your hair torn, to go between tears and cries, in a different direction. Less bitterness then would enter the secret witness of your soul and less tribulation would remain for you, who are going to die, when you do pass from this life.

Once I myself crossed the plains and mountains in the company of our

31. Boccaccio (in *CFW*) tells the tale of how Procne and her sister Philomela were metamorphosed into songbirds as the punishment for Procne's filicide.

32. The inexplicable threads that bind together all the days of our lives from birth to death is a recurrent theme in Cereta; see for example letter XXXV, to Deodata.

33. After this sentence Tom. has a lacuna.

mothers,[34] but my mind was profoundly covered with shame that tortured my soul through the secret witness of my conscience. For anxieties are always mingled together in a wandering mind. But beyond this, we must seek other stairs to God, or perhaps another way in which virtue does not extend her hand in death. Whether you know it or not, one sleep ends all men's lives. Take care, you, that your day does not find you unprepared in your delights. Vale. February 29, 1487/1488.

XXXVII

A CONSOLATION ON THE DEATH OF A HUSBAND

In terms of its humanist themes, Cereta's *consolatio* for her close friend Martha Marcella resembles the consolatory letters of Petrarch, Bruni, and Filelfo.[35] Her letter to Martha contains a number of stock funerary motifs: the instability of fortune, the figure of life as sea voyage, the inevitability of death, the brevity of human life, the anticipation of a better world after death, a desire to die oneself, the pleasure of losing oneself in grief (*voluptas dolendi*), the appeal to the bereaved to cease futile weeping and show fortitude, and finally the exhortation to search not for the passing pleasures of the senses but for true pleasure which is grounded in *virtus*.[36] But Cereta's letter also contains much that is uniquely hers.

The letter to Martha is a sequel to one she had written the previous year to the famous Venetian scholar Cassandra Fedele describing the dream she had had in which she roamed the underworld in search of her dead husband.[37] It is this dream she revisits in her letter to Martha. Just as her letter to Cassandra had suggested that the future might be known through dreaming, so she suggests in this one to her friend Martha that an important remedy for grief lies in the conservation of the past through shared recollection. Cereta's dream life, in which she is able to travel between this world and the next, takes as its departure point Virgil's description of the world of the dead in book 6 of the *Aeneid*. Boiling or stagnant waters, a contagion of fires sporadically lighting up the plains, monstrous apparitions, endless night, and a sense of drowning are dominant images in both letters. This Virgilian land of the dead—Orcus, Avernus, Erebus, or Tartarus or whatever Cereta chooses

---

34. "In comitatu matrum": it is not clear to whom Cereta is referring.

35. Vat. 70 (fols. 54v–56v): Ven. 60 (fols. 96–100v); Tom. 58 (pp. 137–44); Rabil 67. Cereta to Martha Marcella. A consolation on the death of her husband (the title "De morte mariti consolatoria" is present in all the editions).

36. On Renaissance funerary themes see now McClure, *Sorrow*.

37. Vat. 42 (fols. 30v–32); Ven. 37 (fols. 60–63); Tom. 35 (pp. 75–80); Rabil 55.

to call this alien world—is a place of sulphurous rivers, dark lakes, and fetid swamps as well as one of lightning and conflagration. Cereta's dream in this letter, unlike her earlier letter to Cassandra, is told as a memory of the future rather than as a dream prophecy. In this revisiting of her dream of Avernus, a passage on war in the underworld—its compulsive repetitions, its skirmishes without armistice, its soldiers who swim endlessly as in a dream until they drown, its air thick with flying arrows, and its diabolical war trumpets—is evocative of a more personal and more modern memoir of war than anything either in Virgil's book 6 or in her own earlier dream narrative of death. But this long letter is also an appreciation of death as a place which portends not only dread but also that light for which humans wait through the long night watch: *vigilia*—an image Cereta usually uses to describe her all-night sessions of study and writing. At the close of the letter Cereta imagines the work of their—Martha's and Cereta's—joint mourning and collaborative effort to heal themselves as two friends rowing a small boat together through rough waters.

To Martha Marcella [38]

*I*f only Marcus Crassus Parthicus could be a surrogate judge at the inexorable court of Rhadamanthus, Marcella, you and I would both go in a great hurry to the underworld. [39] For gold would be more precious to Crassus than shades would be; thus with a weight of gold we would buy back Pietro and Lelio, the best and most devoted of husbands, whom the chastity of an untarnished honor has guarded with such wondrous uprightness and conjugal purity that the love preserved therein has kept them alive for us through our perpetual memory of days gone by. [40] For the faithful widow does not forget her husband though he lies buried in his grave.

Alas, we pursue the ones we've lost with hearts full of prayers. Why, dear sister, do you weep with bitter sorrow for one who is dead? Do you think the kings of the underworld care about human tears? I remember that last year I was seized and dragged through the perpetual ice of Orcus, the intense flames of the Phlegethon, and the ashy chasms of the Acheron. And though I believe I saw the realms of Tartarus with my own eyes, I might lie to myself in

38. See n. 35.

39. Crassus (d. 53 B.C.). Triumvir and general in the Parthian wars, he was a man legendary for his wealth. Rhadamantus was a judge in the underworld tribunal who decided the fates of dead souls.

40. Note the heavy stress on wifely sexual chastity, even after death; *pudor, castitas,* and *pudicitia* are words that in classical and humanist texts apply to female, not male, chastity.

my dreams. Still, my trembling imagination did see men being cast down and thrown into the furnace of Hades, drowning in eternal night. At that time, in the most profound state of terror, I was seized by grief and fear. I tore my hair and scratched at my pale cheeks, making myself unsightly; I mourned my husband with disconsolate weeping, and I showed the incurable wound in my heart, which felt lacerated and eaten away.

But in the end it was all for nothing. Cruel fate, ever more hostile, stood in my path, while gluttonous Pluto, standing in front of me and leading the way, threatened me with instant death and exile from my home. Shouting hoarsely with a loud voice that was strangled and broken, he said "Girl, watch where you go before the coming of your time, lest a locked gate make a mockery of all your boldness, for once the inexorable procession of the fates leads one thus, all capacity to return is removed."

At first I was stunned, unaware of whether I was alive or dead, such were the fevers of fear that raged deep within my breast, but my less fearful mind, ready for difficult things, soon trampled down the terror that a greater firmness of heart had already mitigated. But an evil demon ordered that I be thrust out of that place, and I, looking for a way not to be further detained, eluded the traps of his attendants and fled the scene swiftly. On the path I had chosen in my haste, I heard the crashing of thunder with battling winds. And, driven by these, shafts of lightning beat upon the entire landscape with a glittering din. Thereupon leaving the path with hesitant steps, I crossed the shoals of the river Lethe without drinking, where the grim Furies sat with hostile eyes at the mouth of a hollow cave.[41] There was an erupting volcano, inapproachable because there were swamps, worms, and fires everywhere; the place was encircled with three ditches, each smeared with poison. Inside the ditches the most horrible battle blazed between the souls, who pierced one another in the side and throat with their swords.

Here sat Aeacus, affecting a judicial rank haughty beyond his means, who, fulminating sentences upon the damned, meted out punishments suited to the gravity of the crime.[42] Here the boatman Charon, shaking his oar and beating the souls with it, gaped at the crowd of souls gathered on the shore. Here, I say, were numerous barking Cenocephali and one-eyed Cyclopes, and they, as if arrogantly boasting about their strength, surrounded the

41. When the dead shades crossed over to the land of the dead, they had to drink from the river Lethe, which enabled them to forget their past lives. Cereta needs to return to life and therefore is careful not to drink from the river.

42. In Virgil only Rhadamanthus and Minos hold the office of judges of the dead; in Propertius, Ovid, and Horace, however, Aeacus (grandfather of Achilles, the greatest hero of the Trojan war) joins Rhadamanthus and Minos' court.

shades and taunted them to do battle with them.[43] In this way, great and ferocious clashes of the demons were stirred up, wherein madness groaned most horribly, and the awful terror of a frightful death was visited upon everyone there, one after another. Some tore other souls limb from limb after their chariots were pulled to pieces; logs driven through the bowels were the implements by which still other souls were tortured, and the dog Cerberus—who even roasted the palpitating limbs of men on a hearth where a huge fire was billowing up—threw other dismembered souls to giant beasts.

I saw those whom Cerberus savagely skinned with a hook, those whom he placed in heavy yokes on the beach, those thrust into prison cells, and those whom he placed in chains and harnesses and forced to undergo the punishment of perpetual servitude under the surveillance of guards. In this way, thousands of souls who were undergoing torture, cried out in pain from their wounds and the fires. Thousands more, assuming an attitude of intrepidity in their desperation, zealously ran to offer their throats to the avenging knife.

The last lot one could draw was that of unfortunate war—a lot that burned many of those who pursued it with brands, and drowned many others who had fled through the remote and rough channels that led down to the sulphurous sea. Others were sent plunging down from the steep precipice of a mountain. In this spectacle of divine retribution, clouds of arrows flew through the air everywhere far and wide; there was never a state of peace, armistice, or cease-fire. Everything blazed with truculent rage. No wonder all hope of putting an end to the evils here was in vain. With no hope of any delay intervening, each person's torments were reborn again. Thus the battle lines were rearmed again on each side, and on both sides, the defeated shades groaned at their uncertain fate. They were crowded together, they creaked and rattled, and they gnashed their teeth in anger. And then the crashing of renewed tumult was heard in the form of diabolical war trumpets.

The sorrow that wells up with these wretched memories saps me of energy and disturbs me terribly. A sense of duty is important, yet also important is the bitterness of the visions which have burrowed into my heart. Still, a certain hope for my dead husband consoles me, because I have never found him whom I've sought in the entire realm of Dis—as though he were one banned from every station along the Cocytus River because of the constancy with which he faced death. But you now, beloved sister and soul mate of mine, why do you waste yourself in grieving? Why do you paralyze yourself for the sake of evil? Why do you make yourself sick with sad toil? Why do

43. "Cenocephali": literally, those without heads.

you sigh and tear our your hair? Ah, take back your courage, for nothing is greater than our minds, and our virtue is the victor over fortune. You don't mourn your excellent husband for your own sake, do you? The innate sweetness we feel towards our own, which is among our first emotions, is the thing that causes this—I confess it.

But the earth demands its own back, and although this grave covers over his pale limbs, still the spirit has not been overcome by eternal sleep. Think about it: will you mingle your soul and the ghoulish bones of a cadaver in one tomb? An exchange of life and death is always going on, but the certainty of death is preferable to life's uncertainty, since the entire space of one's life is a single, brief vigil for death. For sudden death overtakes many even in the midst of laughter. Thus, in the uncertainty of life and in death there is one day which a final hour bitterly interrupts.

I work on, I am restless, and I cannot stand myself because I lost so quickly my companion, the most beloved and precious part of me. But it is dangerous to grieve in this way. For the Epicureans believe that the wise man finds contentment in himself, that virtue is sweeter than any friend, and that our happiness proceeds not from any pleasure, or husband, or wealth, but from virtue. For what good is a pleasure which is tangled and woven with passion? The allurements of the senses are the traps of birdlime, which the burning hour of death turns to ash. What is the point in your caring more for your husband than yourself, or he more for you than himself, when the feelings of lovers are not supposed to be of any use? Friendship doesn't look either for what brings advantage or what follows from it. The stimulus for prudent desire is a pure one. For our love, which is always present in us, stands by us; it is not extinguished by death but softened by absence.

No one is free from toils, such that in human affairs unhappiness is close at hand for each one of us. Indeed, in times of adversity one misfortune is reborn from another. Therefore, let us brush the tears from our eyes and dry them, to the extent that we can. Enough mental anguish—in itself too much to bear—will follow us no matter where we try to flee. We have paid enough honor to our husbands, whom we—dressed in rags and mourning—have surely washed with the waters from one well, that of our tears. Nor should we be so frightened by the changes in fortune that our minds, strung taut with sorrow, may succumb to weakness. I believe that those who died after having lived a prudent life should be laid to rest with songs, not weeping.

Do you believe that God is unjust in his divine and everlasting judgment? He has given the blessed a home in heaven, where the just rest secure in undisturbed tranquility and wondrous peace. There our companions and husbands reside, bound by duty and concern for us. But if those who lived their lives in sedate and moral uprightness of purpose must be mourned with sighs and weeping, what will less fortunate women do who either had no husbands or had husbands whose hands were polluted by crime? For what mind is so distraught that, while ever mindful of the lost object it had cared for, it can forget itself?

Adversity always fosters courage and, at the end of the play, constancy carries the day. But whenever strength of mind goes into the middle of a storm, though its sail may be torn, its ship may be damaged by perilous hail, and the din of the whirlwinds may resonate everywhere, with still greater steadfastness of heart it will not fear the yawning holes in the vessel.

Come, therefore, let us struggle in this deep sea of adversity with stronger oars, and let us raise ourselves up in the midst of danger with steadfast hearts. For wherever the danger is greater, there is more glory to attain and more palms. For the roads to death lead men in many different directions; thus the ultimate end is unequal and uncertain for each.

In the meantime, if fortune should take away any of the things it has granted us, let us bear it with an unwounded mind. Vale. October 8, 1486.

XXXVIII
ON THE INSTABILITY OF FORTUNE AND CONGRATULATIONS
ON MARRIAGE

Cereta's letter of congratulations to Barbara Alberti on her marriage to a man she refers to as Nigrello follows a humanist formula for such occasions. Like the Latin letter and Greek poem that Francesco Filelfo sent Donato Acciaiuoli in 1460 on the occasion of Donato's marriage, Cereta's letter contains all the predictable humanist tropes: the Stoic commonplaces about the instability of fortune, the admonition that reason must be one's guide, the tactful warnings against too much sex, the counsel to the newlyweds to practice moderation, and the insistence that the true road to happiness be through virtue.[44] What is unusual about this *gratulatio nuptialis* is Cereta's near drowning of the marriage theme within a work of self-consolation for the death of her own husband.

44. See Filelfo's nuptial congratulations to Acciaiuoli in a letter dated November 1460 in Filelfo, *Epistolae familiares* (Venice: De Gregoriis, 1502), fol. 119v; see also Filelfo's Greek poem 1.5 to Acciaiuoli in his unpublished Greek opus *De psychagogia*, which is preserved in Codex Laurentianus 58.15, fols. 8–9. For a text and commentary on this poem see my "Unknown Greek Poems of Francesco Filelfo," *Renaissance Quarterly* 37.2 (Summer 1984): 173–206.

To Barbara Alberti [45]

*C*hrysippus, our moral guide, believed that integrity in the good life means that one never lies to another person in order to sweeten the friendship.[46] Besides, although your father's letter came to me as a festive little gift, I do not know how to fashion anything more elegant than the orderliness of the truth; for my tongue and heart have only one appearance, which produces words equal to, and harmonious with, my work.

I congratulate you and I give thanks to our God, who, in taking pity on your barbarous name, has placed you in the hands of a singularly extraordinary husband. Now is not the proper moment for a fuller discussion of him, nor is this the place for such a discussion. But for a long time now this man's divine, exquisite, and distinguished virtue has shown enough in my presence. It is that sort of virtue which (unless I am mistaken) will commend itself to posterity, secure in the eternal nature of its fame.

But you, who are adorned with the purest flowers of youth and whom a modest face and manners gently and innocently embellish, how greatly are you to be preferred to all other women and how much honor would the sure and stable tranquility of a more ample mind lend to you, if only that which fortune has granted would always be ours.

But there is no condition of men that is so firm and stable that it cannot be hard pressed and overturned by fate. Tears run down from my eyes and unseemly sorrow makes me restless when I remember my dead husband. But he, who was kindly and caringly disposed toward his parents, behaved so obligingly towards me in every respect, in accordance with his promise to me of undisturbed peace, that he loved me even while I quietly pursued my studies in literature. For there was between us always one unity, one peace, and one harmony. But death (oh, sorrow) assailed him in the tenderest flower of his youth, and while I would have promised myself better things given my own youth, the iniquity of fortune has stolen everything from me in a brief moment. Fortune always threatens us more when our happiness is most perfect.[47] From this it follows that no one lives secure in his possession of this

---

45. Vat. 72 (fols. 58v–59); Ven. 62 (fols. 106v–108v); Tom. 60 (pp. 154–58); Rabil 51. Laura Cereta to Barbara Alberti. De instabilitate Fortuna et Gratulatio de Nuptiis.

46. Chrysippus (c. 280–207 B.C.) succeeded Cleanthes as the head of the Stoa in Athens, where he devoted his life to reforming Stoicism. See Diogenes Laertius 7.189–202.

47. From this point on in the letter, Cereta pulls out a series of stock Stoic commonplaces on the instability of fortune and the necessity of obeying reason and wisdom: see my article on the uses of Stoic maxims in Quattrocento humanist writing, "Unknown Greek Poems of Francesco Filelfo," *Renaissance Quarterly* 37 (Summer 1984): 173–206.

life, nor does anyone enjoy the good things in life for long. Wretchedness alone is the reward for our anxiety.

Human pleasures are carried to immeasurable extremes, and although we may experience desires that are aroused when the channel for their fulfillment has been removed, there is no satisfaction for greedy minds in any case. Many, who are motivated by the desire for gold, try the sea and sail to foreign shores, while others, who are ready with plans and arms, engage in military campaigns with all their strength, and still others live without laboring, taking their sole comfort in relaxation. But as for me, only the love of literature rages in my heart, and what is more, the very difficulty of my studies is causing my mind to grow and expand.[48]

Thus among the cups of pleasures selected, each person finds his own poison sweetest. Thus restless desire exists in everyone in various forms and noises its presence around in various ways. Happiness does not have the knowledge to appreciate the frailties of humankind; this is because the mind almost always grows weak and ill through having carried the burden of the body.[49] Virtue alone always glistens with its own light; when it ponders temptations that pull us towards luxury, it safely flees from the vanishing smoke of pleasures to the lasting glory of the soul.

Therefore, there is but one foundation and one sheltering roof for human tranquility, so that when all the veils of desire have been peeled away, we can make our way on the right road of innocence to God; and those men who die after voyaging from the turbulent seas of youth to the faultless gate of old age are deserving of him.[50] One must die, most precious sister; certainly it is not necessary that one must live, since no one has ever lived for long. For this life, in which all time disappears and is nothing, is briefer than one speeding day. Because of these things, you and I will go together into one sleep and you will temper the reins of your rising passion with moderation.

After all, the generous and noble mind obeys reason of its own free will.[51] You yourself, who are more learned than I, know how many great men who were once famed for their intellectual and physical strength, or how many married women who were notable for the tenor of their lives as well as their conduct, have been destroyed by an excess of good fortune. For happy are those who die with the innocence with which they were born. It has been

48. "Many . . . others . . ., but as for me": This rhetorical trope is a parody of Horace, *Odes* 1.1.

49. The metaphor of the body as the mind's burden or prison is a commonplace in Greek literature from Plato on.

50. There seems to be a participle, "navigantes" or "venientes," missing in this last clause.

51. The exhortation to obey reason is a Stoic commonplace virtually ubiquitous in Quattrocento humanist writings.

my privilege to write these few bits not to provide premarital counsel but rather to assuage the perpetual sorrow that is strangling me.

I know your kinsmen, the divine Alberti, I know the illustrious Penates of your family, and I know the superb genius of your moderation, which, following wisdom as its leader, raises you to the level of your father and grandfather in terms of the public renown accorded to them.[52] The conjugal auspices that blessed my parents are those that have joined you in prosperity to Nigrello. May the gods bless the just covenant of your marriage with more happiness and favor each day. Vale. November 21, 1486.

XXXIX

ON FRIENDSHIP

Cereta uses the subject of this letter, her attempt to repair a once close relationship now on the rocks, for a pretext to discourse on a standard humanist theme, the meaning of friendship (*amicitia*). The starting point and model for all humanist meditations on friendship was Cicero's *De amicitia*, essentially a Stoic tract that stressed the relationship between two like-minded peers as the fundamental bond on which all other associations in the republic are built. Cereta's approach to the topic of friendship in this letter and elsewhere focuses less on the bond between friends and more on the emotional tensions that pull at the fabric of such relationships. Two images are typically Ceretan and distinguish her particular take on the subject. The first is her use of plant metaphors; friendship is an organic entity that needs to be fed and watered so that it can grow. The second is a related idea: if such a relationship is not nourished, it first grows ill, and a "lethargy" or "paralysis" of one's thoughts and ideas (*torpor cogitationi, stupor opinionum*) comes over it, the two friends stop communicating, enmity and misunderstanding grow up between them, and finally the friendship dies.

To Santa Pelegrina[53]

Those men who have written about friendship have one thought: they see it as a bond that is both extraordinary and by law itself

---

52. Cereta's warm praise extolling Barbara's Alberti kinsmen indicates that Barbara comes from the same clan as Cereta's good friend and correspondent Alberti degli Alberti. Both her injunction to follow *sapientia* (wisdom) and the homage paid to her friend's parents and grandparents are common *topoi* in Roman Stoicism.

53. Vat. 54 (fols. 37–37v); Ven. 49 (fols. 48–49); Tom. 47 (pp. 105–7); Rabil 34. Laura Cereta to Santa Pelegrina. "On friendship" is my own title, though the index to the Vatican manuscript bears a title for this letter that contains "de amicitia" in it.

lifelong, since it springs from the very font of honor.[54] And no wonder, for ethics is that state of being useful which is also honorable.[55] The thing all men seek, however, is that which is useful. And so friendship, though extraordinary in its ethical dimensions and lifelong in its physical aspect, is disregarded among human desires. Since this is the case, a certain torpor of thought sets in, and all of the esteem we have for friends ebbs and flows back to the place whence it originally came. Thus, though the seed of mutual love that was sown between us had already grown strong from a deep root of honor, it suddenly died, as if sucked dry in ground without water: it was as though this seed were stubborn enough to flee by itself from both nature and humankind.

The problem and its solution look to you to say why there has been an interruption in so important a cultivation. Am I to believe that you think that the divine law of friendship is about the exchange of flattery and gifts? What did you really think you would achieve with so long a silence, though not one on my part? Still, if I can be accepted as an arbiter in this situation, I would refuse both flattery and gifts, because both are false tokens, since virtue can neither be counterfeited nor bought. What is more, it is close to impossible to divert virtue from its course.

But if you have anything to say that would refute my complaints, I am asking you, trusting in your wisdom, to write it in a long and elaborate letter.[56] Still, I want this whole matter to be put to rest, and I want this plea of mine to succeed. Only the truth should be taken into consideration, since in our situation it is the case that each one of us should aim to teach, not to defeat the other. For what can it mean for a friend to be victorious over her friend?

There is no place for us to hold a debate, as Carneades did when, taking dubious and inextricable positions in the gymnasium, he argued first on the side of the Stoics and then against them.[57] The question you raise has to be debated, not mocked or belittled, so that the sacred pledge of our loyalty and respect for one another, though now beaten and broken, can be healed, and so that everything—once the sickness in our thoughts about one another has been medicated—may soon be right again between us.[58]

---

54. Cereta here shows her mastery of the genre of the humanist *amicitia* (friendship/patronage) letter. Her vocabulary is flawless: friendship, honor, law, enduring ties, utility—all the right images are there.

55. Her *sententia* about ethics has a terse Aristotelian ring to it.

56. "Ornatissimis litteris": Cereta indicates that what she wants back is perhaps a small oration or treatise, full of learned references and couched in Ciceronian or Senecan Latin.

57. Carneades (213–128 B.C.) was known as the founder of the Athenian Third Academy. He is known for arguing both sides on a question with equal rhetorical skill.

58. Cereta's terms are characteristically Ciceronian and come from the humanist vocabulary of

I am so concerned about you that nothing is more precious to me than my being loved in return by you, who are the most beloved of friends. If you were ever to catch me in some wrongdoing, I have no doubt at all, since you are a person of the utmost kindness, that you would be compassionate and forgiving. After all, this is the hallmark of one's humanity: the ability to recognize one's own weakness. Therefore dismiss the thought of a quarrel as the result of our difference of opinion. Nor should less lenience be reckoned as due the wrongdoer than her wrong. After all, which of us would inflict a punishment on the other, when she might not know the other's heart equally, and when there could be a mutual exchange between pure minds that are inextricably connected in every way? Vale. February 26, 1486.

XL
ON THE COMING OF THE TURKS

After the fall of Constantinople to Mohammed II in 1453, the Turkish takeover of that city and its repercussions in Italy—reports of the atrocities committed by Turkish forces, warnings about Islam's menace to Christianity, fears of a large-scale Turkish invasion of Italy, calls for a crusade to recapture the eastern citadel of Greek civilization and the Christian religion for the West, and a general demonization of "the Turk"—became standard themes for humanist orations, treatises, and letters.[59] In Cereta's letter of December 20, 1485, on the "coming of the Turks," her subject is the Turkish invasion of Apulia in 1480, which she represents as a contemporary event; she also laments the fall of Constantinople and two of Venice's protectorates, Chalcis in Negroponte (1470) and Scutari (1477–78), to the Ottoman empire as though these too were recent developments.[60] Her treatment of the Turkish "threat" differs considerably from that of most humanists; for one thing, the standard polarities of the genre, such as eastern barbarism vs. western civilization and Islamic savagery vs. Christian clemency and compassion, are noticeably muted in her letter, if not entirely absent. After briefly alluding to atrocities perpetrated by the Turks against Christian populations, for example,

---

patronage: "foedus" is the sacred pledge that binds friends (often patron and client) together; "observantia" (respect, loyalty, service) on both sides is the quality that marks friendship ("amicitia") as a relationship that depends on mutuality and reciprocity. But this relationship is always in danger of a breach or fracture (*ictum fractumque*). See Robin, *Filelfo in Milan: Writings, 1451–1477* (Princeton University Press, 1991), pp. 13–30.

59. For an extremely useful and accessible summary of humanist writings on the fall of Constantinople and the menace to the West from Turkish Islam see Robert Black, *Benedetto Accolti and the Florentine Renaissance* (Cambridge: Cambridge University Press, 1985), pp. 224–85.

60. See Rabil, *Laura Cereta*, p. 170, nn. 4 and 5.

Cereta begins—halfway through the letter—to rail against the hatred, avarice, lawlessness, and savagery of the *Italians*. She urges her compatriots not to arms, but to penance, moral reform, and obedience to God, the only hope she sees for Italians.

To Elena di Cesare [61]

ave you heard? The word has now spread: what was only rumored in private is now the talk of the entire city. Nor should the stories that are being bruited about be trusted altogether. The plundering fleet of the Turk has crossed over to Apulia and, alas, it is a bitter thing that, after all that has occurred, he is taking human lives. Who is so foolish that she does not fear the fate that consumes her neighbor? The savagery the tyrant showed to our ancestors is an example to those of us who survive. Do you not feel as though you hear the shouting and tumult of the invasion of Constantinople and the destruction of Chalchis and Scutari, which threw heaven and earth into disorder and silence?[62] The bravest leaders were slain there in battle, if you remember; kings were mutilated, kingdoms overturned, captives were killed in pride and rage, and unburied bodies were thrown into the sea. The barbarian showed the vanquished no mercy; he had no respect for virgins, married women, or nuns; and he evinced no chastity and no religion. The avenging Turk gazed upon the severed heads of Christians with pleasure, he transformed all Greece into one grave and all Pergamon into a conflagration, and he, as victor, surveyed the whole world with unbridled pride.

If we treat these things that he has done as an example for ourselves, then we are pondering the very things he has in mind for us. For the Turk follows in the footsteps of his father's enmity. Indeed, inflamed, this outlaw marks us Christians, enemies of his own faith, with a sword vengeful and dripping with blood. Thus the disciple, rising again as his father's successor, pursues the peoples his father assailed. But if those clouds of bow-carrying Turks should descend on Italy, what do you think would be a sure guarantee for our defense? What will the wretched nations of peoples do, if that Thracian lion, powerful in arms, should come? Will some cities, unprepared for war, go to others for help? Already spirits weaken, and fondness for compas-

61. Vat. 8 (fols. 15v–16v); Ven. 7 (fols. 30–32); not in Tom.; Rabil 27 (pp. 139–40 contain the entire Latin text of the letter). Cereta to Helena Caesarea (Elena di Cesare). Both manuscripts contain the subtitle "De adventu Turchorum."

62. For dates of these invasions see the introduction to this letter.

sion withers. The comfort of a place to hide is no longer an option for us. There is no flight to friends and guardians.

The great things that have been settled can in part be consigned to the future. All of us feel pity for one another's calamities, we console those who have been defeated and show compassion to those whose cities have fallen. Nor is it possible to find one who is still able to offer any assistance. Thus we have all been led astray by hope, blinded by hate, and possessed by avarice. No one stands guard over the Christian realm; no one looks to the interests of the common good. Meanwhile our enemies grow strong; and those who artfully provoke us into war cut us down, plunder our cities, and conquer us. Think, sister, death will be one resting place for both of us. Nor should you think that there can be any home for the conquered other than the grave.

I am no Cassandra who with lamentation could foretell the destruction of Troy long before it fell. I am a more simplehearted girl who—if not present myself—can only be inoculated by previous examples of fidelity. For in the mirror of the past, events of the future can be discerned. One founder alone remains in heaven, one law, and in nature one order. We alone, turned away from god, continue to strive; we alone have become lawless and have shaken off every yoke of humanity from our savage minds. Our pardon, however, comes from heaven. Let us be aware, and let us correct the errors of our ways. Let us prepare our necks for compliance, not the knife. Let us sigh; let us show our tears to god, for the inhabitants of Nineveh washed away God's anger with their tears when they were on the point of death.[63] For that most clement father of men took pity on his own people of Israel. He sent rolling so many helmets of the proudest troops of the Pharaoh, so many shields were seized, so many bodies floated in the blood red sea. For he knows that with dutiful hearts we receive exiles back who exercise the right to return home, if there is contrition for the wrongdoing.

Let us therefore renounce fruitless desires, let us reject all the pomp of the age. Let us, in a timely fashion, know our lord, who by his own mercy saved his more faithful servants from the depths of the ocean, the midst of fires, and the jaws of dire death. Vale. December 20, 1485.

XLI

This is the only piece in Cereta's letterbook addressed to the Venetian scholar Cassandra Fedele, who was probably the most widely known woman writer in Europe at the time. Cereta wrote this letter in 1487, a year after her

---

63. See Rabil, p. 170, n. 7, and Jonah 3:1–10.

husband's death, when she would have been eighteen and Fedele twenty-two. She describes a dream she has of searching for her husband in Orcus, the land of the dead. Imitating Aeneas' journey into the Underworld in Virgil's *Aeneid*, Cereta's letter is intended not only as a showpiece to display her classical learning and her talent as a writer; it is clearly an attempt to enter into a literary friendship with Fedele. A well-ordered essay, the letter demonstrates Cereta's knowledge of Virgil's Underworld landscape and its most famous dramatis personae: its rivers Acheron, Phlegethon, Avernus, and Cocytus; its household characters, Cerberus, the triple-throated dog who guards the gate to the netherworld, and Charon, the boatman who ferries the newly arrived souls across the Styx, and its snaky-haired Furies, Megaera, Alecto, Tisiphone, and Medusa. The letter's crowded tableau includes the most familiar characters and Underworld apparitions in classical literature: the Argonaut trio, Hercules, Orpheus, and Jason; the epic heroes of the Trojan war, Ulysses and Aeneas; the doomed men famous for their punishments, Tantalus and Sisyphus; and the mythical monsters of the ancient world, the Cyclopes, Charybdis, and the Harpies.

To Cassandra Fedele[64]

*T*he learned poets agree that at the center of the earth, far from God, there is a subterranean world spewing fire and smoke; there the dogs of Cerberus bark at souls approaching the gates to Hades. When my senses were lulled to a peaceful sleep, I was summoned to this place. First Charon, brandishing his bloody whip at the gates of Orcus, met me there. And he, churning up filth from the whirling waters, pointed to the gangway to his boat with his oar and his fiery eyes. O ye gods, what terror filled my mind! What fear attacked and hammered away at the virtue of my soul. For, from the dark vapors of the Stygian swamp, a foul odor of pestilence came forth. Sorrowful groans were heard coming from every direction. Tartarean voices rang out, three-bodied shades were seen, and thick darkness rendered everything fearsome, casting a sad dimness over the place.

From the ruptured abyss of Dis they came and returned more boldly, those trembling Furies of the night; nor did the raging shades withdraw at the sight of different species of monsters belching out billowing fire. I advanced, propelled by the approach of a frothing Megaera, and whatever and wherever the terror was, it was exposed.

---

64. See note 37. To the Venetian scholar and writer Cassandra Fedele (1465–1558), the most famous learned woman of her time.

Soon Alecto arrived on the scene, impelled by the winds of madness. Then came the Eumenides, armed with bloody garlands, and adorned with snakes entwined in their hair. Soon afterwards, the head of the Gorgon appeared, roused by Erynnian hydras. Then, coming from below, flying figures were seen throughout much of the night. They encircled the prisonhouses of Erebus; from there the rushing River Acheron flowed with its worms, and next the River Phlegethon, boiling with fire and flames. But one of these rivers, the Avernus, completely filled a basin with a sulphurous lake. Here in a recess below, Tantalus languished, as tortured by hunger and thirst, he strained towards the ever-receding waves. Not far from here Medusa, now blind, was pursuing Perseus with horrible cries. And here the forgetful Lethe hurled itself through Tartarus, smoldering with its hot-white ashes.

Nearest to us was the raging of the River Cocytus, and the lethal sound of trident-bearing Pluto, who roared angrily at Sisyphus and the traitor Ascalaphus. Standing apart from the other souls in an open cafe was Tisiphone, where, bloodied with gore, she shook brands of fire at the shrieking souls.

Next, I was forced to go down into a cavern near us, where demigods and savage kings sat with Rhadamanthus, the avenger of crimes. Nor can I say how many souls there were who were entangled in the wheels of chariots, mutilated by saws, how many were drowned in boiling pitch, and how many limbs were lacerated by birds. Yet how many souls—so cruel to see—did I witness rolling stones eternally?

I saw a thousand souls. Some were breaking up camp to return to Troy, others were setting up pieces of artillery or laying the foundations for citadels; and there were those who caused Apollo to be angry with the Greeks. I saw the arts of Jason and Medea, the judgments of Ulysses and Theseus, and many of their companions who died at sea. Among these was Palinurus, who asked Aeneas to give his body a burial, since he had been thrown overboard.[65] On my right, with hands bound behind his back, lay Priam, who stained the altar of Jupiter with the blood of his severed neck. Among the heroes, a sad funeral was held for Pallas and Patroclus. In the same way, piety touched the hearts of Aeneas' men when they saw the young corpse of Polydorus buried on those greedy shores.[66]

What of the desperate mother who ran through the burning fields, who saw prodigies and portents born again, screaming frantically for dead

65. This conversation between Aeneas and Palinurus—who falls asleep at the helm at the end of book 5 and topples into the sea—occurs in Virgil, *Aen.* 6.337–71.
66. Polydorus reveals his fate in Virgil, *Aen.* 3.22–68.

Eurylus? There followed the crime of Hecuba, the broken treaties, the avenging leaders, the fires crackling into ash in every direction. But above all, fear burrowed into my soul and gnawed at it, when Tomyris shuddered, as though driven insane, at the bloody wineskin from which she drank Cyrus's blood after she slew him.[67] Similarly, Charybdis and Circe, their mouths foaming hideously, filled the dim lands with their barking.

Following the revelation of the birth of the nymph Thalia, Jupiter and Juno were beginning proceedings for a divorce.[68] And Eurydice, who could not be recalled to earth, was mournfully beating her breasts when she heard Orpheus singing to the lyre. And there from a smoke-infested hollow, doleful owls came flying out and also the Harpies, who, uttering cries from their parched throats, stuck their fiery beaks into the half-man, half-goat satyrs. And over here, the cows that were stolen by Cacus were calling to Hercules (the Bryarean hero with his wooly chest) for help by mooing from inside their cave.[69]

From here, I was taken across the boiling shallow waters to the cave where the Cyclopes and Vulcan, that frightening craftsman, were laboring at forging lightning for the gods with constant hammering, din, and the metallic clashing of elements. From this place where thunderbolts were being cut out and beaten, I descended to the gate of horn, next to which Tiresias, who was mounted on a dragon, sang oracles to those who came to consult him. I approached, though quivering with fear of the monster, and I asked sorrowfully, and in the manner of a suppliant, where my dead husband was. He said, "Your husband is far from this place; seek him in other realms. His blessed shade already inhabits the Elysian Fields." When the seer uttered these responses, his wandering and fluid mind began to enjoy the pleasure of divination. Indeed, after his prophecy, when I sought the difficult ascent on the left, being ignorant of the path, I became confused at its precipitousness, after which, roused by my terror, I awoke.

Therefore, although these hackneyed stories may seem to be inventions smelling of the poets who arbitrarily make up silly tales, promising gods and demons and whatever else they wish to invent, still I myself would not dare

---

67. See Herodotus, *Histories* 1.205, for the story of Tomyris, queen of the Massagetae, who led her troops against Cyrus, king of Persia, crushed his army, and slew him, pouring his blood and head into a wineskin (Herodotus doesn't explain why but Cereta takes the story to its gory conclusion). See also Tibullus 4.1.143.

68. Cereta says of the Olympian couple that they "provocabant . . . divortia": The Thalia referred to here was a nymph whom Jupiter had fathered by impregnating Eurynome, the daughter of Ocean.

69. Virgil, *Aen.* 8.194: Cacus robbed Hercules of his cattle.

to improve on nature regarding the content of a dream. In any case, I will not deny the things about the underworld on which there is nearly complete consensus. For I myself profess sometimes the distinctions of the three-bodied Peripatetic, and at other times the uncertain probabilities of the Academy. It is my goal to ask questions, not to settle them or to make the rules about great philosophical issues such as these. Let others who are more desirous of great glory decide these questions. For me the one thing ordained is my wish to search out the Isles of the Blessed, where I may find the Fates and destined resting place of my faithful spouse, to whom mutual affection of a most tender love beyond the vows of human love has joined me.

These are the things I thought I should write to you, Cassandra, whether or not I meant to consult with you as a Venetian prophet or oracle. Nor is it really the case that I have more interest in the dream than I have in you. On the contrary, I have written to you for the purpose of engaging the fineness and precision of your mind in thinking about an issue that requires those particular qualities. And although the miserly character of mother nature has produced in our sex minds that are petty,[70] still you will rouse that brilliant and seasoned mind of yours for unraveling the enigmas of causes in nature, because of which I visited the underworld as I did.

I know you will consider this first gift worthy enough so I won't think that you've rejected me or turned your back on my work.[71] Vale. April 13, 1487.

XLII

The only interesting thing about this letter, other than its representing Cereta's complete about-face towards Cassandra Fedele, is that some of the early manuscripts were doctored to make it look as though the woman Cereta savages in this letter is a certain Gismunda and not Fedele. But Cereta's sarcastic reference to the famous letter that Italy's greatest living Latinist, Angelo Poliziano, wrote to Fedele makes it clear that the woman who has injured and rejected her is indeed Fedele. Cereta works hard in this letter to display her knowledge of the law and legal jargon. The result is a piece that is contrived and repetitious, though some of the authentic hurt she has experienced shows through.

70. Again Cereta displays her sense of belonging to a larger community—the female sex: a sex which she characterizes as *avara*, which generally means "greedy" but here seems to signify something more like "petty," "small-minded," "stinting," or "miserly."

71. Though there are no extant letters from Fedele to Cereta, we should not assume that Fedele never answered Cereta.

To Bonifacio Bembo[72]

*C*assandra attacks me, though no specific charges have been leveled. Possibly motivated by the sting of envy, she takes pains to poke holes in my knowledge—meager though it is—with complicated double-talk. And so it would appear that she either has contempt for her peers or heaps more abuse on people who are more knowledgeable than she.

But the appearance of deceptiveness in a person's speech is often the cover for a fearful heart. This woman doesn't impair the firmly rooted trust that my all-night sessions of study have strengthened in the eyes of everyone regarding me, does she? But merciful gods, what has become of love? Where is that trust which cannot be violated? Where does the old compassion for one's fellow humans lie sleeping? No longer is there a show of friendship among people but only darkness. This sister, whom I praised with such reverence so many times, insinuates that I am a person whose learning is specious. But for long enough now have I filled her ears with the healing nectar of constancy, so that they would not be deluged with hurtful words. My virtuous conduct did not deserve this treatment, nor was this a decent reward for its part: it is better to offer soothing words to one who helps us than to disturb one who sleeps.

It is better for me to keep my own counsel from here on, but I still fear that in the meantime she might come perhaps to believe too much in herself, and attempt something short of the truth, in order for her to think that, in slipping down from the height of heaven, she might go to Catona. And I would want her to have a more confident hope of attaining this honor. But the foundation on which honor is built is not insults but praise. In fact, most men incur blemishes on their character from reproaches and criticism they direct at others. Study and gentleness, however, acquire the best names for their proponents for posterity.

But many voluntarily follow a road full of errors; we, in making our preparations openly, will pursue truth on the correct path to justice, so that things that contradict justice may certainly be known. Of course it is alien to sacred law that anyone should make an accusation against a person who is not present via a third person, especially since no magistrate would hand down a judgment against someone who was not called to testify in court. You your-

72. Vat. 66 (fols. 51–52); Ven. 55 (fols 85–87v); Tom. 53 (pp. 117–22); Cereta to Bonifacio Bembo according to Vat.; to Laurentio Capreolo of Brescia according to Ven. and Tom. This is the one and only time Ven. and Tom. have agreed in a significant variation from Vat. Nonetheless Tom. appears not to have consulted Ven., since he so frequently errs in matters not only in grammar but in common sense as well.

self know that a charge brought by an informer is judged on its merit with the defendant present. For there is one kind of jurisdiction in the court, another in the bedroom, and still another in the street.[73] Hadrian proposed a law according to which no one could be sentenced without charges being brought and there being a trial.[74]

Cassandra therefore gives grounds for abuse, because she believes that the things I have written are not mine but came from the pen of the father who educated me.[75] While I was pondering these things myself and my mind was playing the intermediary in helping me to get in touch with reason, I was amazed that with no evidentiary testimony she should have been moved by what merely had the superficial appearance of truth. But this argument from verisimilitude will work equally well against her, since the two of us are alike in sex and age, unless perchance it should have rained literature in her more intellectually fertile household, in comparison to which my family's house would supposedly have been drier and less cultivated, and thus the place where I grew up would have been at fault, and not Laura. But these things are fictions.

I forgive her: she doesn't pursue these baseless thoughts alone. For the minds of individuals are different everywhere, and the entire sky is illuminated by stars whose appearance is in each case different. But little by little, time has so eradicated such suspicions about me that there isn't anyone who doesn't know of my literary gifts (if one can say such a thing). Indeed this is the truer story, which everyone sees with their own eyes. It is not worth being surprised if illiterate grammarians, who are contemptuous of the work of so many celebrated minds, disapprove of my pen—which in any case is covered with mildew. The opinions of Eusebius and Orosius are said to be utterly obscure, the philosophical position of the one making incomprehensible that of the other, and thus not only Orestes and Phronicus but also even the common people attack me with laughable arguments.[76] For it is by no means easy for the hot and burning throat of envy to quench its greedy thirst for verbal abuse.

In any case, suppose that these things were appropriate charges to bring and not merely the execrations of people who have no shame. Once Cas-

---

73. Vat. and Ven.: "vis" (power, authority, jurisdiction); Tom. erroneously: "vix."

74. She's referring to the second century A.D. Roman emperor and Roman law.

75. Note that she does not say here that her father was either her teacher or ghostwriter; this is Cassandra's claim. See letter I, chapter 1.

76. Orosius (c. 416 A.D.): a Spanish writer who published a universal history in seven books. Eusebius: a bishop in Caesarea in the fourth century A.D. wrote a history of the church and described theological disputes in the early church. Orestes and Phronicus are supposedly contemporary enemies elsewhere in her letterbook.

sandra has charged me in a court of law, I would be delighted if she—who is the gloss and ornament of virtue[77]—would show and tell where the summons of the plaintiff is for a ruling on the allegation, where the scrutiny is for the indictment of the defendant, where contumacy is, and where the confession. If credence must be given to her charge against me, why has there been no preliminary hearing for me to answer her charge? The opportunity to clear oneself in the case of a false charge must always be provided, lest the defendant be punished on a false allegation before the procedures prescribed by the law have been administered. We have written to Chiari, we have written to Brescia, and the case is being referred to Rome.

Here justice does not appear to be in evidence. Surely just as elected judges are not permitted to issue a summons, so no one can be convicted by someone deemed incompetent as long as the judicial canon of sanctions opposes it. For the case, once the proceedings have been initiated, is always concluded with the observance of the canons of the law. For the law, which is concerned with justice, pursues the customs of the place. Thus, when a judgment is handed down, provided there is no taint of collusion, it is published and confirmed as inviolable by an impartial judge, and after that only the treachery of a hatred that is clearly visible on the part of that man allows one to appeal.

But in my view, Bonifacio, you ought not to grieve or be surprised that I have put myself in the path of so many slanderous swords that I felt were stabbing me. For one is on guard against the ecclesiastical principle to the effect that one who does not take care to clear himself of an accusation may be thought to be admitting his guilt.

Wherever the cause of honor is being undermined, one's hand must always be armed with reason; for small lawsuits are sometimes the consequence of great anger. In fact, it was of no small concern to me that certain vulgar senators of the barbershops would shout derisive comments to one another against me. For if the perpetrator in a war of injuries takes his own welfare into consideration, he carefully avoids the weapons coming his way by repelling them.

Thus I am given the chance to exonerate myself from this underhanded calumny, so that those butchers of literature who have been confused about this wrong will understand how arrogant vanity looks after its own interests.

---

77. This phrase appears to be a sarcastic reference to Poliziano's famous pronouncement about Cassandra Fedele in a letter to her which undoubtedly enjoyed wide circulation. He saluted her with the words "O decus Italiae virgo" (literally, O maiden and ornament of Italy). (The letter was eventually published in Poliziano's collected letters (Venice 1553) and Fedele's *Epistolae* (Padua: Bolzetta, 1636, p. 155).

This most distinguished sister of mine should admit that she has been cautioned by a sister that one should speak only about what is either demonstrably or inescapably true. Vale. August 22, 1487.

XLIII

Diana Cereta is one of five younger siblings Laura either mentions or addresses directly in her letterbook. Laura also maintained a correspondence with her sister Deodata, who had taken the veil by 1487, her brothers Ippolito and Basilio, and presumably Daniel, to whom she includes no letters though she mentions him to another correspondent. In this letter, Cereta reprimands Diana for idolizing her and bragging about her, behavior she feels is bound to hurt her image. The letter has an edge to it and she takes a distant, hurt tone towards her little sister, offering high-handed maxims instead of affection.

To Her Sister, Diana Cereta[78]

Yesterday and the day before yesterday I received first the one and then, with more anticipation and longing, your other letter. But a little reading has brought me only a modest amount of pleasure after so much hope. For in these letters first you envision me as a laurel putting out leaves, and then you call me a sister of Apollo, when I'm a small and very fragile tree growing up among the choicest trees, and can hardly even be called an Apollinian magpie among the Muses. So please tell me, how can there be such a happy endowment of genius in me? And from what evidence are you making up these stories? Tall tales (and you know this) are not taken very seriously by learned men, who always delight in testing the truth for the sake of greater wisdom.

   Don't you think it's an unpleasant thing to realize that when you say something about me, people may assume it's coming from my mouth, with you just acting as my messenger? I know myself well enough to know I'm not worthy of such praise. But even if I were to be thought worthy of it, still there are not many men who would believe it was the truth. And suspicions are something to be afraid of even if they are completely untrue. So be careful from here on out about making claims for me, lest you should appear either to be taking the Muses' names in vain or to be overly greedy for my glory.

78. Vat. 22 (fol. 21v); Ven. 21 (fols. 45–46); Tom. 13 (pp. 33–34); Rabil 41; to her younger sister Diana; her letterbook also includes letters to her sister Deodata (Vat. 75), and her brothers Basilio and Ippolito (see Vat. 10, 46, 47).

You yourself know, and I'm sure about this, that if I'm falsely believed to like your praises of me, then the motivation behind your mistake can backfire against me. Our minds are very badly deceived, believe me, when they are dragged headlong, like a chariot without a driver, towards corrupt thoughts. I beg you, sister, not to be in such a hurry for honors. Things of greater weight rise slowly rather than too quickly.[79] For speed can never be praised without the tempering effect of diligence. Those who enjoy the sweetest praises from men, whether they are cheated either by the stain of false virtue or broken by adverse fortune, often incur shameful ridicule for their failure to live up to their reputations. The delight in study should not come from the reward of being praised, but should be exercised for the sake of virtue. I think it is enough that those who embark upon the road to learning are the winners of their own wisdom and glory. Vale. July 1, 1486.

XLIV

Cereta congratulates a woman she addresses as Veneranda on her appointment as the abbess of the Santa Chiara monastery. Her remarks in this letter about Veneranda's immense learning suggest that the abbess may have been one of Cereta's early teachers, or perhaps the instructor she speaks of in her letter to Nazaria Olympica (chapter 1), who taught her how to use her nights to sew and write. On the other hand, the remoteness of Cereta's tone towards the nun and the absence of anything resembling a student's deference or gratitude to her teacher argue against such a relationship. While she does address the abbess as "Mother" (*mater*), Cereta nonetheless plays the role of the older religious woman to Veneranda's novice, teaching, advising, and warning the newly consecrated abbess throughout the letter.

To the Abbess of Santa Chiara, Veneranda[80]

I give great thanks to God for your elevation from a member of an order of the church to Mother Superior of the convent, and I congratu-

---

79. It should be noted that the string of maxims she showers on her sister at this point is not typical of Cereta's style. She seems to be affecting the pose of the older, more successful sister who has wisdom to dispense.

80. Vat. 55 (fols. 37v–38); Ven. 50 (fols. 79–80); Tom. 48 (pp. 107–9); Rabil 62. Cereta to Veneranda, Abbess of Santa Chiara.

late you on this honor. Still, now that you have undertaken this burden, I would like you to prepare to render to God your reason for undertaking this office, and to consider for a little while why God placed Adam, the first parent, in Paradise to live perennially among the greatest delights and pleasures.

Solomon and then David ruled Jerusalem; Pharaoh and Nabuchdonosor, however, reigned in Asia.[81] But not one of these kings has passed you on the road since his departure from God, the Benefactor; you, my Mother, are more plentifully endowed with divine learning than they. For each of these men was punished for his crimes. Not only Jeremiah and Saul but also from among the gentiles, Lycurgus, Empedocles, Pittacus, and Lycophron either refused the kingdoms that were offered them or willingly abdicated from the throne after having succeeded to it; they were motivated, I believe, by a greater fear of God.[82]

Nor do I deny that the good have been as richly rewarded for their virtue as the evil have paid the penalty for their resistance to virtue. Therefore it is equally fitting that each person receives a recompense that is commensurate to his works when he dies. Because of this I would like you, as you wait, now that you have my prayers and supplication, to hear the verdict about you from the tribunal of divine justice, to await the coming of your daughters in Christ as your judges thus far. May there be no liberty, nor any dignity, nor useful thing, pleasure, tranquility, which leads you away from the fear of thought that transgresses the boundaries of religion. This life of yours is the dream of a shade, and our desires exist in vain. Remember that the smoke from burning incense must be dedicated to God; and see to it that your altars do not smoke for you, in some empty fantasy of domination. Think on the place to which we are led when we die, wretched ones, and live in such a way that your death will find you fortunate. Vale. August 13, 1487.

81. Pharaon, Nabuchdonosor: names from the Old Testament. No doubt she means Nebuchadnezzar, the Babylonian king and conqueror of Jerusalem (Kings 24, 25), and Pharaoh, the title of an ancient Egyptian king.

82. Cereta's information about these kings and tyrants may have come from the following: Diogenes Laertius 1.4; 8.52–74.

V

THE PUBLIC LECTURES

There is a tradition that in the period between the death of her husband in 1486 and her own death in 1499, Cereta lectured publicly in Brescia for seven years.[1] Although no evidence remains of Cereta's activity as a public lecturer other than the testimony of her own letters and the early biographical tradition, many of her epistolary essays would have readily lent themselves to presentation in the urban academies and salons of late Quattrocento Brescia and its environs. It is important to remember also that Cereta was writing with a humanist audience in mind precisely at a moment when, particularly in the northern Italian cities and courts, debates about women's nature, women's roles in the family and society, and the education of women were beginning to stimulate unprecedented interest in the "female point of view."[2] While there is no way to know which of Cereta's lectures were actually read in public, this chapter presents a selection of her epistolary orations on the kinds of subjects that could easily have drawn an elite audience to hear her speak in a public hall or private home in Brescia or furnished material for a paper to be presented at the monastery at Chiari where

1. See the Appendix to this chapter; see also Ottavio Rossi, *Elogi isotorici de'Bresciani illustri* (Brescia, Bartolomeo Fontana, 1620); Tom., vita, pp. vi–xvii; *Storia di Brescia: II, La dominazione Veneta (1426–1575)*, ed. Giovanni Treccani degl' Alfieri (Brescia: Morelliana, 1961), pp. 566–70; Rabil, *Laura Cereta*, p. 29.

2. Pamela Joseph Benson, *The Invention of the Renaissance Woman. The Challenge of Female Independence in the Literature and Thought of Italy and England* (University Park: Pennsylvania State University Press, 1992) provides an extremely useful description of northern Italian treatises and dialogues on the woman question written in the fifteenth and sixteenth centuries: important early Renaissance writings on this topic include Cornazzano's *De mulieribus admirandis* (1467); Vespasiano's *Il libro delle lode e commendazione donne* (c. 1480); Sabadino's *Gynevera de la clare donne* (1483); Goggio's *De laudibus mulierum* (1487); Agostino Strozzi's *Defensio mulierum* (1501); Galeazzo Capella's *Della exellenza et dignita della donne* (1525); and book 3 of Castiglione's *Il Libro del Cortegiano* (1525) among other works.

she frequently met with other scholars and writers.[3] Several such orations—
the one on friendship (letter XXXIX), one on the coming of the turks (letter
XL), the topography of Mt. Isola and defense of Epicurus (letter XXXV), the
admonition about the false pleasure of the solitary life (letter XXXVI), the
opinion about entering into the bond of matrimony (letter XVII), and the
defense of a liberal education for women (letter XVIII) among others—are
discussed in chapters 3 and 4. The six epistolary essays of Cereta's introduced
in this chapter include two essays on the wars on Brescian territory and the
origins of war in general; two set pieces on standard humanist topics, one on
the role of fortune or contingency in human lives and the other on greed; a
fifth essay containing a meditation on the sudden death of the baby daughter
of a friend; and a sixth essay offering an urban vignette involving the strange
appearance of a woman who performs a half-naked dance on a street corner
in Brescia, exchanges insults with a crowd of bystanders, and then vanishes.

XLV
AN EXECRATION AGAINST FORTUNE

There is nothing new or original in Cereta's lecture on a theme obligatory for
the humanists, *De Fortuna*. She does not attempt to distinguish between
chance (*fors*) and fortune (*fortuna*) as causative forces, as does Salutati in his
De fato et Fortuna (1396), nor does she engage in a discussion of the human will
or God's providence as he does. To Cereta, Fortune is simply the personification of contingency, and to deify Fortuna is to indulge foolishly in pagan
superstition. Obedience to God's will, the striving to live a virtuous life, and
the acceptance that life for all humans consists of a constant shifting between
good and ill fortune are all that humans can hope for. Cereta's *De Fortuna* is
part rhetorical showpiece and part self-consolation for the death of her husband, a subsidiary theme revealed only at the very end of the letter. Otherwise the work is organized much as are her other formal essays, the one on
entering into the bond of matrimony and the defense of a liberal education
for women (chapter 2, letters XVII and XVIII), with a prologue to introduce
the topic, a central section consisting of exempla, and a concluding epilogue.
As in her other formal essays, here Cereta has selected a single source to mine
for examples, to imitate, or react against. Whereas in her essays on marriage
and the question of higher education for women she borrows her exempla
(and nothing else) from Boccaccio's *Concerning Famous Women*, in this essay she
appears to draw both her exempla and her rhetorical form from Valerius

3. An appendix to this chapter presents excerpts from a selection of letters illustrative of
Cereta's quarrels with her male humanist peers.

Maximus' encyclopedic *Memorabilia*, a book that became as popular as Pliny's *Natural History* and Ovid's *Metamorphoses* in the Renaissance. While Cereta's essay ranges from such topics as the First and Second Punic Wars to the wars between the Greeks and Persians, as is the case in Valerius Maximus' *Memorabilia*, Cereta's moral thematics drive her rhetoric and choice of exempla and not the other way around. Unlike Livy or Tacitus, Cereta presents no narrative or opinion about history or the historical actors she refers to in this essay, which seems at first to be about history; she provides only a list of examples to illustrate one or the other of her two themes, the instability of fortune and the role of contingency.

To Francesco Fontana[4]

Our ancestors located Fortuna in the heavens and built a temple to her in Rome between the Tiber and the Janiculum Hill.[5] In Euboea the Rhamnians used to sacrifice foreigners whom they slew first with a sword to Fortuna the Avenger before they marched out against the enemy bearing their battle standards.[6] When Alexander defeated Darius in the Persian War, he carried a statue of Fortuna on his helmeted head, believing that the sight of this horrifying image caused the enemy to flee. Nor do I admire the deluded pagans for having kept their own counsel each according to his own religion; indeed these peoples earned the contempt of the Christians because they so dreaded this divinity excavated from the dim recesses of antiquity in times of adversity that they seemed to testify to her exalted position as a power and authority over everything else, even though such a divinity is an absurd and empty fiction of the poets and we should consider her cult the earliest form of blasphemy prior to the devil. There is no reason, moreover, why all of us should not be prepared to mock and jeer at Fortuna. For she is our adversary, inflicting us with evils she herself would not tolerate with the profound scowl of her malice. Nonetheless, those who have turned away from God have made her their goddess; but these are men who, having suf-

---

4. Vat. 31 (fols. 24–26); not in Ven.; Tom. 24 (pp. 47–55); Rabil 56 (pp. 84–86); Rabil date: Aril 13, 1487; "ad regium oratorem, Francesco Fontana" (orator of kings) entitled "Execratio contra Fortunam" in Vat. and Tom.; this is her only letter to this correspondent. Cf. Ronald G. Witt, *Hercules at the Crossroads. The Life, Works, and Thought of Coluccio Salutati* (Durham, N.C.: Duke University Press, 1983), pp. 316–41, Salutati's "On Fate and Fortune."

5. An ancient temple to Fortuna once stood in the Forum Boarium in Rome.

6. The Rhamnians ("Rhamnienses"): according to Pliny, *Nat.* 36.17 and Pausanias 1.32.2–8, the people of Rhamnus erected a statue of *Fortuna ultrix* ("Fortune the Avenger") by a pupil of Phidias in their town.

fered worse things, believed that injuries of both a fleeting and long-lasting
sort would befall us as the result of her avenging wrath. It is a different matter,
however, for those who examine, explore, test the truth, and reweave reasons
which allow it to be known that this very goddess is simply the outcome of
things, who—given the inclination of fate—sometimes alters events with
the gentlest of winds and at other times meets them head-on with a hostile
attack. Such unpredictable changes are caused by something which is uncertain and empty, which enfolds the world in doubt and ambiguity, and which
is surely impelled by that force we call Fortuna.

Hannibal the Elder was destroyed by a naval fleet led by Duilius at
Lipara.[7] Hanno, having replaced him, was stabbed to death by Cornelius
Scipio and died on the Corsican sea.[8] But Regulus, who conquered Ham-
ilcar and the two Hasdrubals, died in chains at the hands of the Lac-
edaemonian general Xanthippus.[9] And while Hamilcar plundered
Mauritania, Cotta directed the Roman army's swords against the Carthaginians. And just as Scipio's brother defeated Mago in Spain, so another
Hannibal slew Marcellus and Crispinus after Fulvius died. No otherwise did
Fabius Maximus engage in bloody battle with Cartalo.[10] Thus did another
Hasdrubal defeated by Scipio in Spain breathe his last near the Alps in a disaster like that of Cannae. Similarly, the Consul Claudius lost the Roman
fleet at Drepani, the remains of which C. Junius viewed when that shipwreck was carried out to sea.[11]

Nor did Sempronius lead his troops into Spain any less unhappily than
Marcellus when he surrendered to the enemy in Etruria. Surely even through
the fifty ships of the Carthaginians that were overwhelmed by Roman fire-
power burned within sight of the citizenry and though they were five times
victorious at sea, in the end the Romans remained destroyed, their fleet plundered. However, after Antiochus, who had been defeated by Actilius Gab-
rio,[12] crossed over to Europe to make war on the Romans and the Romans
themselves made war on Macedonia, then Perseus, the son of Philip, who
sank the fleeing Basthernians on the Danube, was led in front of his chariot in

7. Cicero, *Sen.* 44; Quintilian, *Instit.* 1.7.12, Valerius Maximus, 7.3.7: C. Duilius was consul in
260 B.C.; he defeated the Carthaginians in a sea battle at Mylae.

8. Livy, 21.50.2–8 (c. 218 B.C.).

9. Valerius Maximus, 1.1.14.1: Xanthippus assisted the Carthaginians in the first Punic War and
took Regulus prisoner in 256.

10. Livy 22.49.

11. Valerius Maximus, 1.4.3.

12. Valerius Maximus, 2.5.1. Both Livy and Valerius Maximus call this Roman consul (191 B.C.)
Acilius Glabrio.

chains by L. Aemilius,[13] although Aemilius' army had been vanquished by the Lusitanians before that. Nor did the victory of both sides against the Romans in Spain stand in the way; the Spanish also sustained many disasters after the deaths of the Scipios. Thus the Lusitanians defeated Galba, and Galba slew them with tyrannical cruelty when they surrendered.[14] But the son of Amyntas, Philip, who had lost an eye in the battle of Methona, after enriching Macedonia with gold and realms, was killed by the youth Pausanias when he found him without a guard.[15]

Why did those two whirlwinds of war Alexander and Caesar put to flight, subdue, and exhaust so many nations with so many victories, so many triumphs over almost the entire earth? Did not Alexander die from poisons that were prepared at a drinking party? Did not Caesar meet his end in the Senate amid hidden daggers? Was not Seleucus, who had murdered Lysimachus before Pyrrhus' victory, slain amid the corpses of his own men? Proud Xerxes was delivered over with equal turbulence, who, apart from his extraordinary fleet, escaped from Spartan Leonidas with innumerable Persians in Greece at Thermopylae, though he was broken by war and had just been stripped of his camp.[16]

The vigorous warrior Alcibiades, after the Athenian troops arrayed themselves for battle against the Spartans, brought back the greatest glory from his victory over the enemy, but was soon afterwards unlucky when he waged war in Asia, because of which as an exile he abandoned his clemency towards the Parthians.[17] Likewise, when Conon was banished after his defeat by Lysander in a naval battle, he fled first to Evagoras, king of Cyprus, and then to Artaxerxes in Persia, with whose assistance he freed his country from slavery. Yet when Conon, against whom Alcibiades had made war, had been summoned to Artaxerxes and fled from Cyprus, he freed his native city Athens from the yoke of servitude which had oppressed it and his power was recognized by his enemy. Surely that frightening man, Artaxerxes, brought back no magnificent wealth to his father Darius from so many great peoples when, after he had restored Assyria to his kingdom, he destroyed Scythia, Asia, and Macedonia after many losses were suffered by both his own men and those of the enemy. But Miltiades also decimated his troops after many

13. The story of Perseus' (king of Macedon 179–168 B.C.) defeat is referred to in Valerius Maximus, 1.5.3; 2.7.14; 5.1.8.4.

14. Valerius Maximus, 8.1.2.

15. Valerius Maximus, 1.8.9; 8.14.4.

16. Valerius Maximus, refers to Xerxes' defeat at 1.6.1; 2.2.3. The downfalls of Alexander, Julius Caesar, and Seleucus are cited everywhere by the ancient authors.

17. Valerius Maximus, 6.9.4 makes no mention of the Parthians in relation to Alcibiades.

deaths on both sides.[18] Let a noble example make clear that although Cyrus killed Astyages and Croesus when the Lydian king's troops suddenly marched against him, still when he hoped to escape into the mountains he was slain with military expertise by the Scythians whom he had brought together with two-hundred Persian soldiers in a bloody slaughter at the Araxes River.[19] And who would not shudder at the harsh outcome for Ninus, who, flying on the wings of victory all the way from the borders of Libya to the boundaries of Italy, saw himself die finally in the war against Cyaxares from an arrow infected with deadly poisons?[20]

Who of these men, fortunate in his own time, did not remain in the end without glory? Who could adequately consider the madness of those men who are not afraid to worship this slaughterer of the frail human race, against whom no accusation can be too harsh?[21] My campaign against this blood-thirsty idol exhausts and irks me because she continues to contribute to the pollution and degradation of everything shameful. It should seem enough to argue that it is not Fortuna who angers us but rather contingency, for which neither nature nor God is responsible beyond the accidental disposition of events.[22] But really that which we ourselves call Fortuna is nothing other than the image of empty terror about which the pagans have taught us. But as long as we struggle with hatred, as long as we enter into hostile paths and are subjected to misfortunes and immersed in perils, these terrible oscillations and shifts will proceed one after another, because of which fear is born in times of sorrow as is religion in times of fear. It is this species of religion about which nothing worse can be said than that it is practiced in this or that manner. The Persians, for example, did not blush because they worshipped a serpent for their god. The Egyptians venerated a goat and an ox. The Hermontians sacrificed to a bull. The Agregantinans gave gifts to horses. The Heliopolitans worshipped storks. Why was it that the Cretans moaned ecstatically in their worship of a goat? Why did the Indians offer solemn oblations to a ram? Is it not shameful that the Ptonebari sacrificed to savage dogs? Is it not a sorry thing that the shameless Hyrpians prepared a holy ritual for

18. Valerius Maximus, 5.3.3.

19. See Herodotus, *Hist.* 1: King Cyrus of Persia, the conqueror of Astyages and later King Croesus of Lydia, was captured and put to death by the Scythians and their Queen Tomyris in 530 B.C.

20. See Herodotus 1.

21. See Pliny, *Nat.* 28.39, for almost the same phrase: "Fortuna gloriae carnifex" (Fortune the slaughterer of glory).

22. Cereta uses the Tomist term "accidens" to denote the notion of contingency; she appears to be borrowing from Pliny, *Nat.* 17.9 and 19.138, here.

Stygian Dis? Didn't the Pelasgians think it wicked to pray to Sylvanus as the guardian deity of shepherds? Thus did the inhabitants of Memphis decree feast days in honor of Daedalus the craftsman. Thus did the Scythotaurians sacrifice victims to Tartarean Megaera. Thus did the Thracians establish shrines to Mars, a god renowned for his cruelty. Thus did the Titans erect altars to Bryareus the anthropophagite.[23] But I marvel at the things which men worry themselves over whatever the source when I consider the mores and religious practices of the Romans, who established games in honor of the thief Cacus, the inebriated Bacchus, and those impudent women Venus, Flora, and Acca.[24]

Vain is the worship of pagans who believed that insensible and inert things, demons, and corrupt men were elevated to the heavens. But much worse still is our credulity, which pays homage to Fortuna—an imaginary personage—as though she were its own undisputed divinity. Fortuna is, after all, nothing whatsoever and there cannot be anything more worthless than nothing. All the schools of theologians have addressed her; yet she has followed a downward course from the contempt she deserves to the oblivion of philosophy. And although the enormity of Epicurus' and Euripides' being silenced can be laid to their own error—namely, while denying that the care of the world belongs to God, they affirm that all things happen by chance or by some sort of contingency—still all the rest of the philosophers have spat on Fortuna. Aristotle never admitted Fortuna into his philosophy, Socrates denied her, and Plato showed disdain for her. Therefore those men who seek this goddess among the empty deities profane themselves with the direst perjury and they have no god at all.

By meditating on these things peacefully by myself, after a little while I managed to moderate the tearful laments which the intense ardor of my sad bereavement has kindled. Therefore I have seemed to be healed by sorrows, particularly when I consider that in this mortal realm I am a woman. For it shouldn't be much to be saddened with misfortune when nothing among human affairs considers itself stable. A mortal husband was given to me but he gave back his spirit to God before his day. I can have pity and overcome misfortune with my mind, but I cannot accuse God of any harm since the life of the one who is dead and his day belonged to God. If he, however, who is forever omnipotent on his throne of everlasting divinity, did not spare his only begotten son, what causes us to think he would spare us poor beings?

23. Cereta's source for the above catalogue of religious practices is unknown to me.

24. Cacus: a minor Roman deity famed for his theft of Hercules' cattle; Flora: the Roman goddess of flowers; Acca: the wife of Faustulus, the shepherd who reared Romulus and Remus.

Every age loses its flowers, and death is the common fortune of all men: there is but one end for the good man who is fortunate. Fortuna therefore neither curses nor blesses the just, and every outcome in death depends on virtue or vice. Vale. Ides of April.

XLVI
ON THE DEATH OF A DAUGHTER

Cereta's letter of condolence to Giuliano Trosoli on the death of his infant daughter is not a private consolatory epistle. It seems rather to have been composed as a funeral elegy meant for delivery in a city church or at home among family and friends. Written almost entirely in the third person, the letter displays a variety of the more public themes characteristic of Renaissance funerary orations or poems that might be circulated individually but were often gathered together by a member of the family for a commemorative book, such as the volume assembled by the Venetian nobleman Jacopo Antonio Marcello after the death of his eight-year-old son, Valerio.[25] Cereta's use of themes seemingly *de rigueur* in an elegy for a deceased child includes, in addition to the usual threnody on the brevity of life and the instability of fortune, a description of the extraordinary beauty of the child, the reactions of friends and family to its appearance and demeanor, and an account of its funeral cortege and marble tomb. The public context for the performance of this funerary elegy becomes clear when Cereta turns to her audience and begs mothers and fathers who have themselves lost a child to come to the lectern now and speak about their sorrow, a function Cereta cannot perform, not having been a mother herself.

To Giuliano Trosoli [26]

We visited your dear wife, Hecuba, who experienced a difficult delivery after three days in labor. There your little girl, whimpering in her cradle, seemed to call your name. The midwife, who had just arrived, removed the swaddling clothes from the tiny body and placed the baby in a bath of warm water. We all stood around, immersed in our concentration on

---

25. On the genre see Margaret L. King, *The Death of the Child Valerio Marcello* (Chicago: University of Chicago Press, 1994), pp. 24–59; and George W. McClure, *Sorrow and Consolation in Italian Humanism* (Princeton: Princeton University Press, 1991).

26. Vat. 50 (fols. 34–34v); Ven. 45 (fols 69–71); Tom. 43 (pp. 91–94); Rabil 52 (his date: November 30, 1486); to Giuliano Trosoli (Iulianus Trosulus). The letter bears the title "Consolatoria de morte filiolae."

the child. Tranquility united all of us as we gazed at her, for there we saw the most charming flower of infancy born that a divine mind had ever entrusted to homely splendor.

Who could keep from showing the joy in his face at such good fortune? I carefully studied the noble face of your child and looked at each of her limbs in turn. Her thick curly blond hair stood stiff on her head; her face shown, gentle in its beauty. Her eyes looked gratefully at us, her lips had a rosy sheen, and the purity of her cheeks bloomed with small flowers of pink. Thus the highest promise of goodness innocently revealed itself to us, and each of her individual features contributed to a total impression of beauty.

But when the bathwater grew cold from the harmful air, she was immediately dressed in a white embroidered robe and a little cloak. The nurse then offered the baby milk from her young breast. We took turns holding the little girl in our arms. We placed tender kisses on her pure face to quiet her, and when she was almost asleep she was covered with blankets. We ourselves kept quiet so that she would be gently lulled to sleep. Finally, we said goodbye to her, she was returned to her mother, and all of us left the place in silence.

But alas, unutterable is the wound of bereavement: how sad is it that unexpected death has carried away this lily before her time, and sudden illness has destroyed the joys of a budding life. See now how we are cheated without warning; scarcely had this most loving baby girl lived for very long, when this innocent child, who was the occasion for so much happiness and desire, breathed her last breath before her time in the arms of her mother.

She lay silent and pale on a cushion. She was carried aloft with the funeral cortege that went before her; her corpse was laid to rest covered by a small marble plaque. Thus do the cruel fates often hate even those who are as yet unborn. Such darkness is there in human affairs begotten from such disease, and such confusion is there in human life—brief and uncertain though it is.

Now let those parents whose excellent sons and daughters have met the day of their death speak themselves of the causes of tears. I, childless and wretched, will feel your terrible sorrow, though I sense not the toils of your suffering in my inmost being. Alas, this is a parent's love;[27] ponder these things in your heart, and may you who survive your children have compassion; intractable fate has snatched from you the sweet promise of your lineage.

---

27. "Heu, pietas": *pietas* connotes not mere "piety" but love of and duty to parents, children, family, kin, and clan.

The sorrow in my heart stirs my tears—do not doubt it. But grieving, which harms the eyes, does not appease the dead. We are afflicted with vain longing and stricken by the pain of inexplicable death. Nor is there anyone whose promise to live for one more hour can be trusted. For this unforeseen mortality of ours has nothing in it which is certain. Today a gentler fate caresses and soothes us; tomorrow one that barks and cries out hovers over us. Sometimes it strikes with a blow, other times it assails us murderously; elsewhere it rages furiously. Death draws everything headlong in its train. If you recognize that thus it has been decreed in heaven, you will temper a little your ungentle weeping, your tears and your working yourself into a sweat of despair.

I, who am filled with pain and anxiety with you in your grief, would willingly choose to die if I could bring back your daughter. For I myself am but a flickering shadow passing by in this peregrination of increasing years, and I hold nothing more sacred to virtue than adversity. Happy alone are those men for whom the peace of death stands at the end of life's race. Vale. November 30, 1486.

XLVII

ON THE GERMAN CONFLICT

The subject of Cereta's letter to the Brescian magistrate Luigi Dandolo is the incursions of German troops into Rovereto and Calliano, small towns on the Adige River south of Trent, that took place in May and August of 1487.[28] On November 13 of that year, a peace treaty was signed ending the war. In this letter in which Cereta deplores the brutality and senseless loss of life in war on both sides, she criticizes the absence of adequate diplomatic efforts prior to the outbreak of war that might have enabled the Italians to reach a peaceful settlement with the Germans. In what amounts to a eulogy of Venice, Cereta also urges the Brescians to seek an alliance with that city, which had historically been both Brescia's protector and oppressor.

In this letter Cereta strikes a posture skeptical of the aims of all war, an attitude not unusual among the humanists.[29] The enthusiasm expressed by some writers for a military expedition against the Turks was the exception to the general disaffection with war among intellectuals in the fifteenth century.

28. On the German incursions into Rovereto see Rabil, *Laura Cereta*, p. 39.

29. On antiwar feeling among the humanists see C. C. Bayley, *War and Society in Renaissance Florence: The "De militia" of Leonardo Bruni* (Toronto: University of Toronto Press, 1961); and Diana Robin, *Filelfo in Milan* (Princeton: Princeton University Press, 1991), pp. 56–81.

To Luigi Dandolo, quaestor of Brescia [30]

*M*any people complain about the Germans because in recent offensives they had occupied the very gateway to Italy. And now in the midst of increasing signs of victory they have retreated, though no one has forced them to do so. [31] It was as if, in deciding to withdraw from here, they somehow secretly wanted a disgrace greater than the glory they won when they first arrived. For a long period of time I clung to this idea, though I may have erred. I have now reached the opposite conclusion, although insufficient knowledge of military matters does anything but strengthen a woman's judgment. In any case, to pontificate on the business of war is obviously a task for someone more experienced; this is something that I, a young girl, cannot have learned about through experience.

Therefore, whether the Germans came down from the north for the sake of plunder or to avenge themselves in a just war, in the end they did break camp and leave the country, as though the grounds for the hostilities had appeared to have evaporated. Thus, if the Germans put away their ravening arms, if they removed their fortifications from captured towns, and if they put to rest the swords hanging over our heads, who would then dare to level charges against them without being bitterly criticized? Their purpose in returning to their own country perhaps differed from what ordinary people thought it was.

People were saddened and also disgusted (I believe) that Christian souls left so many innocent people homeless, slaughtered so many soldiers, destroyed so many city walls, laid waste so many fields, and lighted the blazing fires of a bloody war. For the war already caused a great many courageous men to come together, and the result is that there has been carnage on both sides and many men have lost their lives. Corpses now lie piled high in carts and are being hauled away on all sides. Was there not time for sorrow and pity—a time when bloodshed might have touched and softened men's minds?

The implacable peoples of the north, whom the Italians have always both hated and feared, tend, because they are skilled in the art of making war

---

30. Vat. 51 (fols. 34v–36); Ven. 46 (fols. 71–74v): Tom. 44 (pp. 94–100); Rabil 65 (his date: August 29, 1487). Laura Cereta to Aloysius Dandolus (Luigi Dandolo), quaestor of Brescia. Entitled "De Theutonico conflictu."

31. Since the Germans invaded Rovereto and Calliano in 1487, Cereta must mean by the "gateway to Italy" any one of the mountain passes the German army would have had to cross to enter Italy via Trent and the Adige River, such as the Mendola Pass, territory that would have been close to home for Cereta.

and trained in military strategy, to attack their enemies frontally, destroying them savagely and brutally. Nonetheless they, who were vanquished in spirit, have gone back again to their native land, and who knows whether it was because they pitied our country or their own people. I am not asking who among us or what soul has become incensed against the enemy. It is important for us simply to reconsider the whole situation, rationally and lucidly. The Germans have returned to the homes they left. Well, I wish they had stayed there longer. The whole of Italy would then have remained peaceful; indeed she has always had too little peace. Our neighbors would have had secure lives; Cisalpine Gaul would not have wept with anxiety, sighing over so many captives, so many dead, and so many fallen under the swords and missiles of the enemy.

During this time, when we were still in a state of bloody fear of the enemy though they at this point were absent—and whether what happened next was because our men inflicted heavier casualties on the enemy or suffered worse ones themselves, or whether it was due to some fate or other I do not know—lo and behold, the Germans, encouraged by popular uprisings in the town of Pietra, initiated new hostilities. Full of fury, they rushed out and surrounded us in an unexpected maneuver, and calling out from their various positions like Bacchantes, they drew their swords and engaged our cavalry in battle, who stood ready to attack them. But the soldiers on our side, who demonstrated their skill both on the battlefield and as strategists, first held one battle line bravely and then a second, and finally only the necks and backs of the foreigners remained—and not their breasts and shields—to receive our men's missiles.[32]

The foreign troops' readiness to flee encouraged the Italians in turn to engage in booty taking. Meanwhile, enemy reinforcements, lying hidden and ready for ambush in a secluded area in the woods, sprang on our soldiers in the midst of their spoils. Both sides took up arms and an intense battle ensued while an enormous din and clamor was raised. The Italian troops spread out in two wings, and thus the enemy, densely packed and caught between the two wings, were slaughtered. Signals calling for help were issued from lookout points on both sides. From one of these points one could see the Adige River and from the other, the city of Trent. The German troops were able to run down to the Adige with a maximum amount of speed; our men with their more powerful cavalry crossed over to the banks on the other side, utilizing a bridge erected for that purpose. The whole sky resounded

---

32. Jettisoning one's shield on the battlefield and "showing one's back" to the enemy in flight was always a sign of defeat, if not cowardice, in classical texts.

with the noise and confusion coming from both sides; and as the tumult grew, fighting erupted, first on one side and then the other.

But the outcome of the battle remained uncertain, and victories were obtained first by one side and then by the other. And alas the hateful bridge collapsed on which fresh companies of soldiers were crossing or returning to one another's shores. After that calamity, suddenly the Germans regained their courage. As for the Italians, some struggled more fiercely and with greater virulence than they had shown in battle; others, who entrusted their lives to little rafts or planks of wood or to the waves, drowned in the basin of the fast-flowing river.

Here envious Fortune offered a miserable sight to our enemies. On both sides, those who were not yet defeated slaughtered one another in a massacre equal to that at Cannae.[33] The wounded and many who were barely breathing lay on the ground like sacrificial victims whose throats had been cut. Here lay a thousand unburied corpses, over whose bodies no grieving mothers sighed, and none wept over the ashes that were collected. On both sides a tearful lamentation rose up for the soldiers who had left their wives widowed. The horror is still fresh over the many dead, whose bodies were rolled and turned by the Adige, as it ran down in ripples that receded into the foaming shoals of the Po and continued underneath its deep waters all the way to the sea, although still the erupting crests of the waves belched forth many corpses from the swelling waves, pulling them back to the sea over and over again with the tide.

In sum, since each army had spent itself in the three battles it had fought in a single day, each succeeded in exhausting the other's strength. The survivors brought back enemy prisoners and captured horses, each to his own side. The remainder of the war was now entrusted to other generals, the troops were deployed for battle, and violent skirmishes ensued. Certainly anger, the avenger of military disasters, played a role in rousing many men to take up arms.

Thus new dangers now face the realms, and again a bloody field awaits the slain and rotting corpses of men. The angry planet Mars blazes at the enormity of the coming disaster. The copious loss of human blood must be mourned, since so many distinguished generals have perished in martial splendor. The injury must also be lamented that has caused so many foreign

---

33. Cannae is the town on the banks of the Aufidus River in Apulia where Hannibal won his greatest victory over the Romans in 216 B.C. As in Cereta's description of what the Italians did to the German army in 1487, Hannibal's troops according to Livy 22.43–49 defeated the Roman army at Cannae by placing his own troops in a crescent-shaped formation surrounding the Romans and finally by bringing the wings of his army together to crush the enemy.

nations to bring an ineluctable Italy to arms and the Ledorian shame of war.[34] I believe there has been far too little consultation among these nations, who in the situation that lay ahead did not adequately take into account the constancy of the Venetians and their moral courage honed by adversity, their sound planning at home, their experience in military matters, and the Numatine patrimonies of their nobles. These men were also unacquainted with the incomparable loyalty of the Venetian citizenry, the fortifications of their cities, the incredible strength of their city walls, and the opulent wealth of this stable empire which long years of battling the Turks have never been able to shatter or threaten.

The Venetians are invincible leaders who, though they might be under siege, are invulnerable to attack; instead they hurl the enemy's weapons back at his head as the appropriate vengeance for his wrongs. They are also leaders who often plunder both provinces and maritime shores with their fleets and the deployments of their troops. Surely this is a nation that should be honored, not tested—one swayed by good will, not injuries. Indeed, there is in their most excellent and renowned spirit a noble and remarkable virtue that enables them to temper the robustness of their bravery with a confidence that they will prevail. Vale. August 29, 1487.

XLVIII
A WARNING AGAINST AVARICE

No humanist worth her salt would fail to include an essay on greed in her collected works any more than she would omit one on the wiles and pitfalls of Fortuna. Warnings against avarice were standard in Roman satire and certainly Cereta was familiar with Horace's treatment of the subject in *Satires* 1.1, Persius' in his *Satires* 2.3, and Juvenal's tenth satire on the vanity of all human desires. Valerius Maximus' compendium of short moral essays bearing such titles as "On moderation," "On abstinence," " "On poverty," "On generosity," "On extravagance and lust," and "On greed" may have provided an example of how to compose such an essay. But as usual Cereta appears to have relied principally on her favorite classical text, Pliny's *Natural History*, most particularly book 33 on the mining and decorative uses of gold and silver, for her exempla of the ruinous effects of the desire for precious metals and gems on men. This essay recapitulates a recurrent theme in Cereta's letters: her contempt for the demand by her contemporaries for luxury apparel and jewels imported from foreign countries.

---

34. The strange phrase "Ledorian shame" may allude to Zeus' rape of Leda, which resulted in the birth of Helen, whose "shameful" seduction by Paris began the Trojan war.

Her addressee is one Lupus Cynicus, surely a fictional name, as is the case with the addressee of many of her public letters. Marking the letter as a typical example of humanist invective, Cereta's choice of name for her correspondent reinforces the insulting nature of her opening remarks since the noun *lupus* (wolf), the masculine form of one of the more pejorative words for a female prostitute in Latin (*lupa*), connotes a lascivious and omnivorous animality, while the epithet *cynicus* suggests an association with the Cynics, a sect of beggar philosophers founded by Diogenes (c. 325 B.C.) who were said to believe in gratifying whatever desires they had in public—like dogs; hence the name cynic from the Greek word for dog, *kuon*—and to be contemptuous of any outward manifestation of material wealth.

To Lupus Cynicus[35]

Why are you alone, who especially hunger for gold, so uncomfortable with yourself? Why do you bite back your half-swallowed mumblings with desiccated lips? Why do you count out numbers on your fingers repeating them over and over? Why with a cocked eyebrow and eyes ready for the hunt do you walk with your head bent over the ground? Do you hope to get everything you yearn for? Or do you perhaps think you are conquering a bigger world than Alexander did?[36] One God produced just one world, and nature made but one Alexander. No accumulation of silver is capable of satisfying the mind; for cupidity causes men to yearn with ever increasing avarice to stockpile their wealth.

It would have suited you better to metamorphose yourself into an ant or a Myrmidon in Scythia and then you would happily carry off on your shoulders the gold you mined in the mountains there.[37] At the least you should purchase nets that would enable you like a fisherman to pull in gleaming flakes of gold from the basins of the Ganges and the Pactolus Rivers.[38] Why should you waste away at home in this torpor of the mind? Why do you burn

35. Vat. 79 (fols. 67v–69); Ven. 69 (fols. 134–37); Tom. 67 (pp. 199–204); Rabil 82 (his date: March 1, 1487). To Lupus Cynicus; entitled "In avaritiam admonitio."

36. Alexander the Great (356–323 B.C.), king of Macedonia.

37. The Myrmidons, famous for accompanying Achilles to the Trojan war, were said to have once been ants; hence their name. The association between ants, diligence, the accumulation of wealth, and the people in western Asia called the Myrmidons has a long history: see Ovid, *Met.* 7.654, and Hyginus, *Fab.* 52. Cereta's ant image is also clearly meant to allude to Horace's famous essay on greed, *Satires* 1.1.33.

38. King Midas, whose touch turned everything to gold, was said to have bathed in the Pactolus River, thereby turning its sands to gold: Pliny, *Nat.* 33.51.

so irresponsibly and with such sloth in this libidinous obsession of yours for property? Summon the strength you possess with your awesome genius and travel to India and Troy; for there you will obtain masses of lustrous pearls which are produced by the shells of the Persian sea. Go, seek out the Arabs and the Bactrians: in their lands you will fill your coffers with the lovely green of emeralds. Adamantine diamonds and blazing gems will burden your shoulders. Go, the precious glory of jewels and pearls that ennoble the avarice of kings awaits you. You will be wary in your trading with the Vandals, untrustworthy in their greedy dealings.[39] If you have need of the celebrated industry of the Phoenicians, the purpose will provide you with counsel. You will also have ready access to the opulent wealth of Alexander. But in fact wherever you wish to travel, whether your destiny is the vast wastes of the desert or you plow the sea in your pilgrim ship from faraway shores, or whether, having measured the provinces on your long journey, you cross over to Taurus, the Caucasus, or Olympus, or if you head back to Spanish Gades via Asia and Tarsas, Assyria and Africa, you must always subject yourself to danger. The affliction of greed can ensnare and contaminate everything with its nets and hooks.

But suppose foreign nations and businesses from abroad should bring their merchandise to Italy, would a mind saturated with riches then rest content? Suppose Crassus, insatiable in his craving for wealth, and Midas, with his avarice for gold, should ask you to take their places; how fleeting, how misleading a pleasure would the possession of these things be for you.[40] And suppose you were to outlive Methuselah, growing older than the phoenix, how would this fleeting, ephemeral, and most transitory pleasure be of use to you?[41] That which is inevitable never ceases to hang menacingly over our heads. Yet few men die even within sight of old age. Old age, however, often brings more sorrowful things to those who live long lives. The aged Priam saw the burning and the fall of Troy. The tragic battle brought on by the aggressor Cyrus resulted in the destruction of Lydia and the death of Croesus in his old age. Xerxes, that most insolent of kings, eager for domination, after the twin disasters at Marathon and Thermopylae, grew old sighing and lamenting his life.

---

39. The *Vandali* are mentioned in Pliny, *Nat.* 4.99; Sidonius *Carm.* 2.369; and Tacitus, *G.*2.

40. The Roman Triumvir Marcus Licinius Crassus (d. 53 B.C.) and the mythological king Midas of Phrygia are proverbial hoarders of wealth in classical literature; see Pliny, *Nat.* 33.133 and 33.51.

41. The biblical figure Methuselah (*Gen.* 5.27), who lived for 959 years, and the rare Egyptian bird called the phoenix, said to live for five or six hundred years, are legendary types that exemplify longevity in Renaissance literature.

But why should I speak of Darius, who was already captured through unexpected treachery in the third war with the Greeks and who mourned the loss of so many of his generals and his mother, a captive forsaken in wizened old age?[42] Why speak of Marcus Marcellus, whose aging body was buried in the raging sea after he had already arrived at the summit of civil glory and had basked in the splendid honors of his fathers before him?[43] A punitive blindness lasting for many years tempered even the hybristic happiness of Lucius Metellus.[44] I would have supposed that Jupiter, sharing in more kindly auspices, might have shown more favor to Caesar and Alexander had not the one drunk poison in the end or the other, being vengeful, met his death by swords.[45]

We have all fled from one fountain of calamity. Our parents were the first to commit wrongs, and restless posterity exacts its punishment. The order of our beginning does not go backwards. The ancient world continues through its offspring; we are all the children of Adam; nor is the sin which nature the corrupter has begotten washed away without tears. Do you believe that Fortune has children whom she would make happy amid life's tribulations? An unjust fate vexes us in our affairs while Fortune rants and rages like one insane, savaging our hopes, which she often mocks with empty counsel.

What good did it do for toiling Hercules to wrench apart the mountains between Europe and Africa?[46] What help did the lofty pyramids bring to the kings of Egypt? What good did the halls gleaming with gold and stars do for Cyrus or Menelaus?[47] What good did Aemilius' monument, Caesar's amphi-

---

42. Cereta's source for the story of the mother of Darius, king of Persia, is undoubtedly her favorite reference work: Pliny, *Nat.* 33.137 and 36.132.

43. Marcus Claudius Marcellus, who drowned at sea on an embassy to Africa in 148 B.C., was consul in Liguria and a general in the war in Spain (169–168). On the legendary wealth of Marcellus and his descendants, see Plutarch's *Lives*, Valerius Maximus, 4.1.7, and a one-liner in Juvenal 2.145 that Cereta surely knew: "generosior Marcellis."

44. Lucius Caecilius Metellus (d. 221) was a general in the First Punic War, consul in 247 B.C., Pontifex Maximus in 243–221, and dictator in 224. Cereta refers to the famous story told in Ovid's *Fasti* 6.436–54 of Metellus' blinding when he saved the palladium, an ancient statue of Pallas Athene believed to have been sent down from heaven by Zeus, from the burning temple of Vesta in 241 B.C.

45. Cereta's point is that both Alexander and Julius Caesar met their ends at the hands of assassins whom they trusted too much.

46. See Pliny, *Nat.* 3.4, for the story that Hercules separated the mountains between Spain and Africa by wrenching them apart to create a channel in between; the promontories on either side of the channel were called the columns of Hercules.

47. Cyrus I (559–529 B.C.), the founder of the Persian empire, was for the Greeks the model of the just ruler and brilliant military strategist who nonetheless died in battle: Cereta's source— Pliny, *Nat.* 33.51–52. Menelaus and his brother Agamemnon were the most powerful and

theater, or Pompey's theater do for them?[48] The ravenous teeth of time have devoured these things and they have departed into everlasting night; thus do all of us traverse our winged course to death leaving behind the things from this life.

But if the body is the onerous burden of the soul, if the brevity of this fleeting life is so short, and if hostile fate is always on the offensive, why do you strive with senseless vows to obtain so much money for so short a journey? If you really seek the Elysian fields for the purpose of eternal tranquility and peace, I do not see how all the gold you have will be adequate for your future life. Listen carefully. If you withdraw at any point from the true path of religion, your prudence is needed so that you can rise up as high in your virtue as you fell from its lofty tower to the lowest abyss of the spirit. For virtue is more fulfilling than any amount of money; it outlasts life and it replaces years of anguish in the end with the inviolate restitution of eternal peace. What mental turmoil so gnaws away at you, therefore, that you constantly lust after loathsome profit as though you were on fire, when among human beings praise is more precious than any coin?

The greedy mind burns to excess in a poisoned heart. Neither does necessity compel you to seek to study, nor does the eye arouse in you a desire to acquire things, and so when the vision of the mind is blocked you harden your obstinate heart to stone. And so it is that we have welling up in us a greater fear of loss than of shame. But you, who await a better end, put on, I pray you, the appearance of a mind free from guilt and of sincere righteousness. Choose frugality over unfairly gotten wealth and, when you think of the future, avail yourself of the examples of our ancestors who flew with speeding wings to death. Look, death keeps its jaws wide open and it devours us in its hunger. It is to this end that we are all led and time is our driver. At this end we all depart on an unforeseen course. For death must draw nearer as life recedes.

I have considered the things I promised you with a faithful heart. If I have any credibility with you, you will receive without difficulty these warnings, which you will accept as true either gladly or out of necessity. Thus, having confessed the intemperateness of your desire, you will prepare the correct way for yourself to heaven through repentance, and thus the light of

wealthy of the Greek kings; Helen, Menelaus' wife, despite this left him, sailing to Troy with the young princeling Paris; Pliny, *Nat.* 33.81, alludes to the wealth of Menelaus.

48. According to Pliny, *Nat.* 36.5; 36.116–117; 34.36, the fabulously wealthy Marcus Aemilius Scaurus (fl. 58 B.C. in Rome) ordered 360 columns to be transported to a theater that was slated to be used for only one month. See also Pliny, *Nat.* 36.102, on the magnificence of the Circus Maximus that Julius Caesar built and *Nat.* 36.115 on the wealth expended by Pompey on the theater he had erected.

immeasurable truth will enter the anxious breast of one who has been estranged from it. Vale. March 1, 1487.

XLIX
A COMPLAINT ABOUT THE BEGINNINGS AND CAUSES
OF WAR, THE BRESCIAN WAR, AND CELESTIAL OMENS

Cereta's letters to the Brescian magistrate Luigi Dandolo and the Veronese
scholar Ludovico Cendrata, a pupil of Guarino Veronese's and a correspondent of Isotta Nogarola's, constitute two of the most important political
statements in this collection. Both reflect her disgust at what she had come to
know were the aims and consequences of war. Her letter to Cendrata has a
focus very different from the epistle to Dandolo. While in the former essay
the invading German army is clearly the enemy, in Cereta's letter to Cendrata
the enemy remains unnamed. In this war chronicle, though she describes the
conflict as a wider one, involving many of Venice's sometime client cities (she
names Parma, Brescia, Ferrara, Verona, Cremona, Bergamo, and Crema), she
dwells particularly on the soldiers' despoiling of the farms, fields, and crops
and their pillaging of the homes and possessions of the local townspeople. In
this essay, it is the armed men, regardless of their allegiance, who are the
enemy and the unarmed citizens in the towns and villages who are their victims, whose houses are emptied of their goods, whose fields are burned, and
who themselves are first to be put to torture and subjected to starvation. As
Cereta sees war, the generals are the ones who start and end battles at their
whim, easily manipulating soldiers who are ready to risk their lives for the
sake of booty.

Cereta sets her account of this war in the larger context of world wars
throughout history. As in Babylonia, Troy, Greece, and Rome, war in Cereta's
world is still a means to power and a subject for the poets. At the close of the
letter she sees a bloody portent in the sky which appears to presage the re-
newal of war in the region.

To Lodovico Cendrata Veronese[49]

Not only the Africans, the Romans, and the Greeks, but also the
Babylonians, the Medes, and the other most excellent nations all

49. Vat. 81 (74v–76); Ven. 71 (fols 139–143v); Tom. 69 (pp. 206–14); Rabil 35 (his date:
March 15, 1486). To Lodovico Cendrata (Veronese). Entitled "De initiis et causis militaribus,
deque bello Brixiano et coelestibus prodigiis . . . conquestio" (A complaint . . . about the beginnings and causes of war, about the Brescian war and celestial omens).

throughout the world built temples and prayed to the celestial god of war Mars. The frightening giant Nembroth and Belus Abantides, father of Ninus, unfurled the flags of war,[50] and as time went on the Indians, and the Scythian nomads, and the fierce Ethiopians followed them. A martial age soon threw into turmoil the peaceful and rustic age of father Liber and Saturn.[51]

The frequent incursions of the Persians and Assyrians after the death of Diocles[52] saw Astyages, the grandson of Phraortes, go into battle. Thus in the course of time pompous Xerxes led out his huge army in an attack on Spartan Leonidas.[53] Savage Alexander surpassed the extraordinary deeds of his father at Thrace, Thessaly, and Thebes, and triumphing over the Persians, Rhodians, Phoenicians, Egyptians, and Armenians, he destroyed the Scythians, Parthians, and Hyrcanians.

Let the poets hymn the Cyclops and the Titans, who challenged the gods themselves to battle,[54] the Lapiths and the Centaurs, and the armed men reborn from teeth sown in the earth.[55] Homer, the prince of letters, sang of the swords of fallen Troy and the ashes of the vanquished city. But a much more expansive volume awaits the cruel massacres of Cyrus and Darius, the deaths of the Pharaoh and Moses, the wars of the Amazons, the punishments of the Arabs and the Lacedemonians, and the sinking of the many Athenian naval fleets sent out against the Romans. The shaking rocks of the Capitolium trembled at the sight of the Gauls, who had invaded Italy with their hoards. In later times the glory of the Scipios in Africa proved fatal, for the extraordinary courage of the Romans no less than their siege works brought great Carthage to her knees in a melee of fire and destruction. Nor would I fail to mention the savage and populous races of Goths who left their homes

50. Belus, the founder of the Assyrian monarchy, was the father of King Ninus (the husband of Semiramis), who extended the kingdom of Assyria from Egypt to Bactria and India. Cereta's patronymic for Belus, Abantides (son of Abas), confuses the Assyrian with the kingdom of Argos, whose founder was said to have been Abas (Ovid, *Met.* 4.673).

51. On the age of Liber and Saturn see Ovid, *Fasti* 4.179; *Met.* 1.89–113. The golden age or the age of Saturn was a mythical time before war and before agriculture, when the earth spontaneously provided the human race with food and drink. Liber, associated with Bacchus, is an early Roman god of wine.

52. See Herodotus 1.97–103: Phraortes succeeded his father Deioces (Cereta's Diocles) as king of the Medes and conquered the greater part of Asia. Astyages was the son of Phraortes' son Cyaxares.

53. See Herodotus 7.206–27: in a famous massacre at Thermopylae in 439 B.C. three million Persian soldiers led by King Xerxes slaughtered the Spartan King Leonidas and his small regiment, who stood their ground and refused to flee.

54. Tom. erroneously: "et praelia"; Vat., Ven.: "ad praelia."

55. See Herodotus, 2.49; Ovid, *Met.* 3: Cadmus, king of Phoenicia, slew a dragon in Boeotia and planted its teeth in a field, whereupon armed men sprang up from the dragon's teeth.

to descend on the Roman empire with so much bloodshed. Later the Roman citizens learned to withdraw from one another in private. Then envy and suspicion grew in the republic to the point of civil uprisings, while the arrogant acts of tyrants violated their neighbors. Still later the blood of vengeance lent new life to savage hearts, fattening them for slaughter on both sides. And such rage, which was without cause since it was not a dispute over the restitution of property or the expulsion of an enemy but rather arose from envy of the other side's rising glory, taught men to surrender the necks of their parents. Finally the lust for domination fed by conspiracies aroused the kings to arms, and then the proud habit of taking spoils sprang up after which the fugitive and robber ships of pirates sailed so many seas.

A leader of peoples never takes action in peacetime but neither does his interest in war become dormant. How do you think a mind can ever sleep when a ruinous fear of poison infects it when night comes? Such a mind is restless nor does it breathe easily, and though it shrinks from action in times of peace and treaty making, once it is agitated it takes pleasure in whatever city it has conquered through war and treachery. Why is it that the vain hope of money often deludes those who are camp followers, even while the savage axes of the enemy threaten them, while the arms of the victors clash around them, and while they view before their very eyes the battle lines of their own men put to flight and slaughtered? As witness to this consider the famous disaster that befell Sulla and the notorious battle at Cannae full of fear and bitter lamentation.[56]

Uncertain hope of victory draws infinite thousands of soldiers to their deaths. Every battle with contending forces is doubtful and dangerous, for while the drums and the ringing din of armor whisper in helmeted ears, every soldier rages with boiling hatred among the bodies that lie in tangled confusion on both sides.

The wound brought to Brescian territory bleeds and drips. Almost the whole of Italy and even populous Calabria have come to despoil the single food supply that is here. The army has grown together into one great people, and having crossed the bridge over the Aglio, it replenishes the plains at night. Because of this both the heavy-armed soldiers and the infantry, who attacked their neighbors with bold and savage sallies, have come together here and there. Their rage at first boiled up suddenly, and with greater daring these men threw themselves on the enemy as though they were running to

---

56. On the mercurial life of Sulla see: Nepos, Atticus; Livy, 75; Valerius Maximus, 12; Plutarch, in vita. In 216 B.C. the Carthaginian leader Hannibal slaughtered forty thousand Romans at Cannae in one of the worst disasters in Roman history (Livy, 22.44).

their deaths for the love of liberty. But when those men whose commitment to the war was greatest allowed the soldiers to despoil certain villages which here and there had resisted, frightened regiments of soldiers from the rural areas began to grow weak. The enemy, encouraged by these events, extorted goods from the townspeople in every way; they sent out edicts, they called local citizens to appear before their tribunals, and they posted lists of those proscribed. A sudden siege ringed the town and hemmed it in with ditches and walls. After this, fear on the part of many and the collapse of trust inclined people towards a civil uprising, kindling in them a zeal for rebellion.

After this, a rebellion at the posts followed and the enemy accepted the surrender of the volunteers. Still, many remained loyal, although they were subjected to many machines of torture, to pain, and the terrible bane of hunger, as though to the extreme test. At this time falling leaves caught by the wind covered the earth, winter sealed the year with frost and ice, but meanwhile the troops of the renowned general Robert returned in full force. Under these most precarious circumstances Robert had quickly anticipated the enemy's plans near Valento. Taking them by surprise and more by terror than by armed battle, he liberated the field and put the enemy to flight, escaping every ambush that had been prepared in this bellicose town.

In the assembling of troops a special agreement was drawn up regarding the hostages demanded. Many atrocities were perpetrated against the prisoners. Our legions were to depart to the enclosed valleys for the winter. The enemy set up camp in nearby positions on the other side of the river. Those who were driven to abandon their oaths because of the killings and the general chaos defected and placed themselves in the hands of the Venetians. Thus this year was more than sufficiently marked with public calamity. In the meantime many men crossed over to the enemy on both sides. Rainstorms protracted what had already been a rainy spring. As soon as the grassy plain burst into flower, a crowd of men carrying scythes returned, and new auxiliary troops joined in, each one with his own legion. The troops were again led down from the hills on both sides into the plain. New skirmishes began anew and the farmhouses closest by were burned down in a new conflagration. While everyone was eager to revolt, at the same time every revolt threatened to bring further danger.

The unequal outfitting of the cavalrymen increased. Great fear of an invasion by the enemy gripped the province. At these developments again some surrendered of their own free will and without signing any agreement. Others who had been pent up behind walls for a long period of time entered into treaties. At this point threats were already causing those who were under siege to quake and tremble; oppressive fear was everywhere palpable, overflowing everywhere; and every place began to be laid waste and destroyed by numerous and frequent incursions; the sword of the enemy prevented the wicked more from shedding blood than from burning and pillaging. This was the reason that houses were being abandoned by those who had lived in them and fields deserted by the farmers who had cultivated them. Well-organized bands of marauders came every day to the detriment of city, but because of all this the people competed with one another to escape from the city, pouring out of the walls and trampling one another, whosoever brave heart had always yearned to protect himself and his city. One species of fortune shook Parma, Ferrara, Verona, Brescia, Cremona, Bergamo, and Crema; everything was ablaze for war, but while the vain hope of a stipend impassioned the remainder of the soldiers, the generals negotiated for peace at the naval locks of the river.

For five years now we have enjoyed a tranquil time of peace. During that time, however, I was living with my father at Lake Iseo, where he was the Pretor of the Sabine coast and the Prefect in charge of restoring the town; indeed the external appearance of the place—which he fortified with a broad ditch, the construction of walls as well as a rampart along the shoreline, and an ever vigilant guard of turrets and a citadel—sufficiently demonstrated how great his expertise was in warding off an enemy.[57]

I was amazed and afraid, I recall, yet I committed everything I saw to my childish mind; and because of this I've more recently stored away certain events in my memory to write to you about, which, though they may be lacking in order, are not without substance, since yours is a more fortunate intellect endowed with the marvelous ability to explain the secret causes of things. I don't know what evil was being augured, but I saw a glittering fire high in the sky that seemed to be wrangling violently with the bristling night, as if a poison might soon stream forth and pour from the star Mars. I saw also bloody stars which had no rays when they rose but a tinge of white and an unusual paleness when they set—as if the cool power of dark Saturn could overcome discomfort grievous to nature. On the left, a fearful body rose from the horn of the emerging moon, which dispersed a trembling cloud of mist through the smoky paths of heaven in the morning.

The improbity of a feminine heart has not dared to interpret such omens. But you, knower and interpreter of the heavens, will do what is hoped for (that is, if we should still rely on the heavens concerning events to come)[58] if you, once you have examined the course of the stars, will dispel

---

57. Tom.: "turrium atque arietum"; Vat. and Ven.: "turrium atque arcis," which I prefer.
58. Tom.: "danda fides est"; Vat. and Ven.: "debenda fides est."

the doubt that steals over me and disturbs, under the impact of such a fateful sign, a mind that would divine the future. March 15, 1486.

L

ON THE APPARITION OF A SPIRIT

The figure of the enraged, snake-brandishing female who emerges as the central character in Cereta's letter to Mario Bono—resembling one of the Furies, or Erinyes—is already a familiar one in Cereta's catalogue of *monstra*. In a letter she wrote to Felicio Tadino (letter XXVI, chapter 3), we learn that a Megaera-like figure surprised her as she wept for her deceased husband and in a letter to Cassandra Fedele she described a second encounter with a Fury in a dream in which she journeyed to the Underworld (letter XLI, chapter 4). The placement in all three editions of her collected letters of Cereta's letter to Bono directly before her letter to Cendrata on the Brescian war, each letter recounting the appearance of mysterious portents, makes it clear that the two letters are companion pieces of a sort. Something has gone wrong in the city of Brescia; the sketch of a madwoman practicing her antics on a street corner that Cereta sends to Bono and the lyrical meditation on the war in Brescia addressed to Cendrata are meant to promulgate this message. But another interpretation of Cereta's letter to Bono should also be considered. The gender of the character under scrutiny in Cereta's street scene, the intensity of the character's anger as reflected in her speech and the dance she performs, and the antagonism that develops between her and the crowd in the course of her performance all suggest that Cereta's apparition may be a figure for the writer herself in her uneasy relationship with the Brescian public.

To Mario Bono[59]

A nervous, noisy, and incessantly babbling woman, a stranger to everyone, appeared today just as the sun was setting and the evening was coming on. And half-naked and holding a snake tightly in her left hand, she danced at the crossroads without embarrassment.

An angry commotion broke out somewhere towards the back of the stunned crowd at this woman making noise through the clattering of her teeth. The woman threatened to punish the people in return, and she turned a deaf ear on those who blocked her path with catcalls. She burned as though

59. Vat. 80, (fols. 74–74v); Ven. 70 (fols. 138–39); Tom. 68 (pp. 205–6); Rabil 80 (his date: February 26, 1487/8). To Mario Bono (Marius Bonus), entitled "De Apparitione Phantasmatis" ("On the Apparition of a Spirit").

she had the flames of Cocytus inside her, and after she had been spat upon with childish cruelty and reviled with abusive remarks on all sides, she employed whatever intemperance she could think of with even fouler hatred of the abuse. At last she vanished from everyone's eyes, and I have no idea what path she took in her flight.

One sense of confusion gripped everyone in the crowd, as though people believed they had been deluded by a deceitful phantasm or the illusion of some portent. For if she was a human being, how did her sturdy body disappear in thin air? We wondered whether she was some spirit from the Underworld or whether her appearance was sanctioned by God.

The earth is the dwelling place for man. Only shades dwell in the Underworld, nor does the wrath of the avenging gods travel to us from that place. This woman therefore, though armed by the Furies, was no Sisyphus, Orestes, Tantalus, or Ascalaphus among men.[60] Nor did she appear to be carried from the deadly throne of Pluto, where the snake-haired Eumenides or the horrifying Gorgons and the three-headed dog blaze up against the world. Nor did she ascend from Orcus, summoned by the Furies like a sorrowful Alecto, Megaera, Scylla, or Hydra, who shriek with their usual savagery.[61]

I do not truly understand what these harsh portents were showing us in so threatening a way. Still a troubled mind knows what ought to make it quake with fear and trembling.[62] Vale. February 23, 1487/8.

APPENDIX

On February 1, 1486, Cereta had written to her father that she had decided to move to Chiari because she felt she could no longer face the continued hostility of the "uneducated public" towards her in Brescia ("indoctum vulgus," letter XVI, chapter 1). But as documents excerpted from her subsequent letters (below) indicate, her move would provide her little if any re-

60. All four of these figures are known for having been sentenced to cruel and unusual punishments in Hades because they either disobeyed divine law (Orestes killed his mother) or because they were themselves cruel tricksters (Tantalus, Sisyphus, Ascalaphus).

61. The Eumenides (or Furies), the Gorgons, Cerberus (the three-headed guard dog at the entrance to Hades), the Furies Alecto and Megaera, and the famous half-human, half-beast figures the Scylla and the Hydra are the most typical examples in classical literature of the legendary monsters and phantasms that inhabit Hades.

62. It is interesting that both the letter to Cendrata and this one end in the same way: with the appearance of a portent, with Cereta's comment that she doesn't understand the portent, and with the vague generalization that the fears of a "troubled mind" (here *consternata mens;* in the Cendrata letter *animus turbatur*) have yet to be put to rest.

lief. These selections illustrate something of the nature of Cereta's uneasy participation in the humanist circles she frequented at the Santa Chiara monastery, at the Ursine monastery, and among the several coteries of literati in Brescia, though much of the nastiness she experienced as personal attacks on her stemmed in reality from a combination of social and intellectual snobbery, the seemingly endemic culture of envy among the literati, the frequent obliviousness to her presence, and, above all, the general disdain for women as a group rather than from contempt for her work itself or any real attempt to engage in a critical dialogue with her about her ideas.

1. Letter LI. To Fra Lodovico de la Turre. Vat. 53 (fols. 36–37); Ven. 48 (fols. 76v–77v); Tom. 46 (pp. 103–5); Rabil 12 (his date August 25, 1485).

*W*hen I arrived at Chiari fresh from my visit at the Ursine monastery, I met Giovio Antonio hurrying towards me as though out of breath in his excitement to explain to me the whole nature of the argument about me at your convent. Instead, he explained the various stock paradoxes in your argument, which caused me to become flustered, and I did blush a little as men frequently do when they become red in the face from indignation. And although I would not have thought it bad or inappropriate to the discussion at hand had it come from you, still I was surprised that you who are philosophers were shocked and thunderstruck, as though you regarded it as something miraculous that I, a young girl, should have absorbed not only the precepts which the art of oratory and rhetoric depend on, but also those that concern the place to which the traveling constellations return, as if you had never heard of something that many men who have read a great deal have heard.

While I'm not the only person who knows about literature, I don't think those men are knowledgeable in any proper sense either. In their eyes, the intellectual capabilities of our sex are so contemptible that they would never voice the opinion . . . that the clever bile of women might enable them to get whatever they might need in order to write. But if you are in the grip of this religious sect, I beg you, look into the mysterious Sibylline books. Look at the sanctions of the laws, which Pallas Tritonia first established for the Athenians. Read the complicated lyric poetry that Sappho sings and the centos of Proba. But I also want to add that I have not woven together these exempla from the ancients in order that I, who am neither their equal nor have the capacity to be so, would want my mind to be compared in any way with that of those extraordinary women. But neither have I done injury to this capacity, since the passion and thirst for knowledge that I've had for a decade of my young life have roused this moral righteousness in me against envy, and this has so liberated my mind from a life of sloth and purposelessness and freed it from every care and duty that I can study furiously and for long stretches of time . . .

2. *Letter LII. To Clemenzo Longolio, teacher of rhetoric. Vat. 26 (fols. 22v–23); Ven. 25 (fol. 49); Tom. 17 (pp. 39–40); Rabil 23 (his date October 31, 1485).*

Cato and the Socratic Xenophon both proposed a rule that people should think before they speak so that their tongues should not out-pace their thoughts. Therefore I have shown you what is being said about you, speaking not in figurative or allegorical terms or in anger, but openly and out of friendship, whether the witnesses who discovered these things were truth seekers or troublemakers, although I consider slanderers no less despicable than adulators, since both are equally harmful to those who be-lieve them. But let those who are malicious bruit their nonsense around. I do believe you are a decent person and I regard you as knowledgeable among those educated in the humanities. Do not alter any further the opinion you have of me. Vale.

3. *Letter LIII. To Orestes and Phronicus. An invective. Vat. 73 (fols. 59–61); Ven. 63 (fols. 108v–113); Tom. 61 (pp. 158–66); Rabil 60 (his date: July 1, 1487).*

We have received the illiterate letters that have come from you and that equally uneducated fool [Phronicus], and although they babble idiotic nonsense, still these letters should by all means call for a beat-ing rather than a forced politeness. But I am quite amazed that you, Orestes, a scarcely human little manikin, without worry that you might be injured, un-armed and totally unfit for war, should march out against me when I'm at least shielded by my pen if not by a sword.

But do tell us please, you unseeing slanderer, you lowbrow prone to mak-ing a scene in public places, how and why it is that I have come to deserve your castigation to the point that you have garrulously excoriated everything in my letters, condemning them to the rod, and you have vomited up muddy sentiments on the subject of envy? Oh how I wish you had at least heard Cicero making speeches, Livy reading aloud, or Plato discoursing on immor-tality . . .

4. Letter LIV. To Fronto Carito. Vat. 58 (fol. 38v); Ven. 53 (fols. 81v–82); Tom. 50 (pp. 111–13); Rabil 59 (his date: July 1, 1487).

*A*s to your writing me that Eusebio has read my letters and thought they were my father's and not mine, I would not have seen either judgment as being at all offensive. Whether he thinks they are my father's, as he asserts, or mine, as he denies, you will come to your own conclusion. In any case, this man's judgment does me great honor, whatever the reasons behind it. Nor do I think it makes much difference whether I am said to be the daughter of an orator thought more eloquent than all others or whether he calls me a stylish and cultivated writer for my tender years.

Eusebio is no more trustworthy on the subject than Orosio, who, though learned on certain small points, is without subtlety and examines minutely the things I have written, going over them letter by letter so that he can contaminate with his monk's hood of envy a single line of my writing that might be sleeping peacefully, oblivious to the incautious slip of a letter. These are the traps of sophistry which the bile of his mind interweaves with threads of envy. Still, the source of his accusation, lambent and furtive, remains unclear to me. Never has my muse concealed herself in a cave. My abilities are obvious to everyone, and the speculation that has surfaced about me, late and unseasonably, serves only to increase not my fear but my diligence . . .

5. LV. To Clemenzo Longolio. Vat. 44 (fols. 32–32v); Ven. 39 (fols. 64–65); Tom. 37 (pp. 81–83); Rabil 66 (his date: October 1, 1487).

*A*ll the men most zealous about the study of literature at Santa Chiara hurriedly rivaled one another to write to me when I first arrived here. You alone stirred up rival factions against me and without cause. Nor have you ceased to wound me in every way with your arrogant talk and your supercilious manner. And as though a war had been declared, you unfurled your standards and marshaled them against me. Still, while I never considered you a stranger because of your reputation (though I don't know you by sight), I used to look to you and converse with you through your works, as though you were present. For the probity of my nature taught me to consider the philosophers important. Nor do I understand what hostility has taught you, who have received an education in the humanities, to speak so inhumanely of a woman who has honored you, Clement . . .

I have at times attributed my slight hesitation in writing this letter to the general uncertainty of my present responsibilities—the kind of thing women are very much involved in—for fear that some awkward discussion of excuses would tarnish my subject. Nor should I fail to mention that it is some pain stemming from anger that impels me to write to you; for a mind that is secure is not disturbed at every storm cloud. But I have done this to win your esteem as though I were going to deliver an essay to an extremely erudite man. For even Philip, the father of Alexander, became intensely preoccupied with the northern peoples of Scythia as though this were his last battle, not because they were people to be looked down upon, but because it was necessary to take extra precautions against them.

VI

DIALOGUE ON THE DEATH OF AN ASS

When a manuscript of Cereta's *Epistolae* was acquired by the Biblioteca Marciana in Venice in 1770, the cataloguer Jacopo Morelli had nothing good to say about her only dialogue, a work which was placed almost at the front of her volume of letters, after her dedicatory letter to Cardinal Ascanio Maria Sforza, and was entitled "In asinarium funus oratio."[1] Morelli wrote that such a trifling piece—on the death of an ass ("operetta . . . sulla morte d'un asinello")—would have been fine for the "anfiteatro di Sapienza Socratica burlesca" but had no business in a serious book of humanist letters and essays.

Cereta may have given her dialogue the prominent place it occupied precisely because she saw it as her most complex, original, and daring composition.[2] Not only did she include in her dialogue a bizarre essay on drugs, ointments, and poultices made from the body parts of asses and their bodily fluids—material she had found in book 28 of Pliny's *Natural History*—she also packed her work with literary references that subtly undercut her interlocutors' stories: to an ancient Latin novel much admired in the later fifteenth century, Apuleius' *Golden Ass*. Cereta modeled the rustic style she adopted for

---

1. Jacopo Morelli, *Della Biblioteca manoscritta di Tommaso Giuseppe Farsetti, Patrizio Veneto*, 2nd Vol. (Venice, 1771), pp. 44–46. Commenting that this work was the first to come from Laura Cereta's pen, Morelli dated this manuscript to the fifteenth century; he described the hand as very beautiful and more accurate than the Tomasini edition; he also commented that it contained all the letters in Tomasini plus eight additional letters not in the printed edition. Morelli's description of the Cereta manuscript appears to be of Venetus Marcianus 4186. Both Cereta's dedicatory letter to Cardinal Ascanio Maria Sforza and the text of the dialogue contained in fols. 5–6v of the Vatican manuscript of her complete works (Vat. 3146) are missing from Ven. Marc. 4186. The Tomasini edition does not contain the dialogue.

2. On the genre see David Marsh, *The Quattrocento Dialogue* (Cambridge, Mass.: Harvard University Press, 1986).

the speeches of her miller Soldus and his slave Philonacus on the idiosyncratic vocabulary and syntax of Apuleius' shepherds, mule drivers, and robbers, endowing her rural characters with a patois starkly different from the classical Latin that characterizes the prose of her letters.

The three interlocutors in Cereta's *Oratio* are the author herself, who delivers the formal consolatory oration and acts as the master of ceremonies presiding over the funeral services for the deceased donkey, whose name is, appropriately, Asellus (Little Ass): Soldus, a miller and the ass's owner, whose speech serves principally as a lamentation for himself; and lastly, Philonacus, the slave boy Soldus employed to drive the ass up and down the mountain, who delivers the eulogy for Asellus.

The most interesting of these interlocutors is Philonacus, whose character and whose tale of Asellus' last days are clearly derived from the story of the miller's boy in book 7 of Apuleius' *The Golden Ass* (in Latin, the *Metamorphoses*: the adventures of Lucius, a man who has been transformed into an ass). Although Philonacus exonerates himself in his speech from responsibility for the ass's death, Cereta's readers would have recognized enough of the details in the boy's narrative to realize that she was imitating Apuleius' story of the guilty miller's boy (referred to by Apuleius' ass as "puer mihi praefectus" (the boy in charge of me), *Met.* 7.17). The number of resemblances between book 7 of Apuleius' *Golden Ass* and Cereta's work about Soldus' miraculous ass is striking. Both Cereta's and Apuleius' narratives feature an ass judged handsome enough to carry on his back a bride attired in her nuptial finery (*Met.* 7.13) and strong and surefooted enough to haul heavy loads of wood and grain down steep mountain trails (*Met.* 7.15: 7.17). Both have as their main character a cruel boy, by his own admission a liar and a thief, who beats the ass until he is bloody (*Met.* 7.17–19) and ties him to a tree in the woods (*Met.* 7.24), leaving him there overnight as bait for a bear whose den is nearby (*Met.* 7.24). In both stories characters intimate that such an ass would be best used if he were killed and butchered for his meat (*Met.* 7.22). But whereas in Apuleius, a shepherd merely suggests that a story could be concocted of a wolf's having eaten the ass to cover his murder (*Met.* 7.22), in Soldus' speech a boy's report of how a wolf ate Asellus is passed off as the true story of his death. And while in Apuleius, Lucius the ass is so demoralized that he ponders suicide by throwing himself off the side of a mountain (*Met.* 7.24), in Cereta the story Soldus reports as having been told to him is that Asellus accidentally slipped off the mountain. While Laura accuses Philonacus of being a liar, the "true facts" in this strange case are never made explicit and there is no omniscient narrator. We are left to wonder whether after his punishment for stealing the wine, Asellus became so weak that he really did tumble off the mountain, thus falling prey to a wolf, or whether instead the ass was mauled to death by a bear after Philonacus tied him to a tree, and whether he had then been thrown from a cliff to make his death look accidental. Certainly this latter scenario is the one book 7 of *The Golden Ass* would have suggested to Cereta's learned readers.

It is important to note that Cereta's character Laura in the dialogue is consistent with the somewhat contradictory figure she scripted for herself in her letters: that of the diffident young orator who hesitates to submit her work to public scrutiny, on the one hand, and that of the exuberantly talented writer who is constantly under attack by men who feel threatened by her accomplishments and her genius, on the other. While the problems of gender and the fictional Laura's anomalous status as a woman orator are not explicitly articulated as issues here as they are in her letters, nonetheless the humanist controversies over women and oratory and women's roles (private vs. public) cannot help but be subtexts throughout the dialogue. Unlike Castiglione's female interlocutors in *The Courtier*, the female subject dominates the stage and calls the shots in Cereta's *Oratio*.

A FUNERAL ORATION FOR AN ASS

Strangers and those of you more familiar to me, throngs and crowds of mourners who have gathered here today, if I were to have consulted the rustic muses for subjects suitable to a country funeral, if I only knew for certain what final homes the fates had arranged for asses,[3] or if the celebrated disputations of my ancestors had resulted in my being learned about Pythagoras' and Porphyry's theories of the transmigration of souls after death,[4] I

---

3. I want to note at the outset a few examples of the recondite and often archaic vocabulary—mined mostly from Pliny the Elder, Apuleius, and Plautus—which doesn't just adorn but fully characterizes Cereta's dialogue and makes the work very different from her letters and frustratingly difficult to read: *asinarius*, belonging to or connected with asses (Apuleius, *Met.* 7.8; 10.19); *conglobare*, to form a ball or form a crowd (Pliny, *Nat.* 2.134, and Apuleius, *Met.* 2.9, 4.26); *fictitia*, artificial (Pliny, *Nat.* 14.98); *friguttienti* from *friguttire*, to utter broken sounds, to stutter (Plautus, *Casina* 267); *dicaculis*, lively, spirited (Plautus, *As.* 511, *Cas.* 529, and Apuleius, *Met.* 2.7, 3.13; *conculcatus*, trampled upon, crushed, despised (Plautus, frag. 163; pseudo-Cicero, *Rhet. Her.* 4.66); the neologistic verb from *re* plus *gyrare* formed from the noun *gyrus*, a circular course for horses (Pliny, *Nat.* 10.59); the noun *garritus*, chattering (Paulus, *Epitoma Festi* p.2.M); and the verb *praefocare*, to suffocate, choke, smother. Cereta's ubiquitous use of impersonal, paraphrastic constructions (which have to be converted into personal constructions in any translation) presents a further obstacle.

4. Rabil, *Laura Cereta*, p. 166, suggests that Cereta may have known Porphyry through Augustine's *City of God* 10.29 or 22.12; in any case Pythagoras' notion of reincarnation was a commonplace among the Quattrocento humanists.

would be the one to call assemblies for the toil of mourning and I would wet this face of mine with tears together with all of you.

But this is certainly a roundabout way of saying that I who am about to speak should consider the end of my speech, lest either my epilogue should be drowned out by a too swift turn in the summation of my argument or my ignorant exposition of the subject matter should get tangled up in its own trivia, causing that which ought to come later in my oration to come first instead. For teachers of rhetoric know that the audience's expectations tend to be dashed if the arrangement of topics in an oration becomes too disorganized and incomprehensible to attentive minds.[5] Similarly, it is the custom of the piper to break his triple-mouthed instrument if its voices fail to respond. Thus, even if I myself am endowed with a gift for public speaking and oratorical display, if I have come here unschooled in the arts and strategems for moving men's minds, then I, the defender of rhetorical majesty, may soon be prohibited from performing the duties of a shining orator.

But since Theocritus, the Stoics, and the Peripatetics seem also to have discoursed upon the immortality of souls, our trust that even the insubstantial soul of a pack animal will be committed to the immortal shades rests enough on their authority. But the condition and cruel fate of animals must not be mourned without you, father Giovanni Soldus, who are the bereaved. Therefore let us all sigh, cry out, and reopen the wound in our hearts. And with a sibilant whispering, let us fill our throats with sobbing, and as though we were unrebellious imitators, let us roll the strangled sounds of repeated syllables around and around in our throats. The beginning of my oration will be fitting enough once I obtain the goodwill I must win from you and the support I must earn so that I can express our common sorrow.

Begin then, old man, you who are afflicted, whom an uncut beard and heavy brow shields from the revelation of a life still more miserable. Tell, so that you don't regret it, tell a sorrowful song. We shall respond in turn. We shall celebrate in song the heroes of the cowherds and the gods of the woodlands, and we who promenade around the funeral pyre shall sing a sorrowful song of our shared troubles and toils. Stand up, you, and let us march forward. Touch the lyre made of rubbed brushwood which has been shown to you. Move the artificial plectra, and absorb once more the words that you have turned over and over with effort and worn thin with the broken utterances of your throat. We shall follow, however many of us are sitting here, and these densely packed crowds will follow us who are first among the

---

5. The reading of the one manuscript we have for this passage, "adaurescat," is surely erroneous; my guess is that *adaugescat* (*ad* + *augescere*, to grow or become) is what the text was meant to say.

people. We shall imitate those melodies from your rustling lyre which you taught us in your spirited songs of mourning.

You soothed the ass as he grew weak, I remember, with broken words and strangled sobs. Lured by those resonant tones, he used to follow you to his stable, when he returned to this trough to eat and drink. Perhaps from these lyric strains he, now a shapeless corpse, will yet know his master. Perhaps the deaf ears of his ruined head will receive in this way your ringing cries. Did not Amphion found Thebes and the Corybantes lay the foundation for Gnossos in Crete with stones that danced to the strains of the flute? Could not the dying Eurydice hear the melodious songs of Orpheus? Nor is that harmonic power far away by which Asclepiades restored to health men who were sick and demented.[6] But Pliny and Seneca have given me too little hope of knowing these things, since these writers believed that substances separate from bodies, not invisible spirits, were put to rest in tranquility after death, during which time these substances passed a period of time without sensation or feeling before being reborn again. This mortality, conferred on all animals, is more deathlike than death. This loss of a life that is gone cannot be retrieved. So there is this sad necessity in nature, and there is also another necessity more blameworthy still—an evil that causes whatever remains of a weakened mind to wither in mourning born of the most regrettable disorder. Therefore though I have no persuasive arguments for the remedying of sorrow, still I lack no songs of mourning whose bitter causes can convert the anguish of death into echoing shouts in this country theater.

Therefore we shall rely on these our strings to arouse pity. And in our despair, let us take for our province the river of mind.[7] Let us unfurl the sails of our troubled eloquence in the midst of the open sea. Rise up, you shepherds, bent over your staffs, and you who are the first among the grooms and you goatherds, shabby in your dark robes, march in front. Let the mulekeepers crusted with squalor follow, let the ploughmen and those who groom the horses go behind, and let those who follow in the footsteps of the shepherds go after; soon may those who tend the cattle join in. And then may an inundation of folk from every farm march beside the body of this beast of burden, pressing densely around it. Let no one wait for a leader to begin the lamentation, let no one wait for a master of ceremonies. Let us look not to good counsel, but to the event. We are convening at this solemn assembly for the purpose of mourning. Now we have no expectation of better things that

6. See Pliny, *Nat.* 7.124, on Asclepiades: a famous doctor from Bithynia who practiced medicine in Rome c. 40 B.C.

7. Cereta's "river of mind" ("flumen ingenii") is one of her most striking and original images.

can lighten our sorrow. Now may the cause of the common sadness which afflicts us all appear clear. The humanity of those who believe that their own lamentations depend on the voice, the expression, and the emotions of the speaker are blighted enough.

For a fountain of piety is opened that emanates from the heart; a path runs from there to the eyes, and from there falls a rain of tears. Look therefore and see for yourselves with your pious eyes that the ground covered with blood. This is where the butchers (so horrible to see) took out their knives to skin the remains of Asellus that were pulled here with a rope and laid out on the ground, and where others scraped the iron shoes from his horned hooves.[8] See how his pack saddle hangs from the ash tree: around it torn pieces of flesh lie in the stiffening straw. Behold, he lies back, his teeth hideously bared and his head twisted to the side. The spoils of his frightful hide are borne aloft on a spear. A bed of rustic straw has been prepared, and there its drooping form will be burned in the fire over this beast of burden. Will you, unhappy companion of your master Soldus, be thus carried away to your pyre, with shaven tail? Who will be able to look on this sepulchral hole with dry eyes, where the ravenous jaws of the earth yawn beneath a dusky pit? Who can view without sobbing the thin body veiled with the chaff of the arbutus tree, spitting gobbets of flame as it burns? Who is so oblivious of praise that he would not write an epitaph for this marble tomb, which will soon be strewn with ashes? Why was it so important for the dictators Augustus and Julius to bury their beloved horses with a monument? Will Alexander surpass us because he led for his horse Bucephalus a funeral procession that had greater pomp? I do not understand why nature made a raven so noteworthy that the Roman people ordered its funeral bier to be solemnly carried in a funeral procession along the Appian Way.[9] And this was solely on account of its special talent: its being able to talk and imitate the human voice.

But alas, you Soldus, plaintive with your long, unkempt beard, how many times, tell us, were there public praises of Asellus? You are permitted to dry your tears. You should recover your strength of mind. Bind up your sor-

---

8. The description of the ass seemingly butchered for his meat and plundered for his iron shoes seems already to belie the cock-and-bull story Soldus is later told about the ass accidentally falling off a cliff and being eaten by a wolf. We are also reminded of Apuleius' shepherd who suggests that Lucius the ass be butchered for his meat in Lucius' tale of his sufferings at the hands of the miller's boy (Apuleius, *Met.* 7.22). Cereta lapses into Italian here: "grafiunt" from *graffiare*, to scrape; "ferros" from *ferro*, iron or iron horseshoes. The text in Rabil has the erroneous reading "ex *urnipedis* ungulis"; Vat. reads *cornipedis*.

9. On a famous raven's funeral in Rome see Pliny, *Nat.* 10.121.

row, lest the serenity of your mind seem dashed by every ordinary cloud. Certainly the infirmity of old age keeps you distant from heartening counsel, and fortune appears to have inflicted a more deadly wound on you than on Asellus. Let prudence suspend your anxiety and may you yourself suspend this dishonorable shame of grief and show a willingness to exercise self-control. Reason warns one of this, and time persuades. Already the fires of the funeral pyre are smoking; already the entrails are breathing, and already the ashy bones crackle in the midst of the fire. Now one always weeps; later one will be obliged to shout over the body that is now ash. Ah, be unwilling, I beg you, to come sadly to the wounds of bereavement. Do not remain suspended wholly in grief. Look, we are obliged to stand. All the sighing mourners have stopped at the arch. Say something. Hold back the sobs that hold sway over your grief. Cease to torture yourself with sorrow. Modulate little by little the whispering phrases, and cutting these short, interrupt them, bending them to your will with your voice.

SOLDUS: O woe is me, o piety. Songs do not make us cry, nor is it appropriate to laugh when one is in the throes of a raging illness. Worrisome weakness is the sign of an ailing mind. I am not able, brothers and neighbors, who were ushered into this place as is the case with ordinary people, I am not able, I say, to bring an end to the mourning amid so much heartrending sobbing. Nor is the feeble power of a weakened mind capable of arming itself against the emotions of a injured heart. I am afflicted, I am drowning in a raging sea of cares, and my heart is freezing to death.

Surely this is not unfitting. For this pack animal was dearer to me than my life. There was a tale among the neighboring villagers that he was born of a she-ass from Arcadia and a male from Salvalaia. On my way back to Brescia from Milan I stopped by chance in the lustral fields of Crema where there was an open-air market;[10] there great numbers of people who came from everywhere had set up shop in stalls and sold their wares for cash. Here I slept among the lowliest folk on a pallet of straw for two nights. On the day after I saw a peaceful little donkey of exquisite beauty who was then scarcely teething, and being well pleased, I spent plenty of gold coins to buy him. Immediately someone standing next to me solemnly promised to pay me twice what I paid in silver if I would sell the animal to him. But I would not have sold him for three times the price. Such a prize he seemed to me.

I led this skittish animal home on a journey that was anything but easy.

---

10. "Octinundinarum": *nundinae, nundinarum* (always plural) is the word for market day or open-air market, which was held every eight days, hence Cereta's "octi-nundarum."

He was like a chorus boy[11] spinning off in a wild dance of his own, moving every which way. At home he grew gradually bigger, and although he did not show his opposition by kicking or biting anyone, still he was a bold little thing and chomped on his bit in such a menacing way that no one but me dared lay a hand on his reins. But when he began to be full grown, he began first to bring the grain down to the mill to be ground with a stone and then to carry the meal deemed good enough to be transported. Sometimes he could scarcely endure the daily staples he bore on his shoulders when he carried his cartload to the marketplace and to the boats on the Sabine lake. You yourselves know from looking out at the monastery from the tower next door how many times our admission that we were short of corn caused Asellus' little saddlebags to go a-begging from door to door and from street to street. Who has not seen me adjusting and balancing the load on Asellus' back a hundred times? You gods, oblivious of the state of human lives, I ask you, what sort of conveyance will carry me after this, withered and elderly, my face pale? Shall I travel the many roads on foot, or will my usual leisurely paddings about in front of the hearth become enfeebled? Alas, how speedily these legs once carried me into the wind, whereas now truly they govern a body that bends but slowly over a staff. Alas, how much my coughings and throat-clearings wear me out. How much do my ears ring as they grow more deaf from the jangling of the yoke. How often do my eyes cloud over with darkness? How weakly do even the teeth in my mouth manage to chew? Look how fever, emaciation, and a pallor destroy this ruined body: a fetid odor comes already from its tainted breast. Now it groans its last breath as life abandons it. Now I should slip down into my grave when nature leaves me. I pray only that nothing worse may befall me when I die. In this way the human condition is more lowly than that of beasts, since we die in a state worse than when we are born because of our sins. All of us overcome the injuries of fortune in the insuperable necessity of death. Alas, besides the interval that remains to the wrinkles of sluggish old age, what time is there left for rest and the restoring of our spirits? What intermission from care, what time for relaxation, what space for thought, what nightly vigils will there be hereafter? Who will do the work? Who will skillfully apply himself to the task should I, who am already ill, or my poor family be in need of anything?

O wretched time, o miserable condition in which I find myself, o life, o sorrow more intense than any other, the most faithful pillar of our poor little home lies in utter ruins. Ah wretched me, I am lost. I have less than nothing

11. "Saltatriculus," the masculine form is not given in the *Oxford Latin Dictionary*, but the related feminine form, *saltatricula*, "dancing girl," is cited as appearing only in Gellius 1.5.3.

left. Already I see where I am being led and where I shall go in my unhappiness to die. Will I survive as a father hated by his own children? Or will a plan that is known and holds our some hope delay me further? Should I meet my end by the noose? The bitter sentence of my decision stands: to ordain my own death, by my own hand and sword.

Thus, trembling at this daring deed, I shall enter the yawning cave of Dis. Thus I shall visit shadowy Tartarus, the shades, and the spirits of the dead. Who does not believe that I'll find myself then in the very jaws of Asellus, who will gladly welcome me, a grieving old man?

LAURA: We all weep over your fate and it saddens us, aged Soldus. But I would not want you to go about collecting themes and stories whose subject matter is pointless. For although I can forgive you to a certain extent for your despair, still I would surely hope that you would consign to praise that which you have cursed so impiously and with such loathing. Certainly I don't understand the sort of rage that has taken hold of you, nor do I understand the nature of such desperation as is yours, which by catching you unawares, causes you to be swept away, to the extent that you disparage both vows inimical to death and also the pieties of gentle folk; and these you have spat upon with the respected beard of old age as though you were cursing the fates and summoning the gods because you were dying intestate. For the power of sadness and melancholy is never so all consuming that it can simply remove the qualities of modesty and fairness of mind from a man who is balanced and just. Instead, you yourself are the real cause of this impious wrong. The throngs of people standing all around you beg you to do otherwise, lest you should attribute crushing misfortunes of this sort to the gods, whom the Giants (who were driven from heaven) used to profane.

Now there has been enough weeping. Nor should the remembrance of the past continue to be a source of torment for you. Restrain your importunate and repeated appeals; do not respond with anger to that which must be. Nor must one mourn the passing of mortal things, since sighs provide no relief for the dead. For who should weep in vain over a thing which is lost? But there are many men standing around me in this great throng who would like to have known beforehand the cause of Asellus' death. However, you, if you expect a funeral full of bitterness, tell it to the nooses and ambushes of fortune, on the altar of which this animal has been sacrificed, so many times and so wretchedly.

SOLDUS: The tattered infirmity of a broken heart proves me guilty. Nor can I be cleansed of my sins in full view of so large a crowd. For the healing balm of words cannot treat the irremediable sickness of loss. I confess, I am ashamed of the compulsion that causes me to suffer pain yet not be able to bear it. But consider, won't you, the inexorable fate that dooms me to die. See the ignorant old man I have become, with my tattered cloak and beard, my speech rambling and embarrassingly bereft of all polish. It has been enough and more than enough that I have beaten this hated breast of mine. Yet apart from all this, something intervenes that causes me, full of the sighs and groans of a wounded heart, to lament the tragedy of misery that has sprung up anew.

It would have been enough and more than enough for me to beat my hated breast, without an event intervening, which caused me, sighing and sorrowing, to speak out against the misfortunes of a wretchedness that is sprouting up in a heart already wounded. But what occurred afterwards was bound to happen, nor should it seem strange to any of you who are distressed and in mourning with me at this service. Namely this: yesterday a woman approached me on the street in great haste, her hair all loose and flowing. Between weeping and cries of lamentation, she announced that my Asellus was dead. I proceeded to walk towards her, my own bellowing mixed with broken attempts at speech when all at once a country lad came rushing up to us and said,[12] "May you be safe from danger, little father Soldus. I don't know whether this misfortune has happened to you because of some vapor from the stars or by some fate, but a calamity, sad to say, has befallen your wrinkled ass. While your mountain-loving ass was grazing along the banks of the river, the remote terrain fooled his reckless feet, and down he came with a sudden leap from the ledge of a rugged outcropping of rock into the steep-sloping bottom of the valley below. No sooner did he land there than a wolf walked up to the mangled body of the dying ass, and proceeded to pluck out his entrails right then and there."

At this point, I fell upon the boy and began in my misery to pour out lamentations that came from the desperation of my heart, "O Furies, O Eumenides, O dog of Cerberus, O long-haired Gorgons, O raging Hydra with all your many maws, what yawning craters of burning Aetna would receive me? I go willingly. How can life be of any use to me and my family now that every remaining bit of hope I had and every help for me and mine has perished with Asellus? Alas, for what does this little field now grow fertile with dung? Who will now carry wood in the cold? Who will carry the grain

12. The whole tall tale that the boy (*puer agrarius*) tells Soldus of how the ass died—the ass's fall from a high precipice into a deep valley and his being eaten by a wolf—comes straight out of the shepherd's speech about how the boys should cover up their murder of the ass with lies once they've killed him (Apuleius, *Met.* 7.22). The boy's story about a donkey who loses his footing on very familiar terrain would strike one as an obvious lie even if we weren't familiar with the parallel passages in Apuleius' *Metamorphoses*.

home after the scythe has mown it? For what purpose are you alive, mad one? Where are the fires of Vulcan hiding? Where does the lightning of Jupiter sleep? Why does not the gorge of Charybdis swallow me up? Why do not the depths of the yawning earth consume me?"

LAURA: Poor grandfather Soldus, already forgetful of your descendants! To what lengths are you going? Where, madman, will so great a sorrow lead you? Where is the lamp of your long experience and all your days? Where is the guiding light of your genius? Where now is the helm of your counsel, which leads you to the proper course? Why do you tear the snowy hair from your head? Who forces you to plunge the days of your life down devious paths? Has jealous fate inflicted sorrow on you alone? All of us are born to know the frequent calamities of fickle fortune. If a more wretched grief overwhelms you or a more stinging onslaught of bitterness, then you could lament with reason, since you, who are a rational animal and one deemed worthy of god, are fleeing this mortal life by precipitous means. If you are moved by any piety towards this beast at all, you ought to be consoled by the fact that his long journey is now over; he is at long last where the painful years of his life have been laid to rest. A father makes a settlement and does not weep, if ever his son sails safe and sound into the harbor after being shipwrecked.

Thus this once very active animal of yours, buffeted by the many and various trials of his labors and having survived the long storms of his toils, finally approached the day full of evil, which one cannot escape through a lengthening of one's life. For the space of one's life, whatever sort of life it is, is one and the same vigil for death.[13] Nor does nature provide living creatures with anything more opportune than death. I grieve more that your life, broken and uneven in its fortunes, has continued to be afflicted so many years. Each person must breathe his last breath. But death is too much the attendant of your old age. The end of our fleeting lives comes quickly and unexpectedly to all men. Therefore let sorrows remain far from your lips and not show in your eyes, lest you be said to be flinging wide the doors to death before your time.

The body ages, but the soul, which as been given the gift of immortality, does not. But be mindful of yourself, lest you show too little respect for the promises of those who respect you. Be flexible, I beg, and change your plan, and pay close attention to the speech of this woman suppliant of yours.[14] But

13. "Mortis . . . vigila": the notion of life itself as a vigil (*vigilia*)—a stolen interlude in the night when most humans are asleep—before the dawn of death finally arrives is typical of Cereta's beliefs and imagery in her letterbook.

14. "Tua oratrix" (your suppliant): note that Cereta calls attention to her sex with this unusual locution.

if you are not affected by these words of mine, may your children's sorrow over your grief win you over. May your wife's feelings move you, since your sadness has reduced her to tears. May you at least be moved by your daughter's likeness to a dead person (when she collapsed) rather than to someone asleep, since mortal pain and bitterness hardened in her when she loosed her hair and robes.

We have proclaimed the causes of our lamentation enough. I would hope that someone would take my place who knew the life and habits of Asellus better than I. Therefore may everyone be silent and listen attentively. Let one who is more informed in these matters speak, so that a more ample, more persuasive oration may take shape and so that the funeral service may return to where it left off.

No delay ensues. A thousand people eagerly arise to speak. But one Philonacus, who was bold from the time he was a boy, descends from a throng of his supporters and steps onto the dais.

PHILONACUS: You are amazed, I see,[15] fathers of the fields, that I, a crude little sheep master—my cheeks still hairless, my feet branded with the marks of a slave,[16] and my head bald in places (as you can see)—have come here to this grassy podium to speak with so insolent a look in my eye.[17] But I beg you—don't think I've come here because I fancy I'm a handsome fellow or think of myself as a decem-king who's better than the other petty chieftains in our country.[18] I've come instead for better reasons, to cleanse myself of sin and wrongdoing and I'm prepared for whatever direction the investigation concerning Asellus the ass may take, since I am someone who knew his toils and service from use and experience. For I've come here myself, an obsequious slave with obsequious ways, from Soldus' household. And I won't tell

---

15. Throughout this speech Philonacus' diction, in comparison to Laura's classical Latin, is full of obviously rustic touches, outdated usages (like the epic accusative of respect), made-up vocabulary, and colloquial omission of the relative pronoun (as for example in Philonacus' opening: "miramini promptum video").

16. Philonacus' "chalk-white feet" (*cretatus pedes*)" according to Pliny, *Nat.* 35.201, the Romans used to mark the feet of their foreign slaves who were exhibited in the slave market with a permanent white chalk brand mark.

17. "Insolenti supercilio": the picture we're supposed to conjure up of Philonacus seems to be the Apuleian character of the insolent, lying young rogue or the Plautian roguish slave. The details from the tale that follows (the ass's carrying his sister on his back to her wedding, the ass's unusual speed, Philonacus's tormenting of the ass, his burdening the ass with excessively heavy loads, his beating him mercilessly, his tying the animal to a tree near a bear's lair, the ass's utter terror at being left out in the woods all night) all come directly from Apuleius' *Golden Ass* 7.17–24, as noted in the introduction to this chapter.

18. Philonacus doesn't think of himself as some "decaregem": presumably from *decemrex* and undoubtedly a neologism (or malapropism) analogous to *decemvir*, the name for the ten high commissioners appointed in ancient Rome to guard and oversee the Sibylline books.

you how this father of mine, after he left the army and took his pension, ran off with this ass's brother, bringing him to this place, as it were. He said he gave our ass's brother to his mother to cook so that the entrails, head, and lungs would be boiled and the leftovers skewered on wooden spits, and afterward an aroma would fill the air and be the herald of what was cooking on the hearth. He wanted a feast prepared with these dishes for his friends who were gourmands, who devoted their bellies completely to eating at the best table. And they drank not from a drinking vessel but a shell, as though they were reveling in the fact that they had never tasted any other animal with so savory a flavor. Such was the power of this dish.

But anyway this miller's ass of ours, who was outstanding in the sweat and hard work he devoted to this duties, always rose to the challenge of his tasks and frequently offered his tired neck to the pulling of carriages; in doing this, he showed wondrous attempts at drawing a hired cart. And although you could see his reactions to the various creakings of the wheels and his fear in his shining and erect ears, his mane, and his haughty nostrils,[19] still he leaned to submit his proud neck to the halter and to cross the more secure roadways leading away from the noisy city's menacing assault.[20] And when he dared to trust himself to the fording of rivers, he never trembled at the crossing of water. Nor was he choosy about which springs he would drink from, and when he was thirsty he willingly applied himself to drinking his draught and didn't have to be cajoled to drink with some sort of whistling. Whenever he leapt from his latticework stall, he met his master while eagerly pawing at the earth. He covered himself with dust, however, when he galloped with his rolling gait, and when he returned home unburdened, his steps were unfettered and his tail curved in the air.[21] Never did he have to be forced with a whip to run, if ever it was necessary to hurry or to return from a journey more quickly. For he was the swiftest and speediest runner, beyond the sluggishness of other animals of his species. Brescia is his witness: for there, under the rapt gaze of every spectator at the August games and with me urging him on, he won first prize in a race. Standing there with a fierce look, he was unable to stand still, but impatient for victory and exulting in his desire to triumph, this bold fellow took his stand against the barbarous and pugnacious horses. What could be more gentle or more submissive than this

19. "Varios rotarum strepitus et pavorem ex micantibus auriculis . . . atque superbis naribus saltuando spirarit" (literally, Asellus exhaled the noise of the wheels and his fear through his shining ears): the epic figure of hendiadys is another "special effect" meant to convey the old-fashioned, rustic character of Philonacus' language.

20. Vat. omits "vel minaci."

21. "Falcata cauda," another rustic figure: literally, his scythe-shaped tail.

animal, who, covered with a tapestry of many colors, straightened his legs gently first on one side and then the other and thus carried my sister to her wedding,[22] her hair arranged in a little tower with garlands braided in between her curls?

Danger made him a creature of even greater dependability and strength, on account of which many people, myself included, now sing his praises for a feat surpassing all others. For when he returned from Breno on his way to Pisogna, he managed to carry a load of five hundred pounds of iron along that whole stretch of winding and torturous roads. And I'll appear to be talking about things beyond belief if I say that this dumb animal's sensitivity to rain was actually a part of his ignorance. His pulsating ears[23] forewarned us so frequently of crucial rainstorms that his predictions never misled me. Is it too small a thing to mention that he went to a smith to have his hooves shod of his own accord?[24] Add that he calmed babies taking their afternoon naps in their cradles with the soothing sounds that wafted from his throat into the breezes. Shortly before dawn he used to waken us when we were still youngsters, those brayings of his rather hoarsely thickening his thin voice.

He went beyond admiration, however, when he, utterly dispensing with sleep, roared out in anger from the beginning of the evening until the rising of the sun as many times as the hours began to be noticed. He was the one vehicle we boys had when we were tired. He carried each one of us away from the fields, often taking three of us on his back from the pits which were overflowing with mud; nor did he ever throw any rider as long as the day was long (not counting when someone who was ignorant of horsemanship fell off him from fear). For he was skillful at turning to either side in response to the rider's hand. Nor should I fail to mention that he, though he was innocent of evil himself, learned to protect me from getting caught for my crime when I would cut the crops with a sharp scythe and steal them from the fields at night. Certainly he was so compliant that he never bore either stings from insects or blasts from the wind with all ill temper. Still, I shall confess an act that needs expiation, and whose villainy distresses me every time I recall it, namely that I, angry scoundrel that I was, punished him by whipping him with sticks when he did not want to soak himself in the river in order to wash

22. See Apuleius, *Met.* 7.13, for a similar tableau of Lucius the ass bearing the bride Charite on his back. "Molliter sub alterno illo crurium explicatu vexit": this description of the ass's gentle, ambling gait, which is called a rack in English, is straight out of Pliny, *Nat.* 8.166.

23. "Auriculae pulsitatae" (his pulsating ears): cf. "vena pulsari" (his pulsating veins) in Apuleius, *Met.* 2.29.

24. *Ferrare*, the verb she uses here, is Italian (meaning to shoe a horse) and doesn't exist in classical Latin.

away the filth from the mange he had on his coat. After this he showed his sadness, looking only at the ground with glassy eyes. He refused to eat for three nights in a row nor did he rise to his feet for those days. But the next day when a few more of us boys returned to the meadows to run around and amuse ourselves on horseback where he was grazing, as soon as one person and then another climbed on him, the revengeful donkey gave a kick with one leg and walked off in the opposite direction down a hazardous path, nor did he stop stirring up and churning the air with his angry feet until he was able to shake each of us—me and as many of the other smooth-cheeked boys as there were—off his back and shoulders. All of us laughed at the timely joke created by this comic figure: a variety of resentments had made for one ridiculous situation.

But an unhappiness much more stinging ate away at my heart, since I was sad about my wounded knee. And Asellus did not move the boys (who were now long gone) to laughter as much as I myself was prepared to move him to tears. And so, burning for revenge, I waited for a long time in silence for evening to come, during which time I left the culprit tied up in the middle of the orchard where he would be exposed to the attack of wild beasts. A ferocious she-bear was wintering in a shady grove in the area and she was suckling her twin offspring there. When this night-wandering creature tracks down her food by its scent whenever the need impels her, she falls on her prey and, while she fends off the raging beast's counterattack with blows and bites, she keeps her awful hunger at bay.

Meanwhile, warned by a dream in which I imagined such a battle, I got up and went out, remaining terrified for much of the night. First I would leave the house and then, after going first in this direction and then in that, I would return to the house. I gazed at the stars in the waning night, which heralded the ruby-red rays of morning in the east. The sun had not yet begun to rise in our region of the earth. But uncombed and not entirely awake, I hastily ran on ahead through the silence of the forest in order to see and observe the fate of this creature with his brazen feet.[25] I looked. I gazed at him still in his fetters. I stepped nearer. Now the movement of his breathing was heavier, and in a final gasp, in which he nearly expired, and as though staring with his eyes rolled back in his head, he let out a stifled sigh through barely panting nostrils. Fear and toil had routed the strength and spirit of the ailing animal. I forced him, released by unexpected hands, from the dimness of the grove into the sunlight. Now his legs were cold and paralyzed with fear and horror.

---

25. "Aeripedis": "having feet of bronze," a common epithet in Latin poetry for hooved animals (horses, deer, donkeys, etc.).

Thus it was a struggle for me to haul this half-dead animal, threatening him with the rod, from that place back to his home. I myself walked ahead of him, staying close by, though I was moving fairly slowly since I was by now exhausted and disgusted, as if I were thinking about what excuse I could use to protect myself in a fight with the ass.

Asellus himself left the city, turning off the main road to the left to a winepress located in a narrow passageway, where he filled his belly with grapes and new wine since he was seized by thirst. Suffused with this vinous potion and the steam from the boiling liquor which he adored, he began first to rush about in every direction in a kind of orgiastic fervor. Afterwards he lay there for two days in a deep, comatose sleep.

This one thought occurred to his cautious master: that the envy of evil men had perchance sprinkled hippomanes, a witch's brew, over the sleeping beast, or that he himself had eaten a mushroom or had come into contact with a viper's venom or the leaves of the livid acanthus with its poisonous juice. For this reason, a doctor was summoned who, with the remedy of blazing iron, succeeded in restoring the sick creature from his stuporous coma to sudden vigilance.

In the meantime the vineyard workers appeared, who devoted a day in court to recover the damages on their master's grapes. There, in an exchange of mutual banter and play between the two parties, the case was fought out face to face before an impartial magistrate. In the end, the judgment of the magistrate against Soldus stood, and the payment of a fine in money was demanded for the workers' loss. Soldus was ordered to comply with the court. He put down his knotty staff, his shepherd's pipes, and his worn sheepskin cloak as surety for his debt.[26] But Asellus, who was still hungry, freed himself of his drunkard's debt for the wrong he did with a month-long fast, while he ground to a pulp thistles, fallen leaves, and thorny brambles with his teeth.[27]

Thus it befalls the wretched that they lose their faith and face[28] in the course of years of servitude. There is therefore this one unspeakable crime, this one terrible arrogance, this one savage and unavenged cruelty that has caused me, a perpetrator of despicable evil, so merciless, so fierce, and so barbarous, to prey upon an innocent creature. Ah, accursed me. I should be plunged up to my mouth not only into the waters of Tantalus but into the swamp of Cocytus. Alas, what land will welcome me into its midst after this?

26. The word "meloten," surely a Latinization of the Greek word for sheepskin, *melote*, is not in the *Oxford Latin Dictionary*.

27. Surely "totundit" (not in the *Oxford Latin Dictionary*) is another antiquarian mannerism from *tundo, tundere* (beat, strike, crush, grind to a pulp).

28. The Latin text reads "fidem frontemque amittant."

What home? Alas, what Nemean lion, what Erymanthan boar, what Hyrca-
nean tiger would rightly seize and devour me with its dire claws and savage
jaws?[29] I admit that I should be seized, stripped, and beaten with a whip because, inflamed with the sin of rage, I inflicted punishment on one who was
innocent. Should this ass, your refuge from us who were the rogues in your
household, have been so bitterly and cruelly tortured? Shouldn't a firmer fortress for this poor little life of yours have been provided by my hands, which
now ought to be hacked off? Why are you men from the same community as
Soldus, many of you soldiers, amazed that the unusual sadness from a loss
suffered long ago and a broken heart has driven this little old man crazy with
grief? We should be more surprised at a man who has forgotten the bitterness
with which he grieved for things he had hoped for in vain.

You, Laura, give us a distinguished speech with the majesty of Demosthenes. Who would keep a bereaved father of a family from weeping
over the death of his own carrier? Who would keep a sick old man from tears
in these circumstances? For death, poverty, and slavery often light the
torches of sorrow and set them on fire in the constant mind. Treat gently
therefore the afflicted. Weep with me instead. With a more compassionate
pen say those things that can elegantly and with lucid reason thrash the
deadly wound of regret[30] that lies in wait to trap us. Take now the rotating
podium for speakers where, filled with the spirit of the age and its volatility,
even if I was imbued with neither the classical authors, nor authority, nor
guided by the look or appearance of polish, still I poured out, in whatever
way I could, a flood of words and tall tales more trifling than trash.

But you, a girl born to true eloquence, who are called to this field for
funeral assemblies and meetings of the mourners' senate, it is your turn to
speak. Remember now, I beg you, that your memorial should have enough
happiness for a kingdom. Now, scatter from your virgin's lips the balm of
Quintilian's nectar, dripping with purity and modesty like a crystalline
spring. Clothe the rest of your speech with this balm because you must
arouse your audience's piety. The herders of the sheep and cattle are expect-
ing beauteous things from the sweetness of your mouth, because they would
dry everyone's eyes and reconcile them at long last to stroking the peaceful-
ness of their minds.

LAURA: You throngs from the countryside and you mountain-dwelling
folk clad in sheepskin, you have heard the stories having to do with the fu-

---

29. These are the mythological monsters invariable called to mind as emblems of the worst
possible savagery by every Latin author.
30. This is vintage Cereta: "paenitentiae vulnus, etc." (literally, the wound of regret, etc.).

neral that this greedy country boy has recounted with labored breath. I myself shall strive for the sake of the sinews of my subject to embrace those
themes with which I may, with metaphors and persuasive arguments, be able
to elevate your minds to a mediation of your sorrow. It will be elaborately
done to the extent that I am able, because I would not bind myself to this
promise with such strings that, if I didn't succeed in persuading you, I would
want my title of orator to be taken away. For in the cases of Aesculapius and
Cicero, although the one was a doctor and the other surpassed all other orators with his eloquence, neither did the former heal all the Hippolytuses who
came to him, nor did the latter persuade the jury with his speech for Milo.[31]

Nor will I fail to mention that this boy, a little fox and spinner of wiles
with scarcely the flowering of down on his cheeks, who, appalled at the awk-
wardness of my speech, tested with the birdlime of false flattery my rustic
genius, my uncultivated gestures, and my pen slow to write because I am a
member of the female sex.[32] And although this fellow rightly lends distinction to many occasions with his wornout species of country charm, his artless
nature, and even his singular demeanor itself, still he harasses and stings me
with the cruel injuries of an oppressive tyrant. For this reason this rustic little
destroyer of humanity deserves to suffer not only the censure of the Porcian
and Sempronian laws, but also the axes of the tribunes' prison as well,[33] since
he would have organized and presented everything aptly and wittily enough
had he, being ill-advised in his asinicide,[34] left those whips and burning
wounds out of the revision of his story.

But because of the insolence of this slave, our father was angrier and
more bitterly aggrieved than he had ever been in any other circumstance: he
felt that in that speech a species of lamentation and mourning was being re-
vived that he for all practical purposes had rooted out of his heart, which was
now placated. Let us consider ourselves what anger would fill our hearts or
what bitterness would cause our minds to seethe if we were to think that he,

31. Hippolytus, son of Theseus and Hippolyte, was so mutilated by his own horses that his torn
body couldn't be put back together again. The *Pro Milone* refers to one of Cicero's most famous
orations, written in defense of his client Milo.

32. "Puer adinvenerit aucupium" (literally, the boy invented bird-catching): *aucupium* connotes,
in general, wiles, deception, the work of a trickster, etc.

33. The Porcian law (*Porcia lex*) permitted condemned Roman citizens to go into exile rather
than go to prison or be executed; the Sempronian law (*Sempronia lex*) decreed that citizens could
not be condemned to death without a full vote of the senate.

34. Cereta's neologism "asinicida," which is not attested in the ancient authors, is analogous to
the *parricida* (murder of a parent). This passage is where Laura of course makes the reference and
comparison to Apuleius' tale of the cruel boy and his readiness to kill the ass he's responsible for
explicit (Apuleius, *Met.* 7.17–24).

who with his continuing labors carried help, protection, and extra supplies to us in our affairs, had been ill-treated with beatings or verbal abuse. Certainly if we were to review the life and exploits of this swift-footed creature of ours, there was never a time when the townspeople had reason to abuse him. This animal, so deserving of his spurs, saddle pads, reins, and saddle, should instead have been preferred to wild asses.

But now that the final hour of Asellus has severed his long life, his body must be restored with exquisite perfumes, indeed rubbed with oils and unguents from Cyprus. Nor will there be any shame in having said that his funeral service should be celebrated with the pomp and circumstance of kings and that he should be presented with his own oration at the rostrum. Nor do I think it seems strange that of two asses born as twins, the gourmands should have feasted on one while the other was purchased by Soldus for a great deal of money; Maecenas after all established the custom among the ancients of dining on asses of this sort and Quintus Asius bought one of them for four hundred thousand sesterces.[35] From all the species of living creatures, it is this one that Silvanus, the god of the herds, protects with his divine spirit. Silenus was solemnly carried on an ass to the god of his mother,[36] and Priapus greatly rejoiced at the immolation of this animal. Apuleius wanted to clothe himself with the features of an ass, and Cornelius Asina led an animal similar to this into the Roman forum, loaded down with a dowry for his daughter's marriage.[37] When he goes into battle, Mars uses the skin of this animal stretched tightly over a drum, and roused by its booming sound, hostile armies running together from different directions bloody themselves with repeated wounds. In addition, Plato seems to have thought that the souls of men who devoted themselves to shameful pursuits for the sake of sensual pleasure were changed into their opposites after they departed from this life.[38] What else? By naming the two small autumnal stars shining in the head and claw of the constellation Cancer the "Little Asses," the religion of a prior era taught (as if it knew) that these asses had been elevated from a life of great punishment on earth to one of caring for human suffering in heaven.[39] The

35. The lore about Maecenas' taste for asses and an ass lover whom Marcus Varro called Quintus Axius (not Asius) comes straight from Cereta's favorite author, Pliny, *Nat.* 8.170 and 8.167.

36. The phrase "ad matris deum" (to the god of his mother) is puzzling and may be corrupt. One would expect something like "ad Midam regem," since Silenus, who was an attendant of the god Bacchus, was once sent on the back of an ass to King Midas (Ovid, *Met.* 4.26–27; 11.90–101).

37. See Macrobius, *Saturnalia* 1.6.

38. On the transposition of souls into their opposite types after death see Plato, *Laws* 905.

39. Pliny, *Nat.* 18.353, on the Little Asses in the constellation Cancer.

consuls celebrated games held in the Roman circus in honor of asses because they were harnessed to the chariot of Apollo, the father of the sun. This thought should greatly soothe and cool your sorrow, and indeed provide a sure road to remembering forever that you possessed such a beast of burden— an animal to whom many simple and uneducated people would make a sacrifice.[40]

But these are matters of faith. Let us talk about the most profitable aspects of the ass, which the more vigilant discipline of medicine has discovered. Among Nero's wives, Poppaea didn't blush to walk in the company of a flock of asses. The great utility of a bath of asses' milk for smoothness and softness of the face is zealously prized. But nature (which lets nothing remain a secret) opines that nothing is more efficacious or healing for the sudden fevers of infants and the aching breasts of a woman newly delivered of a child than asses' milk.[41] Asses' blood is said to be a help in the case of both fevers and jaundice;[42] their flesh when boiled is helpful in the case of consumption and intestinal ailments, and their urine is no mediocre medicine for the kidneys and for warts.[43] Asses' dung and the ashes of their hair are not less helpful in dealing with phlegm than with an excessive discharge of blood and the curling of one's hair.[44] The powder made from asses' hooves is a helpful remedy for little ulcers that form: after the abundant fumigation of these ulcers, hair that was about to emerge grows out in their place, as when an abortion which has been initiated follows the uterus.[45] Also impressive are the results of a drug contained in the asses' liver, which is successful in treating epilepsy in children;[46] and when placed underneath children, the hide of an ass allows them to be healed even from the nocturnal fear of ghosts.[47] Some have writ-

40. "Iumentum cui multae gentes sacrificent": this seems to be inference on Cereta's part based on the extent to which asses are highly prized for various purposes in all parts of the world according to Pliny, *Nat.* 8.167–75.

41. On the curative effects of asses' milk see Pliny, *Nat.* 28.196; 28.251.

42. On the medicinal uses of asses' blood see Pliny, *Nat.* 28.227; in 28.230 the eating of the flesh of a she-ass is recommended for lethargy and melancholia.

43. On the benefits of asses' urine see Pliny, *Nat.* 28.218; 28.244. Rabil, p. 168, suggests for *pthisicis* (another word not in the *Oxford Latin Dictionary* (OLD) "illness" or "consumption."

44. On the medicinal properties on asses' dung see Pliny, *Nat.* 28.200; 28.204; 28.239; 218.251; on the benefits of the ashes from their dung for hemorrhaging see *Nat.* 28.251. "Profluvio sanguinis": see Pliny, *Nat.* 21.169, on menstruation; it's interesting how many of these remedies are female-specific.

45. See Pliny, *Nat.* 28.242; 28.251. "Sicut . . . abortus," etc.: this is a very unusual simile.

46. On the medicinal properties of the ass's liver for epilepsy see Pliny, *Nat.* 28.258.

47. The skin or hide (*pellis*) of an ass placed underneath the boys (*quibus substrata*) acts as a tranquilizer: see Pliny, *Nat.* 28.258.

ten that thinning hair, prone to fall out, is thickened if it is smeared three times with the powder made from an ass's genitals;[48] and a scar is miraculously beautified by smearing it with the fat and dust from an ass's hide, burned and dried in the heat of the sun; cysts and scrofula are improved by this treatment.[49] The vapor from an ass's lungs kills worms.[50] Much is written about the magical properties of asses, in which nothing certain emerges because of the great complexity of these things. Nature has so elevated asses beyond the needs of men and hairy animals that they are impervious to the lice that drove the poet Alcman, the hated dictator Sulla, and the governor of Judea, Pilate, to their deaths.[51]

The fact that Asellus himself was superior to other asses and did many things that learned men will celebrate and hand down to posterity counsels us to lift all the cares and baggage from our minds. Therefore, father Soldus, it will be gratifying to your reputation that so many writers will commend the glorious deeds of this animal to the immortality of letters. So, although you may be driven in the midst of the whirlwinds of horrifying evils between Scylla and the Syrtes, men ought to console you by singing the merits of Asellus who is now buried, because you have had the privilege of enjoying so many years with him. Consider with a more tranquil mind how useful he was to you and how much profit he returned from the benefits he received. Ponder also how this follower of yours always showed you that he enjoyed himself. Pay attention to how many of our provisions he carried in these desolate fields, thanks to the virtue native to his race. Think, I beg you, on what gratitude, goodwill, and enthusiasm this great crowd of those here assembled has shown in embracing, consoling, and encouraging you. This voice is the tearful witness of all who are here, and having pity for the sickness of your soul, it cries out to the heavens with tears and groans.

Let those men beat their breasts for whom dying is not enough unless they think that men who have been shipwrecked will be devoured by fish, that those who die unburied are destined to be the food of birds, and that those whose flesh is rotting will be consumed by worms. This corpse which

48. Pliny, *Nat.* 28.164: recommends asses' testicles reduced to ash for growing thicker hair. *Nat.* 28.261 suggests using an ass's testicles as an aphrodisiac. Cereta: "Si ter a genitalium intersperso pulvere liniantur."

49. Pliny, *Nat.* 28.242: recommends the ashes from asses' hooves for curing spreading ulcers.

50. This comes straight out of Pliny, *Nat.* 28.155: "venataque omnia accenso pulmone [asini] eius fugere."

51. Both manuscripts read "Alemon," clearly a missreading of Alcman, the Greek lyric poet who lived in Sparta (flor. 654–611 B.C.). The information about Sulla's and Alcman's deaths from lice or maggots comes from Cereta's usual source, Pliny, *Nat.* 11.114. The purported immunity of asses to lice also comes from Pliny, *Nat.* 11.115.

has been burned and whose ashes have now been collected is free from such harm. Look, a new urn protects the ashes that have been placed in it. See, the inscription of the ass's name is affixed to these stones that men will visit. And look, these ancient spoils will hang from an ancient oak tree for men of future generations to see. Behold, the very trees long to sing their praises to you. See the herds in the fields, how they encircle us mournfully, as though they were lowing just to afflict you. Why are you destroying yourself, Soldus? Why do you subject yourself to the blows of ineluctable fortune? Why do you go over and over these sorrows of yours in vain? Why do you indulge your grief to such excess? Why do you repeat the unforgettable tragedy of this most blessed animal's death? Is it that his death will make you immortal? You aren't unaware, are you, that Fortune produces happiness that is pregnant with sorrows? Our one happiness comes from the gods and death. All these things bid you, who are too plagued by anxiety, to keep your silence and restrain your lamentation. If you bear your misfortune today with a brave heart, if fortune does not crush you with its adversity, if your heart flies at the harrying passions of your cares and it is well armed, how many and frequent will be the public eulogies of you and your name. Who in the future generations of men will not know this great fire in the world? We now introduce a worthwhile piece of advice into this long funeral ceremony. You accuse Fortune of the abuses that brought harm to an ass who has died when you ought more satisfactorily to be singing his praises for the sake of the immortality of your glory. But so be it. Now, using reason, rise above the circumstances owing to which your humanity has overwhelmed you with emotion.

Look, I have now persuaded everyone; they are returning to their senses. I alone, who came here for the purpose of consoling others, must now be consoled together with you. I beg you: take my advice seriously. Consider of the utmost importance the prayers of those who are mourning. Care tenderly for the thoughts of your friends. I have obeyed the laws of nature, which commend you first to care for yourself, lest you should wish that you, already dying, would depart again from this empty life because of your love for the servant who had been yours. For grieving does nothing for those whom you long for in vain. May this dismal peroration therefore not suffocate you. Look to the barely palpable breath that you draw with your lips. Look, you have dissolved into tears enough times during my speech. We have already defiled our faces enough with our nails. You must free your anxious spirit from this turbulence you have undergone, for its memory has caused you to mourn this dark day so sorrowfully and piteously. Do not howl in grief. Do not beat your breast any longer, aged father who is no more a father. The spirits below do not care for our sighs (trust someone who counts herself among the faithful), and the dead do not hear our cries. It is a fiction that souls go astray when they leave their bodies, wandering aimlessly away. In vain now have you violently shouted Asellus' name in his ear. Only forgetfulness can overcome the past; only reason can smooth away sorrows. Desist therefore from your mourning. Hold back your tears. Restrain your ungentle sobbing. Now that you have been consoled, you have plenty of living to do if you wish. Already the day, darkening under the first shadows, has begun to melt into night. Already, uttered from languid mouths, the restless cries of our hearers have mingled in these funeral rites.

Long enough now have the wailing women torn and defiled their hair in the disarray of mourning. Long enough have sons and daughters-in-law pulled open their torn garments to bare their breasts.[52] See how all the boiling fervor of your bitterness now blazes up among the lines of people. Let us go. Remove whatever verges on black from around you.[53] Rise now at last. The time has come. Look, the buzzing swarms of visitors rise in undulating waves on all sides now, first there and then here. Lead the throngs home. They will follow you regardless of the road you take. Take up the lyre. Tell a story about a cookpot from a cookshop. Their response will imitate yours, and they, like pupils, will sing in whatever meters you choose. Begin. Stir up once again clamorous, alternating songs from mouths that have long been ruminating in silence. Nor should it sadden you to sound your voices together, swarmlike, punctuating your songs with varied and scattered applause.[54] Now, in the closing of this oration, all things resound with the words "salve atque vale."[55]

52. "Diloricavere" (pull apart or open the garment covering one's breast): a rare verb cited by the *OLD* as appearing only in Cicero, *De orat.* 2.124; Apuleius, *Met.* 6.10; 7.8.

53. The *OLD* cites "nigricare" (to shade into black, to be black) only in Pliny, *Nat.* 9.135; 16.186; 26.133; 37.161.

54. Here again Cereta's vocabulary is idiosyncratic: *formiculatim*, antlike, in swarming formation; *deroso plausu*, with half-eaten applause.

55. "Ave atque vale" and "salve atque vale" are traditional closings in Latin funeral orations.

BIBLIOGRAPHY

PRIMARY SOURCES:

Alberti, Leon Battista (1404–72). *The Family in Renaissance Florence.* Trans. Renee Neu Watkins. Columbia. S.C.: University of South Carolina Press, 1969.

Ariosto, Ludovico (1474–1533). *Orlando Furioso.* Trans. Barbara Reynolds. 2 vols. New York: Penguin Books, 1875, 1977.

Astell, Mary (1666–1731). *The English Feminist: Reflections on Marriage and Other Writings.* Ed. and introd. Bridget Hill. New York: St. Martin's Press, 1986.

Barbaro, Francesco (1390–1454). *On Wifely Duties.* Trans. Benjamin Kohl, in Kohl and R. G. Witt, eds., *The Earthly Republic.* Philadelphia: University of Pennsylvania Press, 1978, 179–228. Translation of the preface and book 2.

Beauchamp, Virginia W., Matthew Bray, Susan Green, Susan S. Lanser, Katherine Larsen, Judith Pascoe, Katherine M. Rogers, Ruth Salvaggio, Amy C. Simowitz, Tara G. Wallace, eds. *Women Critics, 1660–1820. An Anthology.* The Folger Collective on Early Women Critics. Bloomington and Indianapolis: Indiana University Press, 1995.

Boccaccio, Giovanni (1313–75). *Concerning Famous Women.* Trans. Guido A. Guarino. New Brunswick, N.J.: Rutgers University Press, 1963.

———. *Corbaccio or The Labyrinth of Love.* Trans. Anthony K. Cassell. Second revised edition. Binghamton, N.Y.: Medieval and Renaissance Texts and Studies, 1993.

Bruni, Leonardo (1370–1444). "On the Study of Literature (1405) to Lady Battista Malatesta of Montefeltro," in *The Humanism of Leonardo Bruni, Selected Texts.* Trans. and introd. Gordon Griffiths, James Hankins, and David Thompson. Binghamton: Medieval and Renaissance Texts and Studies, 1987, 240–51.

Castiglione, Baldassare (1478–1529). *The Courtier.* Trans. George Bull. New York: Viking Penguin, 1967.

Cereta, Laura (1469–99). *Laurae Ceretae Brixiensis Feminae Clarissimae Epistolae iam primum e MS in lucem productae.* Ed. Jacopo Filippo Tomasini. Padua: Sebastiano Sardi, 1640.

———. Vatican manuscript. Vat lat. 3176. cart. 3. XVI in 73 fols. Contains eighty-three items; the only source containing all Cereta's extant works. Sixteenth century.

————. Venice manuscript. Marc. Cod. Lat., XI, 28 [4186] mbr. XV, 154 fols. Includes seventy-four items containing many lacunae. The manuscript begins on folio 11; according to the index of the manuscript, folios 1–10 once contained her dedicatory letter to Cardinal Ascanio Maria Sforza and the opening of her dialogue on the death on an ass. Fifteenth century.

Elyot, Thomas (1490–1546). *The Defence of Good Women: The Feminist Controversy of the Renaissance.* Facsimile Reproductions. Ed. Diane Bornstein. New York: Delmar, 1980.

Erasmus, Desiderius (1467–1536). "Courtship," "The Girl with No Interest in Marriage," "The Repentant Girl," "Marriage," "The Abbott and the Learned Lady," and "The New Mother," in *The Colloquies of Erasmus.* Trans. Craig R. Thompson. Chicago: University of Chicago Press, 1965, 86–98, 99–111, 111–14, 114–27, 217–23.

Fedele, Cassandra (1465–1558). *Clarissimae feminae Cassandrae Fidelis venetae epistolae et orationes.* Ed. Jacopo Filippo Tomasini. Padua: Franciscus Bolzetta, 1636.

————. *Oratio pro Bertucio Lamberto.* Modena: 1487; Venice: 1488; Nuremberg: 1489.

Filelfo, Francesco (1398–1481). *Epistolae familiares.* Venice: ex aedibus Ioannis et Gregorii de Gregoriis fratrum, 1502.

Kempe, Margery (1373–1439). *The Book of Margery Kempe.* Trans. Barry Windeatt. New York: Viking Penguin, 1986.

King, Margaret L., and Albert Rabil, Jr., eds. *Her Immaculate Hand: Selected Works by and about the Women Humanists of Quattrocento Italy.* Binghamton, N.Y.: Medieval and Renaissance Texts and Studies, 1983; 2nd revised paperback edition, 1991.

Klein, Joan Larsen, ed. *Daughters, Wives, and Widows: Writings by Men about Women and Marriage in England, 1500–1640.* Urbana, Ill.: University of Illinois Press, 1992.

Knox, John (1505–72). *The Political Writings of John Knox: The First Blast of the Trumpet against the Monstrous Regiment of Women and Other Selected Works.* Ed. Marvin A. Beslow. Washington: Folger Shakespeare Library, 1985.

Kors, Alan C., and Edward Peters, eds. *Witchcraft in Europe, 1100–1700: A Documentary History.* Philadelphia: University of Pennsylvania Press, 1972.

Kristeva, Julia. *Desire and Language. A Semiotic Approach to Literature and Art.* Trans. Thomas Gora, Alice Jardine, and Leon S. Roudiez. Ed. Leon S. Roddiez. New York: Columbia University Press, 1980.

Kramer, Heinrich, and Jacob Sprenger. *Malleus Maleficarum* (ca. 1487). Trans. Montague Summers. London: The Pushkin Press, 1928; reprinted New York: Dover, 1971.

Labalme, Patricia H., ed. *Beyond Their Sex. Learned Women of the European Past.* New York and London: New York University Press, 1980.

Lionnet, Françoise. *Autobiographical Voices: Race, Gender, Self-Portraiture.* Ithaca: Cornell University Press, 1991.

de Lorris, William (1225–40) and Jean de Meun (1273–80). *The Romance of the Rose.* Trans. Charles Dahlbert. Princeton: Princeton University Press, 1971; repr. University Press of New England, 1983.

de Navarre, Margarite (1492–1549). *The Heptameron.* Trans. P. A. Chilton. New York: Viking Penguin, 1984.

Petrarca, Francesco (1304–74). *Rerum familiarium. Libri I–VIII.* Ed. and trans. Aldo Bernardo. Albany: State University of New York Press, 1975.

de Pizan, Christine (1365–1431). *The Book of the City of Ladies.* Trans. Earl Jeffrey Richards. Foreword by Marina Warner. New York: Persea Books, 1982.

———. *The Treasury of the City of Ladies.* Trans. Sarah Lawson. New York: Viking Penguin, 1985. Also: Trans. and introd. by Charity Cannon Willard, ed. and introd. by Madeleine P. Cosman. New York: Persea Books, 1989.

Poliziano, Angelo (1454–94). *Opera Omnia.* Ed. I. Maier. 3 vols. Turin: 1971.

Spensere, Edmund (1552–99). *The Faerie Queene.* Ed. Thomas P. Roche, Jr. with the assistance of C. Patrick O'Donnell, Jr., New Haven: Yale University Press, 1978.

Teresa of Avila, Saint (1515–82). *The Life of Saint Teresa of Avila by Herself.* Trans. J. M. Cohen. New York: Viking Penguin, 1957.

Vives, Juan Luis (1492–1540). *The Instruction of the Christian Woman.* Trans. Rycharde Hyrde. London, 1524, 1557.

Weyer, Johann (1515–88). *Witches, Devils, and Doctors in the Renaissance: Johann Weyer, De praestigiis daemonum.* Ed. George Mora with Benjamin G. Kohl, Erik Midelfort, and Helen Bacon. Trans. John Shea. Binghamton: Medieval and Renaissance Texts and Studies, 1991.

Wilson, Katharina M., ed. *Medieval Women Writers.* Athens, Ga.: University of Georgia Press, 1984.

———. *Women Writers of the Renaissance and Reformation.* Athens, Ga. University of Georgia Press, 1987.

Wilson, Katharina M., and Frank J. Warnke, eds. *Women Writers of the Seventeenth Century.* Athens, Ga. University of Georgia Press, 1989.

Zanelli, Agostino. "Laura Cereta al Vescovo Zane." *Brixia Sacra* XIV (1923): 173–78.

SECONDARY WORKS:

Bayley, C. C. *War and Society in Renaissance Florence: The "De militia" of Leonardo Bruni.* Toronto: University of Toronto Press, 1961.

Beilin, Elaine V. *Redeeming Eve: Women Writers of the English Renaissance.* Princeton: Princeton University Press, 1987.

Benson, Pamela Joseph. *The Invention of the Renaissance Woman: The Challenge of Female Independence in the Literature and Thought of Italy and England.* University Park, Pa.: Pennsylvania State University Press, 1992.

Black, Robert. *Benedetto Accolti and the Florentine Renaissance.* Cambridge, Eng.: Cambridge University Press, 1985.

Bloch, R. Howard, *Medieval Misogyny and the Invention of Western Romantic Love.* Chicago: University of Chicago Press, 1991.

Brown, Alison. *Bartolomeo Scala (1430–1497), Chancellor of Florence. The Humanist as Bureaucrat.* Princeton: Princeton University Press, 1979.

Caccia, Ettore. "Cultura e letturatura nei secoli XV e XVI," in *Storia di Brescia. II, La dominazione Veneta (1426–1575)*. Ed. Giovanni Trecanni degli Alfieri. Brescia: Morcelliana, 1961), 477–527.

Clark, Elizabeth A. *Ascetic Piety and Women's Faith; Essays on Late Ancient Christianity.* Lewiston, N.Y.: Edwin Mellen Press, 1986.

Clough, Cecil H. "The Cult of Antiquity," in *Cultural Aspects of the Italian Renaissance. Essays in Honour of Paul Oskar Kristeller.* Ed. Cecil H. Clough. Manchester: Manchester University Press, 1976), 33–67.

Cremona, Virginio. "L'umanesimo Bresciano," in *Storia di Brescia. II, La dominazione Veneta (1426–1575).* Ed. Giovanni Treccani degli Alfieri. Brescia: Morcelliana, 1961), 542–66.

Davis, Natalie Zemon. *Society and Culture in Early Modern France.* Stanford: Stanford University Press, 1975. Especially chapters 3 and 5.

Davis, Natalie Zemon, and Arlette Farge, eds. *A History of Women in the West. III, Renaissance and Enlightenment Paradoxes.* Cambridge: Harvard University Press, 1993.

Dixon, Suzanne. *The Roman Family.* Baltimore: Johns Hopkins University Press, 1992.

Felisatti, Massimo. *Isabella d'Este, la primadonna del Rinascimento.* Milan: Bompiani, 1982.

Ferguson, Margaret W., Maureen Quilligan, and Nancy S. Vickers, eds. *Rewriting the Renaissance: The Discourses of Sexual Difference in Early Modern Europe.* Chicago: University of Chicago Press, 1987.

Freud, Sigmund. *Collected Papers.* Trans. and ed. Joan Riviere. New York: Basic Books, Inc., 1959.

Gardner, Jane F. *Women in Roman Law and Society.* Bloomington, Ind.: Indiana University Press, 1986.

Gay, Peter. *Freud: A Life for Our Time.* New York: W. W. Norton, 1988.

Greenblatt, Stephen J. *Renaissance Self-Fashioning from More to Shakespeare.* Chicago: University of Chicago Press, 1980.

Grendler, Paul. *Schooling in Renaissance Italy. Literacy and Learning, 1300–1600.* Baltimore: Johns Hopkins University Press, 1989.

Gundersheimer, Werner L. "Women, Learning, and Power: Eleonora of Aragon and the Court of Ferrara," in *Beyond Their Sex. Learned Women of the European Past.* Ed. Patricia H. Labalme. New York and London: New York University Press, 1980), 43–65.

Herlihy, David. "Did Women Have a Renaissance? A Reconsideration." *Medievalia et Humanistica*, n.s. 13 (1985): 1–22.

Horowitz, Maryanne Cline, "Aristotle and Woman." *Journal of the History of Biology* 9 (1976): 183–213.

Hull, Suzanne W. *Chaste, Silent and Obedient: English Books for Women, 1475–1640.* San Marino, Calif.: The Huntington Library, 1982.

Jardine, Lisa. "Isotta Nogarola: Women Humanists—Education for What?" *History of Education* 12 (1983): 231–44.

Jed, Stephanie. *Chaste Thinking. The Rape of Lucretia and the Birth of Humanism.* Bloomington: Indiana University Press, 1989.

Jones, Ann Rosalind. *The Currency of Eros: Women's Love Lyric in Europe* (Bloomington and Indianapolis: Indiana University Press).

Jordan, Constance. "Boccaccio's In-famous Women: Gender and Civic Virtue in the *De claris mulieribus*," in *Ambiguous Realities. Women in the Middle Ages and Renaissance*. Ed. Carole Levin and Jeannie Watson. Detroit: Wayne State University Press, 1987, 25–47.

―――. *Renaissance Feminism: Literary Texts and Political Models*. Ithaca: Cornell University Press, 1990.

Kelly, Joan. "Did Women Have a Renaissance?" In her *Women, History and Theory*. Chicago: University of Chicago Press, 1984. Also in *Becoming Visible: Women in European History*. Ed. Renate Bridenthal, Claudia Koonz, and Susan M. Stuard. 2nd ed. Boston: Houghton Mifflin, 1987, 175–202.

―――. "Early Feminist Theory and the *Querelle des Femmes*." In *Women, History and Theory*.

Kelso, Ruth. *Doctrine for the Lady of the Renaissance*. Foreword by Katharine M. Rogers. Urbana, Ill.: University of Illinois Press, 1956, 1978.

King, Margaret L. *The Death of the Child Valerio Marcello*. Chicago: University of Chicago Press, 1994.

―――. "The Religious Retreat of Isotta Nogarola (1418–1466), " *Signs* 3 (1978): 807–22.

―――. *Venetian Humanism in an Age of Patrician Dominance*. Princeton: Princeton University Press, 1986.

―――. *Women of the Renaissance*. Foreword by Catharine R. Stimpson. Chicago: University of Chicago Press, 1991.

Klapisch-Zuber, Christiane, ed. *A History of Women in the West. II, Silences of the Middle Ages*. Cambridge, Mass.: Harvard University Press, 1992.

Kristeller, Paul Oskar. *Eight Philosophers of the Italian Renaissance*. Stanford, Calif.: Stanford University Press, 1964.

―――. "Learned Women of Early Modern Italy: Humanists and University Scholars," in *Beyond Their Sex. Learned Women of the European Past*. Ed. Patricia H. Lahalme. New York and London: New York University Press, 1980), 91–116.

Labalme, Patricia H. "Venetian Women on Women: Three Early Modern Feminists," *Archivio Veneto* 5.117 (1981): 81–108.

Laqueur, Thomas. *Making Sex: Body and Gender from the Greeks to Freud*. Cambridge: Mass.: Harvard University Press, 1990.

Lerner, Gerda. *Creation of Feminist Consciousness, 1000–1870*. New York: Oxford University Press, 1994.

Lochrie, Karma. *Margery Kempe and Translations of the Flesh*. Philadelphia: University of Pennsylvania Press, 1992.

Maclean, Ian. *The Renaissance Notion of Woman: A Study of the Fortunes of Scholasticism and Medical Science in European Intellectual Life*. Cambridge: Cambridge University Press, 1980.

———. *Woman Triumphant: Feminism in French Literature, 1610–1652.* Oxford: Clarendon Press, 1977.

Marsh, David. *The Quattrocento Dialogue.* Cambridge, Mass.: Harvard University Press, 1986.

Matter, E. Ann, and John Coakley, eds. *Creative Women in Medieval and Early Modern Italy.* Philadelphia: University of Pennsylvania Press, 1994.

Mayer, Thomas F., and Daniel R. Woolf, eds. *The Rhetorics of Life-Writing in Early Modern Europe: Forms of Biography from Cassandra Fedele to Louis XIV.* Ann Arbor: University of Michigan Press, 1995.

Mazzuchelli, Giovanni Maria. *Gli scrittori d'Italia,* 2 vols. In vol. 6 (incomplete). Brescia: Giambattista Bossini, 1753–63).

McClure, George. *Sorrow and Consolation in Italian Humanism.* Princeton: Princeton University Press, 1991.

Monson, Craig A., ed. *The Crannied Wall: Women, Religion, and the Arts in Early Modern Europe.* Ann Arbor: University of Michigan Press, 1992.

Morelli, Jacopo. *Della biblioteca manoscritta di Tommaaso Giuseppe Farsetti, Patrizio Veneto.* 2nd Vol. Venice: 1771.

Najemy, John. *Between Friends. Discourses of Power and Desire in the Machiavelli-Vettori Letters of 1513–1515.* Princeton: Princeton University Press, 1993.

Okin, Susan Moller. *Women in Western Political Thought.* Princeton: Princeton University Press, 1979.

Pagels, Elaine. *Adam, Eve and the Serpent.* New York: HarperCollins, 1988.

Palma, M. "Cereto, Laura," in *Dizionario biografico degli italiani,* 23 (1979): 729–30.

Pantel, Pauline Schmitt, ed. *A History of Women in the West. I, From Ancient Goddesses to Christian Saints.* Cambridge, Mass.: Harvard University Press, 1992.

Pasero, Carlo. "Il dominio veneto fino all'incendio della loggia," in *Storia di Brescia. II, La dominazione Veneta (1426–1575).* Ed. Giovanni Treccani degli Alfieri. Brescia: Marcelliana, 1961, esp. 182–222.

Pesenti, G. "Lettere inedite del Poliziano," *Athenaeum* 3 (1915): 299–301.

Peroni, Vincenzo, *Biblioteca Bresciana.* Brescia, 1816.

Perosa, Alessandro. "Sulla pubblicazione degli epistolari degli umanisti," in *La pubblicazione delle fonti del medioevo europeo negli ultimi 70 anni (1883–1953).* Rome: Istituto Storico Italiano per il Medio Evo, 1954), 327–38.

Pomeroy, Sarah B. *Goddesses, Whores, Wives, and Slaves: Women in Classical Antiquity.* New York: Schocken Books, 1976.

Quilligan, Maureen. *The Allegory of Female Authority. Christine de Pizan's Cité des Dames.* Ithaca: Cornell University Press, 1991.

Rabil, Albert Jr. *Laura Cereta: Quattrocento Humanist.* Binghamton, N.Y.: Medieval and Renaissance Texts and Studies, 1981.

Ricci, Ludovico, "Notizie di Giovanni Olivieri," *Nuova raccolta d'opuscolo scientifici e filologici.* Venice: Simone Occhi, 1770), vol. 20, opus 6: 3–18.

Robin, Diana. "Cassandra Fedele's *Epistolae* (1488–1521): Biography as Ef-facement," in *The Rhetorics of Life-Writing in Early Modern Europe: Forms of Biography from Cassandra*

Fedele to Louis XIV. Ed. Thomas Mayer and Daniel Woolf. Ann Arbor, Mich.: University of Michigan Press, 1995), 187–203.

———. *Filelfo in Milan. Writings. 1451–1477.* Princeton: Princeton University Press, 1991.

———. "Space, Woman, and Renaissance Discourse," in *Sex and Gender in Medieval and Renaissance Texts: The Latin Tradition.* Ed. Barbara K. Gold, Paul Allen Miller, Charles Platter. Albany: State University of New York Press, 1996.

———. "Unknown Greek Poems of Francesco Filelfo," *Renaissance Quarterly* 37.2 (Summer 1984): 173–206.

Rose, Mary Beth, ed. *Women in the Middle Ages and the Renaissance: Literary and Historical Perspectives.* Syracuse: Syracuse University Press, 1986.

Rossi, Ottavio. *Elogi istorici de' Bresciani illustri.* Brescia: Bartolomeo Fontana, 1620.

Rubinstein, Nicolai. "Italian Reactions to Terraferma Expansion in the Fifteenth Century," in *Renaissance Venice.* Ed. J. R. Hale. Totowa, N. J.: Rowman and Littlefield, 1973), 197–217.

Russell, Rinaldina, ed. *Italian Women Writers. A Bio-Bibliographical Sourcebook.* Westport, Conn.: Greenwood Press, 1994.

Stuard, Susan M. "The Dominion of Gender: Women's Fortunes in the High Middle Ages," in *Becoming Visible: Women in European History.* Ed. Renate Bridenthal, Claudia Koonz, and Susan M. Stuard. 2nd ed. Boston: Houghton Mifflin, 1987, 153–72.

Tetel, Marcel. *Marguerite de Navarre's Heptameron: Themes, Language & Structure.* Durham, N.C.: Duke University Press, 1973.

Toscani, Bernard. "Antonia Pulci (1452–?)," in *Italian Women Writers. A Bio-Bibliographical Sourcebook.* Ed. Rinaldina Russell. Westport, Conn.: Greenwood Press, 1994), 344–52.

Treggiari, Susan. *Roman Marriage: Iusti Coniuges from the Time of Cicero to the Time of Ulpian.* Oxford: Oxford University Press, 1991.

Walser, Ernst. *Poggio Florentinus. Leben und Werke.* Leipzig, 1914.

Walsh, William T. *St. Teresa of Avila: A Biography.* Rockford, Ill.: TAN Books & Publications, 1987.

Warner, Marina. *Alone of All Her Sex: The Myth and the Cult of the Virgin Mary.* New York: Knopf, 1976.

Wayne, Valerie. "Zenobia in Medieval and Renaissance Literature," in *Ambigious Realities. Women in the Middle Ages and Renaissance.* Ed. Carole Levin and Jeannie Watson. Detroit: Wayne State University Press, 1987, 48–65.

Wiesner, Merry E. *Women and Gender in Early Modern Europe.* Cambridge: Cambridge University Press, 1993.

Willard, Charity Cannon. *Christine de Pizan: Her Life and Works.* New York: Persea Books, 1984.

Wilson, Katharina, ed. *An Encyclopedia of Continental Women Writers.* New York: Garland, 1991.

Witt, Ronald G. *Hercules at the Crossroads. The Life, Works, and Thought of Coluccio Salutati.* Durham, N.C.: Duke University Press, 1983.

Index